T0208275

MINDS OF
REASON

IT IS NOT WHAT IT IS

Dr. Feridoun Shawn Shahmoradian

authorHOUSE®

AuthorHouse™
1663 Liberty Drive
Bloomington, IN 47403
www.authorhouse.com
Phone: 1 (800) 839-8640

Published by AuthorHouse 07/19/2019

ISBN: 978-1-7283-1982-7 (sc)
ISBN: 978-1-7283-1981-0 (e)

Print information available on the last page.

*Any people depicted in stock imagery provided by Getty Images are models,
and such images are being used for illustrative purposes only.
Certain stock imagery © Getty Images.*

This book is printed on acid-free paper.

About the Author

Dr. Feridoun Shawn Shahmoradian showed an avid interest in learning about other cultures from a very young age. Shawn's love for people, as well as his need to quench a thirst for learning about others' way of life, inspired him to travel extensively to many parts of the world, including the Middle East, Persia, Turkey, (Istanbul, Ankara), Europe, West Africa, and North America. His travels have rewarded him with an invaluable wealth of knowledge and experience, allowing him to acquire realistic views in the context of diversified culture, philosophical, social, political, economic, and psychological endeavors.

Dr. Shawn attended many spiritual and callisthenic seminars in different parts of the world, including Morocco (Rabat, Marrakesh city, Fes, and Casablanca), Oslo, Paris, Amsterdam, Dublin (Ireland), Toronto (Canada), and Monroe (California), Santiago (California), New jersey, Orlando (Florida), Dallas, Houston, and Galveston (Texas) In the United States of America. He then visited New York, Washington, Las Vegas, San Antonio, Austin, El Paso, Corpus Christi, Texas, New Orleans, Miami Beach, Mexico (Mexico City, Cancun, Cozumel), and Bahamas.

At the age of Seventeen, Shawn attended Crawley College in Crawley England, for three consecutive years, and also attended boarding school at Birchington-On-Sea a village in northeast Kent, England. He visited London several times, resided at Brighton England for a while, and visited Hasting, Canterbury, and Sheffield England. Dr. Shawn then traveled to Fresno and San Francisco, California, and went to Lake Tahoe, Nevada, to teach. Dr. Shawn then left to study at Stockton College in Stockton, California, for two full years, taking philosophy and other social science courses. He then transferred to Galveston Texas College for one more year. A couple of years later he received his electronic engineering degree from

Texas Southern University in Houston Texas. He furthered his studies at Texas A & M and received his master's degree in economics, a minor in finance. His love for social science motivated him to attend the University of Texas at Dallas in Dallas Texas, and there he obtained a master degree in public affairs, with a minor in psychology.

Dr. Shawn obsession with sports and a relentless pursuit for excellence in the art of self-defense that he pursued while facing insurmountable challenges over many years makes him a true embodiment of wisdom and strength. After extensive and thorough research in a variety of arts, Dr. Shawn finally created the Pang- Fang system a very unique and extremely practical system approved by well-known authorities in the field of self-defense. Dr. Shawn's system is highly recommended since it conveys decisive tactics with utterly significant strategy in a life and death situation. Dr. Shawn holds a nine- degree black belt in Hapkido, a Korean martial art, and holds a tenth-degree black belt in the Pang-Fang system of self-defense, second-degree black belt in Judo, first-degree black belt in Tae Kwan do, and third-degree black belt in Wu Shu Kung-Fu. He is acknowledged a prominent figure and as a holder of a non-conventional doctorate in the sport and the art of self-defense. Dr. Shawn is the author of the book Mind fighter, the book of The Anatomy of wake-up calls volume one & volume two, The book of God and the system and the book of Incorporeal God: An Insight into the higher realms.

In the name of the Omnipotent, Omnipresent, Omni-temporal, Omnibenevolent, and the Omniscient God. The most merciful, the most gracious, and the most compassionate. The proprietor of patience, time, space, and beyond. The Fiduciary, Custodian, the Adjudicator (the Arbitrator, the Judge) to all there is and the nonexistence. In the name of the almighty God.

This collection of essays are strikingly informative since phenomenal strides are taken in search of truth, abating speculation. The well-thought interdisciplinary essays are rare, since they can quench the thirst for studious-minded people in search of knowledge and can bring that inquisitive mind closer to the reality of universal existence. The book is entitled *Minds of Reason* and sub-titled *It is not what it is*, which divulges the most arcane (enigmatic) issues of our time, clarifying imperative subject matter like why there is a God and why not many gods, why we are here, what happens after we die, what existed before the big bang, is our living purposefully driven, if a mind or matter is responsible for creation, and so on.

The book *Minds of Reason* delves into exploring for truth; it unveils the awesome traces of God while leaving no stone unturned, convincing the reader that there's more to life than meets the eye. Quintessential discourse on emerging fields for groundbreaking ideological, spiritual, philosophy, scientific, cultural, psychologic, social, political, economic domains, and the rationale behind these intriguingly intricate subjects, are clearly discussed.

The refined methodology is executed to carefully manifest the essence of what matters, to play a catalyst in intuitively abstract findings, to muster a dynamic form or variation of clear cognizance for illustrating key arguments, to better fathom the essentials of existence. The aim is to insightfully navigate the uncharted territories to further deter obtuse debates; where dogmatic theoretical views can transcend to higher perception planes to further avoid vain acrimony (altercation) for a paradigm shift in meaningful communication, quantifying manna (gratuitous benefit) outcome from both sides of the aisle.

Turn your passion into glory.

1

WHERE DO THE FALLACIES LIE?

Not believing in the Magnificent Designer, the awesome Creator of all there is and all there ever will be, with unimaginable potency as the true reason for existence, bearing infinite wisdom, the superbly intelligent cause behind the majestic universe, the Maker of the exalting cosmos and beyond; and when not realizing the phenomenal traces of the Almighty, and unable to attune to non-anthropomorphic (humanoid, anthropoid) God. And further, unreservedly (reticent, openly) denying the truth, and when demurral (skepticism, reluctant) to essential attributes of the Omnipotent, Omnipresence and Omniscient Ahura Mazda (God, Lord, Spirit.)

One needs to rigorously challenge one's own mind, since one is not fathoming the conscious-oriented universe, literally awakened, as one is not perceiving the miraculous impetus force of God as the sole reason for existence. Where the ambivalence, the mistrust should absolutely not imply to the flawless Creator, or for one to act delusional towards the breathtakingly sacred creation, but to delve into one's own blunt mind.

Or perhaps because someone's diluted (weak) belief is due to extreme hurt facing humanity, blaming God, one ought to further reassess one's paradoxical (unsound) findings since, in good faith, the Merciful Provider has utterly endowed humanity with all of the gratifying resources to live in luxury, in which I am afraid the goods are ungratefully ruined and on the verge of annihilation by mankind without any remorse.

The reality implies the infinite traces of God, where complexity in nature and the immaculate universe are undeniably directed at a splendid designer; and since we are the product of habits, we have the potential to become accustomed to varieties of the atmosphere, we become acquainted with our surroundings, we take even the most wondrous things for granted, acknowledging them as self-propelling, or perhaps gifted by nature, believing that the universe provides, and yes, that is a fact; in the meanwhile, not making much sense when not perceiving the power of intention behind such an astonishing state of being.

It is sad when not realizing that we are the nature, we are an inseparable part of the whole being and the amazing universe; we are part of the cosmic energy, the particles, the electromagnetic forces, the interstellar dust, the nebulas, and beyond which much of the space between the stars is filled with atomic and molecular gas (primarily hydrogen and helium) and tiny pieces of solid particles or dust (composed mainly of carbon, silicon, and oxygen). In some places this interstellar material is very dense, forming nebulas, as we undeniably are made of the same agents which nature, the Milky Way, and the cosmos are comprised of.

We couldn't survive a couple of minutes if we do not breathe, not being able to inhale oxygen and exhale carbon monoxide; we cannot survive a few days with no water, and perhaps a week or two with no food, and if not activated to reproduce, as these events and much more are nature-driven, our survival branches out from the environment that we live in, as it should enlighten us to honor the cause, the almighty God, preserve life, respect nature, validate cooperation, work in unison with nature, believe in collectivism, value mankind, while shedding light on the fact that all men are created equal.

We should be aware of such purveying (provision) and remarkable existence that offers convincingly countless evidences of a mighty cause. And unless we can overcome the notion of acting indifferently towards the miraculously oriented events literally happening around us, then we have acted as blindly as a bat, not showing prudence towards the actual cause of existence and depleted of any reasoning power. Hence, one's wisdom should mature to heighten mental dynamics, avoiding mind traps to further meditate on one's own thoughts for cultivating the facts.

But there is hope, since the human mind is potentiated to unquestionably one day break through the web of uncertainty to truly realize God. Taking enlightened steps toward the right direction, the physicists already have unveiled the absentia world, better known as the subatomic realms empowered by quantum physics.

Making humanity aware of an entirely different set of rules that must be applied in lieu of Newtonian laws are only doable in the empirically oriented world of cause and effect and within the action and reaction events, as they are obsolete in the higher domains, and as scientists are facing mind-boggling dilemmas in the quantum world, while experiencing exciting dare for a thrilling and promising future.

It seems that the secret of God lies in infinite beauty, since everything created in nature is beautiful, indicating that without a doubt, God is a beauty-oriented Being. And since man is made in the image of God, man is also innately attracted to beauty, like beautiful thoughts, beautiful words, beautiful conduct, beautiful songs, attractive bodies, beautiful faces, attractive features, beautiful scenes, beautiful climate, beautiful colors, good-looking creatures, beautiful nature, and so on. Referencing beauty, Aristotle rejected Plato's theory of forms. Aristotle stated that "properties such as beauty are abstract universal entities that exist independent of the objects themselves. Instead, he argued that forms are intrinsic to the objects and cannot exist apart from them, and so must be studied in relation to them."

The next secrets of God are infinite intelligence, infinite wisdom, with an infinitely brilliant imagination. So is man, because we have an idea about absolute perfection and have a notion about the pinnacle of invincibility; we have an idea about quintessential (flawless) being, as if the ultimate characteristic, the most perfect model is imprinted in our mind.

Then, man as imperfect seeking completion searches for knowledge and information, mindfulness, cultivating wisdom, trying for the ability to learn, also with infinite imagination, looking for innovations, abhorring evil, insisting on fair allocation of resources, where covetousness and irrational pile-up of wealth can be stopped. Wanting to dispel violence, persisting to end corruption and ill-behavior.

The next secret of God is doing the infinite good, infinitely resourceful; where divinity finds its meaning. And so is man, as an imperfect being, wanting to do good, seeking perfection, looking for freedom, democracy, justice, peace, and human rights; in which the human heart and brain are the two organs that are infinitely based, since our heart unboundedly desires to the day we physically expire, and our mind infinitely craves progress, is curious, and inclined to acquire wisdom until the day we die.

Where beauty, intelligence, consciousness, mindfulness, imagination, goodness, and God are concept-oriented phenomena, so is heresy, demons, and ill conduct. But the secret is that destructive behaviors are overcome by virtuosity, compassion, caring, through constructive actions in which the overall good reflects living, since virtue overcomes evil; otherwise, life would have been terminated long before, and wouldn't have lasted billions of years and be still in the making.

The hidden issue is that we do not die; yes, we do expire physically, but because we are the only creature that by nature has the outside body experience, as we cannot be found anywhere in our physical body—we cannot be located in our brain, in our heart, kidneys, lungs, bone marrow, in our nerves and veins, or any other part in our anatomy. Because we are conscious-oriented, we are ideas; we are energy-based entities circulating for infinite time, linked to cosmic energy, with much higher frequency rates than any other creature, or substance. We exist to experience higher realms, and we comparably are much in tune with the universe, persisting in revealing the secret of life.

Some so insensibly claim that existence, that we have originated from matter; if so, then we would have no souls, as we would be exhausted of any spirit, and definitely without prevailing to the higher realms. And that would be the end of it, as we perish into dust, since all matter is destructible, as no matter can ever exist forever. But the fact is that the entire existence, that life is thought-oriented, that everything is either animated or not, are energy-oriented with different frequency rates.

There is no nothingness, no impermanent, no impertinence, as all and everything is connected, as human beings are part of nature, spiritually, and through the human consciousness, linked to the universe. Human awakening gives meaning to existence, since there are only consciously based experiences, and an idea-driven universe designed to transcendentally last, architecturally vibrant with the intention to elevate the human spirit to the higher domain, and for the human soul to face a renaissance, a revival, an ecstasy, a trance, a new beginning, an ascendancy.

Further, it would be utterly wacky to accept that an unintelligent, mindless matter, without any emotion, exhausted of any feeling, without sensibility or any wisdom, basically an unanimated being, to create an intelligent, conscious-oriented, thought-driven entity. It is in vain to credit lifeless substance for making an animated being with emotions and feelings, exuberantly pursuing a living; a rational being with the infinite potentiality for progress, and definitely with purpose, that intends to conquer the universe and beyond.

It is acting credulous (gullible) to fancy such tremendously inspiring, highly thought-provoking, infinitely imaginative, immensely curious human beings to be made from decayable matter, without any willpower. If so, that is absolutely a miracle; otherwise, it would be nothing short of a mockery.

You might ask why would anyone believe that matter, an inanimate substance with no mind, no sense, no intelligence, depleted of any knowledge and information, impermanent by nature. Since all matter is perishable, as they can be manipulated, altered to liquid, transferred to steam, gas, and also hardened, to be the cause of existence, as the matter is unstable, and hence, contingent to various circumstances.

The naivety takes over since many believe that what we witness as matter, the world around us, and in what we experience, is the answer. Mainly because science can deal with what is visible and tangible, and so-called the practically experimental issues.

Forget that science is the byproduct of the unseen conscious, where mind utterly governs, enlightening us to disregard such empty manifestos, and in vain doctrines, other than the belief that God rules. In which it believes the matter is the cause of existence, that matter rules? Ignoring that science solely discovers new inventions, as it exploits novelties via intelligence and curiosity, looking at things that are already hidden in nature, since our world is already potentiated with decisive matters, unbounded with disciplinary ideas, and gloriously promising a future, waiting to become exposed.

Furthermore, it is practical to scientifically turn matter into energy, as the scientists have even experienced it with the atomic bomb, but in no way probable to turn energy into matter; it is just not possible. No one can materialize our thoughts, ideas, or substantiate our feelings, our emotions. Because we are a closer part of God, as the Almighty is energy-oriented and beyond reach for such undertakings, we are part of the cosmic energy, part of a holy concept, made because of a sanctified thought.

Intelligence, wisdom, awareness, curiosity, imagination, ambition, rationality, mindfulness, inspiration, love, sacrifice, empathy, dreams, will, intention, and a host of other feelings and emotions, are some of the essences that make us humans. And for punishments and reward, we either are ascended to the higher realms for rewards or descended to the lower domains for chastisement.

2

THE INFINITE FOOTPRINTS OF GOD

"The subtlety of nature is greater many times over than the subtlety of the senses and understanding." (Sir Francis Bacon)

The world's scientific views curiously explore the cosmos, the universe, they cultivate life, delve into the human brain, as they often are eager to know about the human conscience, the mind, and the mysteries of God.

Consciousness is sought, as the quality or state of becoming insightful with something and further awakened within oneself, looking for the awareness with philosophical, scientific, spiritual, mental, psychological, biological, physical, cultural, social, and political concerns, searching for the reasons behind often meandering concepts relating to humankind, through which is the state of being characterized by sensation, emotion, learning, thought, mind, enlightenment, volition (will, the power to make one's decision and choices), and cognition further develops.

In the cosmos, we are perplexed, wanting to know what is the nature of the universe, where the universe came from, and where it is going. In life, we want to know if there is a soul. We struggle to understand the creationist's view, the evolutionary concept, genetics, the effects of the environment on a human's upbringing, and the origin of life. We are inquisitive to know if there are extraterrestrials; why do we think we aren't alone? (Extraterrestrial means originating, existing, or occurring outside the Earth or its atmosphere.)

Extraterrestrial refers to any object or being beyond (extra) the planet Earth (terrestrial), it is derived from the Latin words *extra* ("outside," "outwards") and *terrestrial* ("earthly," "of or relating to the Earth").

Intelligent life may refer to extraterrestrial intelligence – intelligent extraterrestrial life originating from outside Earth's planetary boundaries, whether theoretical, having existence in the past, present or future, yet not discovered by terrestrial intelligence as of today.

Scientists tell us that the chemistry of life may have begun shortly after the big bang, 13.8 billion years ago, during a habitable epoch when the universe was only 10–17 million years old. The scientists further acknowledge that soon after the big bang, primordial protons and neutrons were formed from the quark-gluon plasma. (Quark-gluon plasma is a state of matter in which the elementary particles make up the hadrons of baryonic matter.)

Baryonic matter is made of protons and neutrons that are freed of their strong attraction for one another under extremely high energy densities. Also by definition, baryonic matter should only include matter composed of baryons. In other words, it should include protons, neutrons and all the objects composed of them (i.e., atomic nuclei), but exclude things such as electrons and neutrinos, which are actually leptons. These particles are the quarks and gluons that compose baryonic matter of the early universe as it cooled below two trillion degrees.

A few minutes later, in a process known as big bang nucleosynthesis, nuclei formed from the primordial protons and neutrons. (The plural for the nucleus is nuclei; the atomic nucleus is the very dense central region of an atom. And on the contrary, now that science has relatively advanced, more fundamental and perplexing issues have surfaced leaving scientists and the physicists in awe, since the more they dig into the unknown, the more they face puzzling agendas.)

For instance, in the subatomic world, everything is being quantized, as in the atomic world, energies are also quantized. This means it can have only certain values. In mathematics, physics, to restrict (a variable quantity) to discrete values rather than to a continuous set of values.

In physics, to change the description of (a physical system) from classical to quantum-mechanical usually results in discrete values for observable quantities, like energy or angular momentum. In physics we apply quantum theory to, especially form into quanta, in particular, restrict the number of possible values of (a quantity) or states of (a system) so that certain variables can assume only certain discrete magnitudes, as light is quantized into packets of energy.

In electronics, approximate (a continuously varying signal) by one whose amplitude is restricted to a prescribed set of values distortion is caused when very low-level audio signals are quantized. The physicists are facing pixels, in which a pixel is simply the smallest element in a visual display, billions of times smaller than an atom, where molecules would be too complex to be compared to the relatively simple pixel (any one of very small dots that together form the picture on a TV screen, computer monitor, etc.).

Atoms have smaller components and have too many properties to be compared to pixels, in particle physics, an elementary particle or fundamental particle is a particle not known to have any substructure, thus it is not known to be made up of smaller particles. Quarks: up, down, charm, strange, top, bottom. Leptons: electron, electron neutrino, muon, muon neutrino, tau, tau neutrino. Composite subatomic particles (such as protons or atomic nuclei) are bound states of two or more elementary particles.

For example, a proton is made of two up quarks and one down quark, while the atomic nucleus of helium-4 is composed of two protons and two neutrons. Then the atom was discovered, and it was thought indivisible until it was split to reveal protons, neutrons, and electrons inside; these also seemed like fundamental particles, before scientists discovered that protons and neutrons are made of three quarks each.

Today, we know that atoms do not represent the smallest unit of matter. Particles called quarks and leptons seem to be the fundamental building blocks—but perhaps there is something even smaller. Physicists are still far from understanding why a proton has about 2,000 times more mass than an electron. They've found that an atom has a nucleus, that a nucleus contains protons and neutrons, and that those particles, in turn, are made of quarks and gluons—particles that bind quarks together. But most physicists believe quarks to be the smallest building blocks of matter.

What's smaller than a photon? Smaller than photons include quarks, gluons, electrons, and neutrinos. Then there are the forces that join those things up: light is one of them. Light is carried by little particles called photons. And there is the Higgs boson particle, which scientists recently found that is also smaller than an atom.

The particle duality means being a particle at the same time as being a wave; that they can exist in different places at the same time has further complicated the situation, which implies that the world we live in is apocalyptic, or full of prophecy. Denoting the truth about the world-view spirituality, believing that the invisible wholeness underlies all of the creation, and ultimately it is this hidden realm that matters the most.

Passive observation and probably ignorance render ways to active participation and brilliant new discoveries, telling us that we are part of God's creation while blessing God's creatures with much more pleasant surprises to come. Giving humanity a hint that perhaps our Maker is a God-like computer infinitely imaginative, so genius, simulating a computer-like effect.

A computer made of meat, neurochemical-driven, deciding how we feel genetically, determining how we grow, live, and then die, having an invisible programmer, an unseen analyst dealing with our software department known as the mind, apparently endorsed with the hardware known as the human brain, and lump sum of meat, fat cluster, with seemingly no intelligence, without a CPU (central processing unit) does not make any sense. Ironically, the neuroscientific approach is that the mind is merely a by-product of the brain.

In the meanwhile, long before knowing the true nature of our universe and the world we live in, we were told by the prophets and sages, like Noah, Abraham, Moses, Jesus, Mohammed, Buddha, Rumi, Lao-Tzu, and so on, that a transcendent domain exists and resides beyond the everyday world of pain and suffering; for instance, nirvana means freedom from all sufferings, as Buddha taught.

The ancient *rishis*, or sages, of India suggested that the knowledge of the cosmos is locked inside the human mind. They taught us no sin can go unpunished, where the penitence (contrition, sense of sorrow for one's transgression) should be felt, and one's righteous behavior and humility (modesty, humility, not arrogance) will be rewarded, and that justice will be sought.

The wise remind us that even though the eye beholds the physical world and observes the external existence, this is solely a veil drawn over a vast mystery and the hidden universe that is beyond our five senses and human nervous system, to realize the infinitely unseen realm of possibilities, with the understanding as bio-centric, or Bio-centrism considers all forms of life as having intrinsic value.

In the meanwhile, the core of our curiosity and questioning should focus on what is the reality. Is the reality the consequence of natural laws rigorously operating through cause and effect, or is it something else? Either reality is bound by the visible universe, or it is not.

Either the cosmos was created from an empty, meaningless void, or it was not. Either a programmer, a magnificent designer, and superb analyst is in charge of this super-complex simulated computer called life or not. We can rationally address the whys of the universe, which are gradually answering hows and whats of the universe as they open more doors to the unknown behind the closed doors, eventually shedding light on the mysteries of the universe.

What is even more imperative besides our due diligence persistence on discovering the unknown is that we should not deny ourselves the power of reasoning and the essence of correct thinking. We are not to act like primates; if we do, it will eventually depreciate us into machine-like robots with senseless programming.

We need to be careful of the environment we are living in, since a material-intense society can make people into consumers with one-track-mindedness, veiled and blinded by the industrial societies, hardened by greed, obsessed with material wealth and the thirst for excessive pleasure of the flesh, where every other vital issue can become secondary and not a priority, even as far as doing very little to preserve an innocent human life, as if we are just numbers.

With that said, we ought to be thankful for science, because it is through science that many possibilities for a better world are taking place. For example, science has created a humongous social network that instantly connects the world we live in.

It is through technology and scientific notions that we have conquered many mortal diseases and have the ability to rewire the globe to reach the most remote places and hear the cries of those in pain poking our consciences to do something decisively humane about the victims of countless tragedies and to affect each other often for the best to create a planetary civilization, where cooperative endeavors are gradually replacing competitive agendas. Ironically, it is via science that we are able to know the awesomeness of the almighty God, since it is via science that the wonders of the universe are being incrementally discovered. Scientific methods are deeply rooted in nature; it is the way to comprehend the physical world, as it cannot be falsified.

We also should know that science cannot explain the meaning of life, or why are we here, and if we have a soul, why we feel love, and why we sacrifice and are sometimes sacrificed, gambit (losing oneself) to save another human being. Science cannot tell us how to locate consciousness, nor how to measure consciousness, because consciousness is a concept that cannot be seen, it cannot be sized.

It is not plausible; no magnifier or telescope of any kind can locate the mind. Consciousness is a dilemma that truly has perplexed science, without which, no scientists can ever experience anything, deliver any dependable scientific notion or any reliable output, where nothing is ever possible, since no meaningful communication is ever probable without consciousness.

Bottom line: it is because of consciousness that we experience, discover philosophy (the whys of the world), science (the hows and the ways of the world), and so on. Consciousness can explain science, while science cannot explain consciousness. We are all about intelligence, imagination, emotions, and feelings. Imagine a beautiful face, or let's say Whitehaven Beach in Australia, the sunset, the sunrise, the face of your elementary school teacher, imagine you are walking in the moon, or imagine anyone or anything that you wish to conceptualize or fancy.

The point is that as true as one's imagination is, no picture, no scene, no occasion can ever be located in anyone's brain imagining them. What takes place are known as electrochemical activities manifesting episodes where the mind resides. In reality, we are having a subjective experience, as science cannot describe how electrochemical pursuits manufacture such pictures beyond anyone's imagination, which can solely denote that we are conscious beings.

All of our experiences happen in our consciousness, without which, no experience is ever possible, hence making life as we know it impossible. Where in our brain are memories stored? Making matters more complex, why can we imagine? Why are we creative? Why do we have free will? Why do we have empathy? Why do we care? Where do the laws of the universe come from? Who created them? Why can we not measure the unit of either mass or energy? Why can we turn matter into energy, but are unable to turn energy into mass? Why are we not able to measure reverence? Why do we not have a scientific explanation for consciousness? Is human conscious linked to cosmic conscious? Where in our brain are the experiences made? As Einstein puts it, "If it is a rational world, then it must have a rational source."

In Rene Descartes' *Cogito Argument*, which ultimately results in the famous saying, "I think, therefore, I am," Descartes argues that anything we learn or infer from the senses can be doubted. This is because all sense perception can be deceived. The "I think, therefore, I am" debate can also be interpreted as you and I are concept-oriented beings because we think, therefore, we are, and the only creatures endowed with the out-of-body experience in which, without thinking, we might as well be a piece of rock, dull and with much lower frequencies, without active senses to interact with the energy-based universe.

Our thoughts are energy-based, as nature is, since we are an inseparable part of nature; that is exactly why when our ideas, our thoughts are not constructively managed, then, in one way or another we become punished, since there is nothing unorderly or destructive in our universe except when man's ill-doings take over, often without any remorse, and that is sad, proving the expression of "what goes around, comes around." Which manifests the laws of karma?

Science believes that all sensations come from our brain; they are the byproducts of our brain, insisting that mind, our memories, thoughts, experiences, are the attribute of the brain. Science further says that by titillating (exciting, arousing, stimulating) certain parts of the brain, particular reactions can occur. Yes; of course it is quite natural for the brain to respond when certain parts are triggered, since our brain manages to connect us to the world, just like a smart Samsung or Apple cell phone does.

It seems that as realistic as scientific notions are, even science occasionally can be blinded. It is science that revealed all matter is energy-driven; solely energy-oriented frequencies are operating in subatomic realms where quantum physic is active, as the physicists, the scientists, can observe wavelike particles maneuvering in strange ways.

Particles simultaneously show up at several places and cannot be evaluated, since they show a vibrating, wave-like manifestation, and as delicate as the brain is, it certainly couldn't be an exception, because for the brain to act as an energy-based organ, it would be impossible to connect to the energy-oriented environment.

The human mind is energy-oriented; otherwise, our brain couldn't have so cogently (soundly, rationally) been in tune with our mind, as our brain and mind are vibrantly interconnected, so magnificently in unison, it wouldn't be an easy job to discern which is subordinate to the other.

The dilemmas are that the relationship between neurochemicals and electrochemical activities are utterly not detectable, since any situation, picture, or scene that one is imagining cannot be found in one's brain. There is so far no explanation of any idea to decipher how electrochemical pursuits generate subjective experiences about one's picturing things in one's head.

Hundreds, if not thousands, of subjective experiences happen every day in our consciousness without ever being located by scientists, because consciousness is doing the observing; we are searching for the consciousness, while the consciousness is doing the looking. The mind of science is meshed in with what science is looking for, only making the self-awareness possible.

Most of all science has challenged religions about things that are superstitious and not true, as science has unlocked the secrets that are often beyond anyone's imagination. Science has exposed how the human brain functions, how the universe initiated, how it expanded and exploded to immeasurable reach, how the universe is growing at a very high rate, and how it is going to end. Thanks to God that we live in a world that is hungry for scientific wonders and spiritual longing.

It is because of science the Omnipresent God becomes known because science reveals that an infinite universe was instantly created by the big bang that at the same time showed up everywhere, since cosmic radiation becomes prevalent where radiations impact existence from all sides. Scientists tell us that the big bang did not happen in a particular time or place, since before the big bang there was neither space nor time; it was after the big bang that existence appeared everywhere, radiation coming from all sides, proving the Omnipresent God.

The awesome mechanism of how the big bang was created should make any inquisitive mind wonder about the magic which started with a dot smaller than the tip of a tiny sewing machine needle and stretching it across billions, if not trillions, of light-years of space and time, which should prove the Omnipotent God.

Many sages and enlightened philosophers have redundantly made clear that a universe operating with absolute accuracy, with laws so precise that even the tiniest flaw, does not happen. Because if miscalculation happens for a fraction of a second, no universe, nor any life-driven planet, would ever be possible; which needs to remind us of the Omniscient God, a magnificent Designer absolutely free of any kind of mistake.

Further, what makes the reality of our lives possible is that everything has its opposite, even to the core of existence where matter and anti-matter operate, leaving the concept of good and evil intact. One might ask, why should we have demonic behaviors at all? The answer again lies in the nature of beings, as it seems that without opposite forces, no life is ever possible, and the universe would have been meaningless, as no living is possible without death; telling us perhaps this is a test before entering the next sacred realms or not, where our good deeds should truly matter.

The reality is that opposite forces are constantly at work to make what we know as nature possible, leaving inquiries as such to God's territory since they are beyond human comprehension.

In the meanwhile, the secret lies in harmony, which, along the line of peace and tranquility comes beauty, love, truth, goodness, virtues, justice, equanimity, compassion, forgiveness, transcendence, cooperation, and many other spiritual concepts, since they give meaning to what God is about, rather than evildoings, which signifies satanic behaviors.

Lower selves should be challenged, in which individual's consciousness needs to be refined so that it may reach the radiance of truth, from which one will be cut off by ordinary activities of the world, substantiating that man is made in the image of God where good deeds, clear conscious, and purified souls reside.

To give meaning to human intelligence for understanding that the infinite God cannot conform to human's finite perspectives, but to celebrate our free will, let us either choose destructive impulses to bring out the worst in us, where lower selves and the human flesh is served, or select constructive behaviors, reaching the divinity of mind and manner, and in seeking God.

What should urgently be noticed is that science devoid of spirituality has brought about irresolvable ills condemning humanity with the rise in global warming, Darwinism's survival of the fittest mentality, which dictates kill or be killed behaviors, ethnic cleansing, despicable war crimes, imperialistic exercises, extreme income inequality, precarious living standard for the poor, defunding public education, cutting off social welfare, predatory lending, attacking solidarity movements seeking justice, encouraging digitally oriented violence, placing humanity at the verge of atomic destruction and vulnerable to extinction, arriving with military industrial complex, wherein the wars of aggression globally take many innocent's lives every day, where many bystanders lose their lives and are ignored as collateral lost.

Such atrocities occur because thousands of culprits are spiritually and emotionally disconnected from the grave tragedies they are causing, which should alert humanity that, if we are to expect a mass extinction in our modern era, it would certainly be because of potentiated modern behaviors linked to primitive conduct and savage actions. Therefore, we are left with no choice but to urgently follow the footsteps of God and take the right course for thinking virtue, with good deeds, and with good words, to persist on high caliber moral and spiritual standards, since hoarding wealth, sex, influence, power, and violence have completely blinded us, as we are not noticing the destruction of planet Earth as literally is happening all over the globe.

3

FREEDOM

No capital-intense society can feel true freedom, since capital-driven environments by nature stratify (classify) societies where the poor have to relentlessly struggle to make ends meet and the rich are worried about their wealth and position that might become endangered by those deprived of even the basic necessities in life. It is a no-brainer that millions without financial security will defend themselves against the ravages of poverty through undesirable tactics, where moral depravity can become the norm. Mahatma Gandhi said poverty is the worst form of violence.

I believe poverty is the root of most evil, because of the horrific socioeconomic ills it creates. A free society should mean a society where not only the elites and the super-rich are protected, but the unpopular, the indigent, and the deprived can also feel safe.

The economic onslaught takes the breath out of predominantly poor neighborhoods, leaving them gasping for basic necessities to survive without any life support. The idea of the you are on your own mentality should only work where there are no few robbers among us which, through abracadabra tactics and in the name of the business and law take more than 90 percent of global resources, leaving the majority of the people with dirt to live on.

With so many being exhausted of financial security, neither freedom nor other sacred-oriented concepts, such as liberty, human rights, and the pursuit of happiness, make any sense, reminding us that nowhere in the world should freedom be bestowed to any dictatorial regimes or relinquished to fake democracies where the governors of force under false pretenses arrest, torture, and even kill the crusaders of truth.

"Freedom cannot be bestowed — it must be achieved."

Elbert Hubbard (American writer, publisher, and artist)

You cannot bring out the worst in people and expect to be renowned for protecting freedom, liberty, and human rights; that is hypocrisy in action. You'd be better to refer to intelligence, responsibility, accountability, dignity, trustworthiness, thoughtfulness, which all individuals should uphold.

Yes, any sensible mind ought to agree; but then, put the life of superb luxury you moguls are having in question, and imagine yourselves, your loved ones without food, shelter, clothing, and exhausted of medical necessities, no available schooling; either laid off, or with no promising jobs, having no reliable transportation, and constantly being tempted by luxury living and material extravaganzas in life, and so on.

I am sure you as well would think twice when wanting to talk positive, and acting optimistic, and I doubt that you'd take advice to behave righteously. I sure am not defending any misbehavior, nor am I encouraging uncivilized conduct. Neither am I in any way belittling motivational songs; what I am saying is that desperate times call for desperate measures. It is basic human nature to survive; even if it is at the expense of others, I am afraid.

Conduct that might seem extreme under normal circumstances might seem appropriate during hard times and adversity, which can exert pressure on so many to do the unthinkable. But one cannot even understand what desperate means unless one has experienced it.

I believe that the worst type of moral turpitude (moral turpitude is conduct that violates common moral standards) is to globally inflict a penalty on billions with the crime of poverty they did not commit. It is perhaps true that even in the most perfect world, humanity will fail to deny inequalities, but I am certain that relatively the less class differentiation, the fewer inequalities, the more avoidance of strife (dissension, conflict, wrangling) and bitterness, since seeking balance is always the key.

As in an economically lopsided environment, freedom can manifest its full meaning neither for the poor, as people in need are yoked with having no means to survive, as it makes them worry not knowing where their next meal should come from or how to pay their past-due bills; and for the rich, who employ mercenaries to protect themselves and their wealth, which might find those very guardians to one day turn on them, constantly leaving them with anxiety of how to stay safe.

In an individualistic society is not favorable to the well-being of the society that every member exploits, all of one's talents for personal gains, which the overall intention should be for the common good. The grinding poverty, beggary, starvation, and economic deprivation will eventually afflict all ranks of society, since the millions' desperate struggle for basic needs renders them insensible to all feelings of decency, without right and wrong sensitivity concern, even to the extent of losing self-respect. Nelson Mandela overcoming poverty is not a gesture of charity, it is an act of justice.

We live in an era in which the survival of the fittest attitudes have unfortunately fueled the fire of wrongful competition, deviltry, diablerie (reckless, mischief, sorcery), iniquity, suicides, homicides, genocide, misdeed, offense, sin, wickedness, greed, jealousy, fraud, lies, dishonesty, sexual misconduct, theft, conspiracy, rape, murder, inferiority complex, superiority complex, and other ill-oriented conduct, frequently leading to a crime-infested atmosphere, especially with hardcore criminals that do not mind playing Russian roulette to protect themselves from the hazards of financial insecurities.

"Freedom is nothing but a chance to be better."

-Albert Camus (French author,
journalist, and philosopher)

Occasionally, the rich get caught in this ugly game of greed as they also break the rules, but end up with a slap on the wrist for punishment, since they do have the means to break loose from the clutches of persecution because in a capitalist system, money is the king, playing the role of in God we trust. Dwight Eisenhower said, "You do not lead by hitting people over the head, that is assault, not leadership." I believe no assault is greater than keeping the actual producer of wealth distinctly poor.

It is not a hidden fact that pecuniary (fiscal, monetary) policies run by the few have accumulated most global resources to benefit themselves, where billions are literally being ignored as if they are cursed to tolerate filthy living. The globally rich elites have manufactured scarcities at the cost of human lives, taking the world financially hostage, which it seems they do not even bother to peacefully resolve the issues of predatory lending, hunger, global warming, the wars of aggression, genocide, toxic foods, harmful environment, crippling sanctions—which, in reality, affects the poor and the helpless—the threat of nuclear mayhem, and hundreds of other malaise that have already endangered the very planetary existence.

Critical thinking, unity and mass cooperation, sympathy, moral and legal imperatives, caring, and seeking justice should prevail to deny those mighty few who push the idea of whatever it takes to make money, since I am afraid they have abused their power, utterly neglecting the underlining principle and the morale of the system to exploit and suppress the actual producer of the amassing corporate wealth.

William Shakespeare said, "If the money goes before, all ways do lie open." On the other hand, with financial depravity, all ways remain shut, as well as leaving doors of freedom in question.

4

IS GOD AN ABSTRACT ENTITY?

A concrete noun refers to a physical object in the real world, such as a cat, a person, a building, or a car; an abstract noun refers to an idea or concept that does not exist as concrete nouns in the real world, and cannot be touched, like freedom, virtues, happiness, numbers, brain malleability (elasticity, ductile, flexibility), subconscious mind, mind, atom, subatomic particles like electrons, quarks (which is the basic block of hadrons, as there are two types of hadrons: baryons three quarks, and mesons one quark, one antiquark, and neutrinos with a very tiny mass smaller than any subatomic particle), the universe, the cosmos, infinity, etc.

The sacred concept of the infinite God means there is utterly no limit to Omnipotence, Omnipresence, and the Omniscient God. Rendering no position, leaving absolutely no room for any being or any existence to take over, since infinity is an open-ended expression without any boundary.

Abstract concepts are ideas that cannot be seen, since they cannot be exhibited via concrete (real) examples, but we cannot live without them. Concrete nouns are people, places, or things that we can experience with our five senses; the abstract nouns are the opposite. We can't experience these nouns with our senses. If a noun is abstract, it describes something you cannot see, hear, touch, taste, or smell.

It can be difficult to know when a noun is abstract because there are so many words that can function in different ways, for example, some words might function as verbs in some cases and abstract nouns in other cases; love and taste are two examples. Abstract nouns can be countable or uncountable (mass), they can also be singular or possessive, love, anger, hate, peace, sympathy, pride.

Simply put, describing the progression of logic in a computer program will be possible only if the reader can correctly visualize (imagine) it in his or her mind; therefore, the logical development in computer programing can only be substantiated if the programmer could thoroughly and mindfully imagine.

Abstract reality is a sense tool that empowers us to clarify the world through expressing quality or characteristics apart from the specific object, such as love, hate, anger, frustration, craving, happiness, thrill, hope, desire, imagination, creativity, courage, justice, obedience, honesty, bravery, excitement, poverty, devotion, and other emotions that are abstract nouns, as with so many other feelings that are abstract entities.

A sense of abstract reality is a tool that empowers us to make sense of the world in terms of ideas; this abstract theoretic world can come to appear more real and reliable than the everyday particular world from which it is abstracted. The adjective abstract for things that are not materially oriented objects, or they are general and not related to specific examples, with a word or a phrase naming an attribute added to or grammatically related to a noun to modify or to explain it.

They literally are inseparable from who we really are; also, with the concept of God as an abstract reality that is imprinted in our mind, seeded in our spirit, potentiating humanity with the power of consciousness, empowering us with intelligence, wisdom, freedom, will and the ability to choose, in which if they are activated in the right ways, they clearly distinguish human beings from the beasts.

They are inevitable sources that often flare up in our mind, soul, and body in a variety of ways, as they are not concrete words that can only be sensed. One's senses cannot see, smell, taste, hear, touch, or perceive an abstract noun, since, in essence, an abstract is a quality; concepts are ideas imprinted in our very existence, in which abstract ideas activate thoughts that are not about worldly things, such as reliability, trust, education, faith, knowledge, happiness, empathy, cowardice, freedom, self-expression, peace of mind, safety, etc.

They are the issues that one cannot touch but one can feel them. The existence of abstract objects initially seems like a deep metaphysical inquiry. The view that abstract objects do exist is called Platonism; the view that they don't is nominalism; those who think they do exist, but only in the mind, are conceptualists. Concrete nouns or ideas can normally be experienced with our five senses; concrete nouns are contrary to abstract nouns, which reference concepts that cannot be felt or experiences via our senses.

A concrete thinker will count 50 projects, while a more abstract thinker will meditate on the numbers, for instance, size, length, width, magnitude, scope, volume, amplitude, diameter, depth, radius, and height, are all measures; they are an abstraction in the sense that they do not exist in and of themselves, but they nevertheless explain the real qualities of physical objects. Time is no different; the more one's understanding of physics, the less sense it makes to think of time extending in any direction.

We should utilize the adjective abstract for something that is not a material object. An adjective is a word that modifies a noun or a pronoun to make it more specific: a healthy baby, a sunny day, a humid evening, a kind lady, or a warm glass of milk. You use adjectives to give your nouns a little attitude or to communicate clearly.

The abstract is from a Latin word meaning pulled away, detached, and the basic idea is of something detached from physical, or concrete, reality; and as far as numbers, it is globally understood that numbers and the other objects of pure mathematics are abstract, since numbers cannot really exist without accompanying a concrete object, like 8 books, 12 men, 6 women, or 100 plants, 7 dolphins, 20 monkeys, etc.

Abstract thinking is the empowerment to think about objects, principles, and ideas that are not physically present. It is linked to symbolic thinking, which uses the substitution of a symbol for an object or idea. A variety of everyday behaviors make abstract thinking, like the abstract concept of time.

It begins with awareness and consciousness, as thoughts of the past and future are conceptual ideas that exist in the mind. They are ideas that filter and contort (deform, distort) our realization of factual time. The reference of a word is the relation between the linguistic expression and the entity in the real world to which it refers. In contrast to reference, the sense is defined as its relations to other expressions in the language system.

Thus, there are words that have a sense, but no referents (the person, thing, or idea that a word, phrase, or object refers to) in the real world. Generally, a concept is a function whose value is always a truth value. Concepts are mental representations, abstract objects, or abilities that construct the fundamental building blocks of thoughts and beliefs. They play an important role in all aspects of cognition. In today's philosophy, there are at least three advancing ways to understand what a concept is:

1. Concepts as mental agendas, where concepts are entities that exist in the mind (mental objects.)
2. Concepts as abilities, where concepts are abilities anomalous (strange, deviant, aberrant) to cognitive agents (mental states.)
3. Concepts as Fregean senses (sense and reference), where concepts are abstract objects as opposed to mental objects and mental states.

Concepts are studied as components of human cognition in the cognitive science disciplines of linguistics (the scientific study of language and its structure, including the study of morphology, syntax, phonetics, and semantics. Specific branches of linguistics include sociolinguistics, dialectology, psycho-linguistics, computational linguistics, historical-comparative linguistics, and applied linguistics), psychology and philosophy, where an ongoing debate asks whether all cognition must occur through concepts.

Linguistics is the study of language and its structure; morphology and syntax are two major sub-disciplines in the field of linguistics. The main difference between morphology and syntax is that morphology studies how words are formed whereas syntax studies how sentences are formed.

Concepts are used as formal tools or models in mathematics, computer science, databases, and artificial intelligence, where they are occasionally called classes, schema, or categories, while in an informal situation, the word *concept* often means any idea. An abstract object is an object that does not exist at any particular time or place but rather exists as a type of thing (i.e., an idea, or abstraction). The term *abstract object* is said to have been instated by Willard Van Orman Quine.

Abstract and concrete are classifications that denote whether the object that a term describes has physical referents, as abstract objects have no physical referents, whereas concrete objects do. They are most commonly used in philosophy and semantics. All human feelings and emotions are non-concrete words; they are abstract nouns that can only be sensed, as abstract words may mean two different things to two people or have a different meaning in different contexts, and abstract words are used to describe notions, concepts, and things that can't readily be observed by your five senses.

Abstract words include terms like good and bad, or bravery and cowardice. Abstract objects have no physical referents, whereas concrete objects do. They are most commonly used in philosophy and semantics, the branch of linguistics and logic concerned with meaning. There are a number of branches and sub-branches of semantics, including formal semantics (which studies the logical aspects of meaning, such as sense, reference, implication, and logical form, lexical semantics, which studies word meanings and word relations, and conceptual semantics, which studies the cognitive structure of meaning, the meaning of a word, phrase, sentence, or text.)

Platonism philosophy states that there are such things as abstract objects, where an abstract object is an object that does not exist in space or time, and which is hence utterly non-physical and non-mental. In brief, Platonism refers to the philosophy that affirms the existence of abstract objects, which are believed to exist in a third realm distinct both from the sensible external world and from the internal world of consciousness, and is the opposite of nominalism.

Nominalism doctrine believes that universals or general ideas are mere names without any corresponding reality, and that only particular objects exist; properties, numbers, and sets are thought of as mere features for considering the things that exist. Importantly in medieval scholastic thought, nominalism is particularly linked to William of Occam. The philosophy or Platonism doctrines believe that physical objects are ephemeral (transient, temporary) representations of unwavering (consistent, unchanging) concepts and that the ideas alone render true knowledge as they are known by the mind.

Platonism about mathematics (or mathematical Platonism) is the metaphysical view that there are abstract mathematical objects whose existence is independent of us and our language, thoughts, and practices, just as electrons and planets exist independently (resilient, self-sustaining) of us, so do numbers and sets. Mathematics expresses values that reflect the cosmos, including order-lines, balance, harmony, logic, and abstract beauty. Deepak Chopra.

We ought to realize that the entire beings and whatever is in existence leads to an intelligent designer, as there wouldn't be painting if no drawer, as there is no shape, sketches, and figure of any kind if exhausted of lines, where the fundamentals lay. The term is often applied to movements during the Middle Ages and Renaissance that were set forth by Neoplatonic doctrines; all Neoplatonists, regardless of religious orientation, believe in the superior quality of intangible (ethereal, bodiless, incorporeal) reality, and they consider Plato as the greatest of ancient philosophers.

It is imperative to note that the very essence of our beings, the atom, which is the building blocks to all there is, are not seen with the naked eye, they are irrelevant within our conscious, since they exist independently, as they are not plausible. An atom cannot be felt in any way or shape, but without it, no existence is ever possible. Then, why should anyone be blurred or blinded in seeing God the Creator of the universe and beyond, when one is not even able to notice the very essence of one's makeup, the atom?

Come to think of it, we are all in an abstract, energy-oriented universe, since the entire cosmos and beyond is governed by God, an abstract concept, referencing ideas which serve as the building blocks of what we know as mental delineation or metal rendition (colloquially understood as ideas in the mind), where thoughts are the fundamental cause for the entire existence. Mental portrayal (representations) are the building blocks of what is called propositional attitudes (colloquially understood as the stances or perspectives we take towards ideas, be it believing, doubting, wondering, accepting, etc.). These propositional attitudes, in turn, are the building blocks of our understanding of thoughts that inhabit (dwell, populate) everyday life, as well as folk psychology.

In the philosophy of mind and cognitive science, folk psychology, or commonsense psychology, is a human capacity to explain and predict the behavior and mental state of other people, through which we have an analysis that connects our common, everyday comprehension of our mind, leading to the scientific and philosophical understanding of concepts. Referencing the human brain and mind, as they are analogs (parallel) to an operational computer, we are basically made similar to a computer comprising of hardware and software.

We are programmed through our software (mind), which literally controls every decision and all the activities that we do. Obviously, living will not be possible without an intelligently designed software (mind) that is certainly potentiated to one day conquer not only galaxies, but the entire universe. But contrary to a computer, which must have an independent programmer to function, our brain is set to relentlessly program our mind and to activate our physical body to execute all sorts of tasks, instruct and manage our body without an external programmer. Meanwhile, it is imperative to know that our mind and our brain are energy-oriented entities, which is the very reason they can relate to the energy-oriented world.

The puzzling issue is that we cannot locate the programmer inside our brain, nor are we; e able to find the consciousness anywhere within. The savvy minded creator who invented computer hardware must have based it on the human brain manifesting magnificent imagination, conceptualizing computer software to simulate the human mind, from simple programming to the most intricate outlets. Yes, we live in a computer-simulated, abstract world, designed by an Omnipotent, Omnipresent, Omniscient Programmer which governs everything from infinitely micro beings to infinitely macro entities in existence.

5

THE ONTOLOGICAL CONCEPT

I suppose therefore that all things I see are illusions; I believe that nothing has ever existed of everything my lying memory tells me. I think I have no senses. I believe that body, shape, extension, motion, location is functions. What is there then that can be taken as true? Perhaps only this one thing, that nothing at all is certain.

— Rene Descartes

The idea of how to integrate concepts into an extended theory of the mind, what functions are permitted or not by a concept's ontology. There are two main philosophical aspects of the ontological concepts: (1) Concepts are abstract objects, and (2) concepts are mental icons. Generally speaking, ontology is a branch of philosophy that is concerned with metaphysics and the nature of existence. What exists their cause, the essence of things, their being and identity.

There are three assumptions in research: epistemological, ontological, and methodological, for instance, in computer science and information science, an ontology encompasses representation, formal naming, and definition of the categories, properties, and relations between the concepts, data, and entities that substantiate one, many, or all domains.

Complicated questions like those are part of a branch of philosophy known as ontology, in which ontology, at its simplest, is the study of existence, but it is much more than that too. Ontology is a part of metaphysics, a branch of philosophy that looks at the very nature of things, their being, cause, or identity.

Epistemology is the study of knowledge, where the methodology is the systematic, theoretical analysis of the methods applied to a field of study; it comprises the theoretical analysis of the body of methods and principles associated with a branch of knowledge. A methodology does not set out to provide solutions—it is, therefore, not the same as a method.

In the simplest terms, a concept is a name or label that regards or treats an abstraction as if it had a concrete or material existence, such as a person, a place, or a thing. It may indicate a natural object that exists in the real world, like a flower, a tiger, or a plant, etc. It may also name a man-made object like a table, car, or a house, etc.

Abstract ideas, knowledge, and domains, such as freedom, democracy, happiness, virtue, equity, science, sadness, etc., are also symbolized by concepts. It is important to understand that a concept is merely a symbol, an indicator of the abstraction. The word is not to be mistaken for the thing. For example, the words Milky Way, Mars, Pluto, or Moon are concepts that represent celestial objects.

Plato was the definite proponent of the realist thesis of universal concepts. In Plato's view, concepts (and ideas in general) are innately inhabited; that was the elucidation (clarification) of a transcendental world of pure forms that lay behind the actual physical world. In this view, universals were described as transcendent objects, in which this form of realism was insightfully tied to Plato's ontological projects.

The concept of mathematics, like Derivative, integral, and so on, are not referring to spatial or temporal perceptions of the external world of experience. Neither are they related in any way to arcane (mystic) limits in which quantities are on the verge of nascence or evanescence; that is, coming into or going out of existence. The abstract concepts are now considered to be totally autonomous, even though they originated from the process of abstracting or taking away qualities from perceptions until only the common essential attributes remained.

It should by now be explicitly clear that the almighty God is an abstract concept beyond space and time, where God's autonomous existence is over the grasp of any mortal, since the realm that we operate in is limited to the human nervous system by which we become aware of surroundings, and the environment we live in; until perhaps the day that our software, the human spirit, the soul, can actually maneuver in transcended heavenly realms.

To further clarify abstract concepts, for instance, it is an abstract idea to question, where did we come from? Why are we here? Where are we heading after we expire? One can answer that we are here to seek beauty, to seek wisdom, to become enlightened, to do good, to gradually progress, to further evolution and reach the pinnacle of perfection, to become part of God, and then, it seems that nothing seems certain, except for what amuses us in our minds, and if so, the mind should not be controlled.

> For, after all, how do we know that two and two make four? Or that the force of gravity works? Or that the past is unchangeable? If both the past and the external world exist only in the mind, and if the mind itself is controllable – what then?
>
> — George Orwell, 1984

The Catechism (confession, creed, dogma, credo) of the Catholic Church says: By his sin Adam, as the first man, lost the original holiness and justice he had received from God, not only for himself but for all humans. It could not be a savvy notion, since this type of interpretation does not correlate with human nature; it does not comply with who we are, as it makes sense to say one as a human being is potentiated to either do good or evil, to act sinful or virtuous, since these, of course, are relative terms.

Furthermore, we first know that we are here, that we are not perfect, we are by-passers that should reach our full potentials, to fill our brain with as much knowledge as possible, to do brilliant works, to be the best that we can be, to do no evil, to do right. Yes, for the afterbirth to fill our clean slate with golden content, on our mind, which should always remind us with the invaluable maxim, to live and let live, and to certainly pass on the good thing we have learned to others before leaving for the next realms of existence.

It seems that we already have an imprint in our mind about God; the concept of beauty, about smiling faces, not liking anger, disdaining pain and suffering, not fond of ugliness, not fond of harsh and rough noises, not attracted towards scary features and ill situations, enchanted with pretty faces, liking good scent, despising fetid (bad odor), pleased with good words, attracted to good behaviors, liking good thoughts, wanting to be educated, trained, seeking perfection, tilted towards a healthy environment and serene atmosphere, as we instinctually are attracted to breastfeeding as infants, since babies innately perform suckling to survive.

6

ONE GOD OR PERHAPS MANY GODS?

One God or perhaps many Gods? The obvious answer to questions as such is that anyone in one's right mind cannot claim seeing God, either seeing one God or many. The closest thing in seeing God is the reasoning power through which the human mind can discern facts from fiction, by which one can identify what makes sense and what does not, since fortunately, the human brain has already reached an evolutionary stage where our resourceful mind can detect decisive issues and meditate on robust discoveries to progress further.

It is true that diabolical behaviors and devil's advocacies are often exhibited by the very human mind in which the same mind is also potentiated with awakening forces which can quash (abrogate, void, overrule) the dark side of its nature, to nullify the mind's ignorance and to acolyte (usher) human beings to enlightenment and guide to where God resides.

Some argue how anyone should know if there is one God in charge, many gods, or perhaps a network of gods that operate in unison. Well, a thorough, logical talk, speech, or statement is expected to make sense and have no discrepancy in what is meant to address. No matter what literary work or dialogue one follows, and no matter in what language that work is presented, it needs to substantiate a clear and viable point.

The whole contextual concept ought to have no disparity or the slightest contradiction, as it is a logical fallacy for instance to say a rectangular circle, rounded square, or deafening silence. There isn't any congruency in the statement. According to Aristotle, the principle (or law) of non-contradiction is the firmest, believing that the principle of non-contradiction is a principle of scientific inquiry, reasoning, and communication that we cannot do without. No one in one's right mind can claim seeing God, as we are utterly left with no choice, as we should steadfastly rely on reasoning power for making sense.

Further, when we say Vahdat Dar Vojood', meaning unity in existence, it means a mighty God that has no cause will absolutely not deteriorate or lessen in any way, which by all means is perfect, that is not contingent to space, time, or any other inhibiting factor; furthermore, one should not extenuate (mitigate, palliate) any disparaging suggestion or claim that otherwise needs to keep up the true meaning of the word unity and the word existence. What unity in existence should mean is that everything from micro to macro, from the tiniest, from the minuscule to infinitely large, are an inseparable part of God.

Here we are accentuating on the word *unity* and the word *existence*. Unity in diversity is used as a popular motto as an expression of harmony. The phrase becomes a deliberate oxymoron when we say or acknowledge unity in existences. There is solely one existence, since the essence of all that exists is latticed (meshed) in God, which adheres to the entire existence, since without God, no existence of any kind is ever possible. For instance, no matter how diversified things or objects are, they are all made of atoms, regardless of their nature or any attribute that each might carry. Everything is made of the atom; our world is apparently unified within the commonality of carrying atom, atom is the common denominator for the entire physical beings.

It means a position whose effect fully identifies with the multiplicities, the entire material diversities, and the spiritual realms. Unity in existence means all existence is interwoven in God, in their actual cause, as everything and everyone is an inalienable part of God's existence.

Either rhetorical or what is literally seen and exercised in every day's routines and work should remind us of the unity in the oneness of God and the existence.

We observe no conflicting manifestation in our universe, since everything in nature and beyond is as patented (not concealed) with absolute discipline, significantly coordinated, where every being is blessed with a purpose. All creatures are mandated towards one goal, as if the designers, architectures, engineers, the surveyors, foundation workers, the roof men, bricklayers, stone and concrete laborers, carpenters, painters, plumbers, electricians, the landscapers, etc., are collectively laboring to build a fine home for its residents to enjoy the serenity of mind with comfortable living.

Furthermore, the whole is made up of the parts, and if the parts have destiny and purpose, in which everything and all is undeniably meant to serve their objectives, then logic dictates that the whole, which comprises of these parts, also has a destiny and purpose. To say we come from nowhere and we are going nowhere simply does not add up, and is both wrong and utterly contradictory. Even the famous phrase the survival of the fittest presupposes the arrival of the fit. If Darwinists wish to maintain this purely biological theory, that the entire vast order around us is the result of random chance and random changes, then they are also saying that nothing of any empirical evidence can ever be confirmed, and no empirical science can be demonstrated, which basically is as good as saying no experimental scientific findings are ever valid.

We are endowed with intelligence, enriched with consciousness, memory, imagination, willpower, and the freedom to choose, and have the ability to discern right from wrong, as we are utterly distinguished from the lower species, from the beasts, that are either devoid of such dynamics, or relatively speaking, have much lower frequencies in comprehension. Therefore, it would make no sense to punish animals, which for humans, contrary to the beasts, it makes whole lots of sense to be reminded of our existence as a test because demonic and bad behaviors shouldn't go unanswered, where good deeds should definitely be noticed and rewarded.

Death does not experience human beings, rather human beings experience death, where everyone according to their deeds will either ascend to higher realms or descend to lower phases of existence, where nominal symbolic such as hell, heaven, and other domains for retribution or reward should be expected to exist. The point is, because we are all organically connected, one's righteous doings, or committing wrongs, will affect the rest. Therefore, it is imperative to behave as mankind is made in the image of God, and definitely not as seeing God in man's image.

The overwhelming complexity in the universe and the awesome precision in design would challenge any inquisitive mind that no polygamy-oriented thoughts about the existence of God can have the unanimity (consensus, assent, union) to agree with all the intricacies that the universe carries. Such genius and the spectacular design can only be manifested from a sovereign mind, a sole Omnipotent, Omniscient Creator, and not creators, since the reality of all beings and the attributes of God do not in any way conflict.

Furthermore, it is not far from reason to fathom that everything starts from one and then expands to multicity, where complexities and further exponential processes occur. No matter how far any phenomenon travels, and how complicated all processes become, they all begin from one; oneness is a common denominator for all there is, and all there ever will be; oneness is the root cause of the entire existence.

Everything in existence is sound and superbly unified without any interruption, propelling from the dawn of time to present days that can only attribute from an absolutely infallible mind. Otherwise, this intricate evolutionary process would have been extinguished in its inception, and couldn't have had lasted for so long as it has and still roaring forward full of zest and absolutely without any interruption, imbued with an extremely intelligent guide, so resilient beyond mankind's comprehension.

Let's maneuver like the sun does, where everyone and everything enjoys its warmth, its goodness, regardless of their biological or social status. Let's make the moral and the legal imperatives universally prevalent so that one can expand onto where God resides in one's soul. Therefore, let's act like eagles, where the eagle can look directly into the sun as a test for their chick's worthiness; the eagle holds them up facing the sun. Let's be worthy of the sun.

The birds that cannot stare into the sun and turn their eyes away are cast out of the nest. Let's not be cast out of fruitful existence, as we should look straight into the eyes of the living, to cultivate prosperity, happiness, caring, peace, and always hope for a much better life; where nothing, even thinking of death, couldn't constrain us to live life to its fullest. Let's believe in God.

7

IN SEARCH OF DEMOCRACY

When adamant to make a free society, and for democracy to be unleashed, there must exist boundless professional counselors, skillful training instructors, quality social services, adept management, and plenty of devoted social workers to educate those in need of mental and behavioral hygiene; when the intention is to build a civilized and rational-minded society. Be aware that in the absence of an informed nation, no democracy can ever flourish except resulting in irresponsible criterions where violence will surely go rampant.

I say it is difficult to implement true democracy when people are famished, where the disease of hunger is prevalent, when illiteracy must be cured, when homelessness and lack of proper medical care must be terminated, when joblessness is often the case, and when transportation is frequently problematic. If the intention is to sincerely lessen the proliferating crimes, ending in too many ills from the criminals, then the above moral, social, and legal imperatives need to be met. I honestly believe that not only is it immoral, but it should be illegal to waste a mind, to force people into unemployment, and not to cure the sick, not feed the poor, and not financially subsidize the needy.

Let me be clear; there is no ambiguity about having freedom and an education going hand in hand for prevailing a civil society. The cultural short-sightedness of extreme inequality has entrapped billions, and is the leading cause for sabotaging a fair and just society as it should be dealt with head on to expose the faces of the underground masterminds behind the very reason for people's misfortune and hellish situation.

The society should be able to absorb the seed of freedom just like a fertile ground that needs irrigation, proper sun, nutrients, and care to grow into a fruitful tree. Priorities should be rendered to those that earnestly believe in acting as true human beings with good conscience. if not, rest assured that our beasty side is to prevail and behave corrupted and become nothing but destructive elements of society.

God endowed humanity with the miracle of brain and mind, so question more to manifest and make good use of your intelligent, your positive emotion, your goodwill, and constructive actions. Nehru puts it this way: "Democracy is good I say this because other systems are worse. So we are forced to accept democracy. It has good points and also bad, but merely saying that democracy will solve all problems is utterly wrong. Problems are solved by intelligence and hard work."

And Thomas Jefferson said, "When the people fear the government there is tyranny; when the government fears the people there is liberty." I say: "The more educated, civilized and opulent the nation, the more democracy is practical and freedom should make sense."

Here is the bottom line: to avoid chaos and bloodbath, we either have to put up with a dictatorial regime of governing, or we must relentlessly work hard to treat and take over our human beastly side, since it can erupt at any time if not fundamentally mended.

This can be manifested through viable education and effective training; and humanity should professionally aim for a gradual introduction of democracy, human rights, liberty, and freedom through which the pinnacle of goodness can be nourished and reached. A sacred realm of existence in tune with the image of God promised can be attained and secured; it is then when human worth and dignity are truly recognized.

8

IN SEARCH OF TRUTH

Many scientists, philosophers, and faith-oriented individuals are engaged in an uplifting quest for truth. Yet, what is the truth and how do we locate it? With the birth of relativistic mechanics, wave mechanics, which in turn evolved into quantum mechanics, the entire classic physics where Newtonian laws govern went topsy-turvy as scientists discovered new dimensions which have perplexed the best minds of our times, as they are not able to grasp the magical world of subatomic particles, where it seems their vibrating, dance-like maneuvers give meaning to the reality of our lives.

Even though quantum mechanics apparently provides the best explanation presently available on a microscopic level, neither the unseen realms of the subatomic nor future scientific discoveries can bring us to the truth. Bear in mind that quantum mechanics took place out of the need to provide explanations for a horizon (domain) of physical phenomena that could not be done by classical physics: blackbody spectrum, photoelectric effect, spectra of the elements, the specific heat of solids. Through the work of Planck, Einstein, and others, the idea shaped that electromagnetic and other forms of energy could be exchanged only in definite quantities (quanta.)

With the work of de Broglie, the concept arose that matter could show wave-like properties. It was Einstein who proposed that waves (light) could behave like particles (photons). Heisenberg proposed the first victorious quantum theory, but in terms of the mathematics of matrices—matrix mechanics. It was Schrodinger who came up with an equation for the waves predicted by de Broglie, and that initiated the wave mechanics. Schrodinger also showed that his work and that of Heisenberg's were mathematically equivalent. But it was Heisenberg and Born who first understood that quantum mechanics was a theory of probabilities.

Einstein would never agree with that, even though he assisted in discovering it! It was the work of Dirac, von Neumann, Jordan, and others, which eventually exhibited that matrix mechanics and wave mechanics were but two forms of a more fundamental theory—quantum mechanics.

Quantum mechanics is a theory of information. It is a set of laws about the information that can be assessed about the physical world. The first hint for a modern physics lay in understanding the genesis (creation) of the blackbody spectrum: A blackbody is an object that captivates all radiation, with whatever frequency, that falls on it. The blackbody spectrum is the spectrum of the radiation released by the object when it is in heat.

Yet, recent experiments and new calculations and theories have manifested the existence of finer divisions into much tinier entities— quarks, bosons, leptons, etc., as they are made of even finer strings, as per the string theory. Physics is ever expanding as the reality it attempts to unveil continues to shift. But that reality continues to stay out of the grasp of the latest scientific theories.

Even Einstein seriously doubted its methodology and probability predictions, stating, "I am sure that God does not play dice." It seems that God votes for gradual progress because as every scientific theory runs its course, a new innovation, a fresh discovery replaces it, as the latest one brings humanity a bit closer and in tune with the mysteries of the universe.

For instance, the equation exhibiting the gravitational attraction $F = Gmm'/r2$ between two masses, in conjunction with Kepler's laws of planetary motion, when dissected on the scale of the universe, has a huge problem. There is apparently not enough mass in the universe to account for the entirety of the gravitational attractions calculated and observed in the universe.

Hence, scientists postulate that there is an elusive element known as dark matter. This hidden dark matter is required to balance the equations of motion for the planets and stars. Yet scientists are baffled as to where this matter is or what it actually is. They can notice its effects by looking at the bending of light from distant stars. In other words, they fathom that the presence of some matter is there, but what that matter is escapes them.

Einstein has proven in his famous theory of relativity that nothing can travel faster than the speed of light or even close to that. Of course, in the contemporary world, it has become the norm to find science fiction-like exceptions to this rule. Truly, it is quite hard to tell if we are dealing with fiction-like scenarios or facts. Either way, NASA spent billions of dollars, and so much time and effort, researching time warp drives—a concept made famous in the popular science fiction show *Star Trek*. The warp drive was utilized to empower the Star Ship *Enterprise*. Another movie, *Contact*, is where a space machine passes through a wormhole, exhibiting a means of travel.

Yes, it is science fiction, perhaps utopia, or exaggerated imagination, but unless our mind can fathom and grasp such so-called dreams, it would be impossible to manifest it, as it couldn't be far from the reality, turning human's passion for magical discoveries into glory. Perhaps movies as such are science fiction, but the best science fiction is always oriented on the actual science and is merely extended by brilliant dreams.

Wormholes are anticipated and learned by moderate physics as doable constructs. They are not fictional—the physics of wormholes is viable in theory. Miguel Alcubierre Moya is a Mexican theoretical physicist who is famous for his paper "The Warp Drive: Hyper-fast Travel Within General Relativity," which stowed the theory of the time warp as a realistic concept.

A great number of scientists mandated his theories viable, although far-fetched to put into practice in any case. The idea of such theoretical physics was regarded practical enough for NASA to explore time warp as a probability as a means of space travel, since they dedicated themselves to such research. Later on NASA halted the endeavor, and stopped their plan. The contemporary science is not progressive enough to resolve many issues of our time. Yet the physics involved in the idea of time warp space travel seems real and theoretically possible. Not all scientific theories materialized through a systematic study of nature, applicable to precise scientific laws of nature, since many wacky imaginations and weird intuition have also ended in great scientific inventions.

For example, the benzene molecular structure was conceived by Friedrich August Kekulé, a German chemist, from a strange dream of a snake chasing its tail. He did not ignore his thoughts from this dream but applied them to his research and thereby reached a great breakthrough.

Many discoveries occurred by those who were not looking for them. For instance, Viagra was discovered by lucky accident, an unexpected but useful side effects from drugs. Saccharine, the artificial sweetener in Sweet'n Low, was discovered by a Russian chemist who forgot to wash his hands after a day's work. Often world-altering findings are the result of creative minds noticing that material or invention could be changed for a different purpose.

The microwave in 1946 was founded by Percy Spencer, an engineer from Raytheon Corporation, as he was working on a radar-related project. While he was testing a new vacuum tube, he realized that a chocolate bar melted in his pocket a bit faster than expected; his curiosity led him to aim the tube at other things, like eggs, more chocolate bars, popcorn, etc., where he drew the conclusion that heating the object experienced was because of the microwave energy.

X-rays

In 1895, a German physicist named Wilhelm Roentgen was working with a cathode ray tube when he realized that a nearby fluorescent screen would keep glowing in the dark room while the tube was on. He replaced the tube with a photographic plate to capture the images, creating the first X-rays. When he put his hand in front of the tube, he could see his bones in the image that was projected on the screen. The technology was then adopted by medical institutions and research departments—unfortunately, it took a long time before the risks of X-ray radiation were learned.

Penicillin. In 1928, Sir Alexander Fleming, a professor of bacteriology, saw that mold had grown on his Petri dishes of Staphylococcus bacteria colonies. While looking for the colonies he could salvage from those infected with the mold, he noticed something intriguing. Bacteria wasn't growing around the mold. The mold actually happens to be a scarce strain of Penicillin notatum that secreted a substance that inhibited bacterial growth. Penicillin was then employed in the 1940s, helping open up the age of antibiotics.

The pacemaker was accidentally invented in 1956 by Wilson Greatbatch, as he noticed the wrong fitting resistor emitted electric pulses, which made him think of the timing of the heartbeat.

The effort that led to the discovery of insulin was an accident.

Albert Hofmann studied Lysergic acid (LSD), a powerful chemical that was first isolated from a fungus that grows on rye, which he first synthesized in 1938. These chemicals he researched were going to be utilized as pharmaceuticals, and many derivatives of them are still used as of today.

Teflon and superglue were accidentally discovered, and thousands of other inventions happened because of accidental discoveries.

This line of reasoning illustrates that the frontiers of science are still vastly short of solving many of the challenges facing them. They are stifled by their small world of limited perception and are further restricted by that science available as tools for their understanding. In general, scientists restrain themselves to the formal thought process, a process that does not allow them to be openminded when considering metaphysical topics in the realms of spirituality and religiosity. Bear in mind that innumerable ideas, like the Pythagorean theorem, the binary number system, decimal system, zero infinity, mathematics, the so-called language of God, evolution, and thousands of others, have their origin ingrained in ancient knowledge and information.

In other words, this ancient system of knowledge was familiar with and illustrated many methods and constructs of math and science that were not even idealized nor founded in the rest of the globe until several millennia later, in which most very old text has eloquently shed light on that. When Heisenberg and Bohr debated about inexorable (certain) disturbances in any conceivable measurement, it was evident to them that this uncertainty was a property of the system, not of the apparatus (machines, devices). In essence, this very important Principle of Uncertainty suggests that we cannot really measure things on a microscopic level with absolute certainty.

Furthermore, Kurt Gödel's Incompleteness Theorem shows that there is a constraint on all but the most basic mathematical systems. These theorems boundlessly show that Hilbert's program for finding a complete and consistent set of axioms for all of mathematics is impossible. These incompleteness findings of Gödel shook the very underpinning (foundation) of twentieth-century mathematics, just as the theory of relativity and quantum mechanics redirected contemporary physical research.

Gregory Chaitlin of the IBM T. J. Watson Research Center takes Gödel's incompleteness results a bit further, and shows with algorithmic (a process or set of rules to be followed in calculations or other problem-solving operation, especially by a computer) information theory that mathematics has more extensive and serious limitations than hitherto (formerly, previously) suspected.

9

IN SEARCH OF HEAVEN

We live in an era where I am afraid hell and heaven play a significant role in innumerable people's psyches, entangling so many with the yoke of uncertainty, nudging believers to do what's right and making non-believers aware of their insensible actions toward religion and God, promising that non-believers will be denied the heaven above and perhaps punished by ending up in hell. "Mankind is not likely to salvage civilization unless he can evolve a system of good and evil which is independent of heaven and hell." George Orwell.

Oddly enough, not too many look into the mottos for what is right and wrong, which have fundamentally topsy-turvied the entire socio-cultural, socio-economic, and socio-political agendas for the worse, globally denying billions of social and economic justification, forcing millions into doing wrong just to survive. This, I am afraid, has manufactured cut-throat societies beyond correction, as violence has become the norm, as it seems no safe haven is left for the needy to refuge to.

Leaving so many violators with the impression that they shouldn't be a concern with the after-death punishment, as if the retributions would not be so real, that reprisal (payback) will be as fake as voodoo magic (a black religious cult practiced in the Caribbean and the southern US, combining elements of Roman Catholic ritual with traditional African magical and religious rites, and characterized by sorcery and spirit possession) spilled on those wrongdoers. Instead of morally malfunctioning and/or not abiding by the law, the very victims of this whole civilized shenanigans called capitalism must peacefully fight for their rights via non-violent means.

No one should deny that we live in a monetary-oriented environment, where global tendencies are significantly attracted towards the love of money, and rightly so. No proper living is ever possible without it, as so many simply do not have it, where billions are internationally poverty-stricken and without hope for living a decent life.

Wherein the business name has replaced God's name since unduly corporations have even yoked the state and the governments to do as they say is right and wrong, and what is ethical or not, where moral and legal imperatives have shifted to serve the bosses' interest, and not the republic.

The epistemology (the investigation of what distinguishes justified belief from opinion) and meaningful linguistic literature are apparently not intact, as so many interactivities are dubious and incoherent with what is fair and just practice among many social and financial layers of societies; giving meaning to the expression that everyone has a price.

Everybody has a price means that everybody will eventually sell out and do something unethical if they are paid enough. (It doesn't necessarily mean with money—it could be the promise of a great job, higher position, legal protection, sexual favor, or anything else which the culprits might have craving for.)

This is especially true in poverty-stricken atmospheres. If anyone believes otherwise, let them experience having no job, dealing with an empty stomach, no roof over their head, deprived of any education, without viable transportation, with no proper hygiene and medical availability, and without any kind of savings.

Especially when someone's loved one is in need of immediate lifesaving surgery or medical attention, since in many capitalist systems there are no adequate social, medical, or practical economic programs to protect the needy, the elderly, disabled, and the unemployed, making the expression that there is no free lunch a reality. No matter how desperate one's situation happens to be, the real problem is that the capitalist system so cleverly plays double standard, and it is beyond the layman's grasp to detect the cunningly deliberate designs aiming at making the rich richer and the poor poorer.

Institutional religions undeniably play a huge part in feeding consumers with wrong prophecies as well, not finger-pointing the misleading issues to deter believers from such path that leverages the capitalist system to ruthlessly exploit the workers and the actual producer of wealth. Through hard work and backbreaking productivity, the laborers have already created so much wealth for the capitalist's bosses beyond anyone's imagination.

The institutional religions should remind people that hell is here, since billions are deprived of living in peace, as believers are just happy with the promises of the afterlife; reminding them of the ill consequences of hell, and denial of heaven if they dare to do otherwise and as instructed. Placing masses of people in a hard place and a rock, striking them with the double-edged sword of unjustified living conditions and for awaiting the punishment of hell. Like Dante's *Inferno* manifesting a fictional novel which comically draws on the afterlife, just an imaginary fiction not taken as truth.

Many religions capitalize on manufacturing fear and anxiety in a world that is already compounded with stress and pain caused by financially ruling elites. Religion's redundant conditioning of masses promising them hell and heaven should not go any further than Dante's *Inferno* comedy, and many other fictionally based stories uttered in human history.

Accepting that many variables are responsible for one's character and attributes, in which the environmental effects, wrong or right, upbringings are extremely decisive and have a lot to do with one's personality makeup. Therefore, instead of trying to make people fearful and threaten them with the anxieties of the afterlife comedy-like ordeals, promising to torture the sinners in hell, and the expectancy to reward the righteous in heaven.

It would make much sense to establish a thorough social program which could financially sustain citizens in time of need without having paralyzing worries when out of work, or when hit with the recession, depression, and when one has to struggle with a devastating illness, or is faced with any other tragic outcome. By the way, if a society is equipped with proper social welfare and makes sensible social and economic programs, it would significantly lower crime rates.

Perhaps in Dante's allegory, the story of divine comedy can shed some light on the journey of the soul towards God, with the *Inferno* explaining the concession (admission) and the refusal of sin. The *Inferno* tells about the trek of Dante through hell, guided by the ancient Roman poet Virgil, in which Dante the poet perceives to be on the universal Christian quest for God. Concluding that Dante's character is anchored in the everyman allegorical tradition: Dante's billet (position) is meant to show that of the entire human race.

In Dante Alighieri's hell-fire, the poet and pilgrim Dante embarks on a spiritual odyssey guided by the soul of the Roman poet Virgil. Dante travels down through the nine circles of Hell and witnesses the castigation (chastisement, punishment) eternally endured by the souls of deceased sinners.

First Circle (Limbo) Dante's First Circle of hell is virtuous non-Christians and unbaptized pagans who are chastised with eternity in lesser heaven; where they live in a seven-gated castle denoting the seven virtues. Circle 1: Limbo. Resided in by virtuous non-Christians and unbaptized pagans. Circle 2: Lust. The souls here are chastised by being blown about violently by tremendously strong winds, devoid of peace and rest. Circle 3: Gluttony, Circle 4: Greed, Circle 5: Anger, Circle 6: Heresy (eccentricity, nonconforming, dissent), Circle 7: Violence, Circle 8: Fraud.

Being a Christian, Dante adds Circle 1 (Limbo) to Upper Hell and Circle 6 (Heresy) to Lower Hell, making 9 Circles in sum; incorporating the Vestibule of the Futile, this leads to Hell containing 10 main divisions. Thus, Hell has in total 24 divisions. In Canto III of the hell-fire before arriving at the Acheron River and approaching hell, Virgil guides Dante through Hell's Vestibule, where the futile are committed, where those who have exhibited hesitation, indecision after indecision, are forever hustling and bustling (spinning) about without certain objective, exhausted of any goal with indefinite end; they simply are not able to rest eternally.

The Vestibule is the abode of the weather-cock mind (an erratic person, unstable, fickle-minded or often changeable) the obscure (vague, shadowy, puzzling, abstract, opaque) tolerance which will neither ratify nor damn (condemn) the leery, timid, cautious (cowardice) for which no say so or determination is ever final. The spirits rush pointlessly after the aimlessly spinning banner, spurred by the thought that, in doing anything whatsoever certain, they are losing on something else.

Dante conceptualized the recorded entrance to hell: abandon hope all ye who enter here, inhabited by pursuers of pointless endeavors. After going through the gate of Purgatory, Virgil led the pilgrim Dante through the mountain's seven terraces (grandstands.)

These tally (agree, correspond) to the seven mortal sins or seven roots of sinfulness where abomination and wickedness are done, starting with Pride, Envy, Wrath, Sloth, Avarice (greed), Prodigality (spending too much, extravaganza), Gluttony (too much eating or drinking), and Lust (sexual desire, eroticism, libido.)

Historically speaking, the powerful and the financial bullies have always played active roles in setting up states, the way governments ought to be running and how laws should be dictated, since concentration of wealth, which no doubt leads to concentration of power, influencing politics either with direct hands-on or affecting it via covert activities.

Classified societies often leading to extreme income inequality strikes global victims with financial insecurities, leaving them no choice but to sometimes do the unthinkable for subsistence. The powerful and the influential unfortunately have turned living into survival games, where the so-called fittest with the evilest and inhumane ideas conspire against commoners, devouring all of which belongs to the poor. You might ask if greed has anything to do with it.

The answer is yes, but we are faced with a system which relentlessly fuels the fire of temptation, misleading consumers through potently toxic media by setting financial traps with deceiving tactics, which lures millions into a buying spree, continuously brain-storming consumers to hoard things they do not need, and eventually they cannot buy the things they often desperately need. This whole dilemma compounds when people become laid-off or become unemployed, forcing them into the survival mode to the extent of even selling their souls.

The economic insecurity plays like the eye of the storm, whirling so fast into tornado-like worries, bellowing the victims off their feet with anxiety and fear, leaving them with little hope for survival; it is a no-brainer that eventually, every trick in the book is used to cheat, lie, steal, corrupt, and even murder to secure one's monetary position. Especially when there are no meaningful social networks offered in the very unstable capitalist system to temporarily rescue citizens from sometimes horrific financial situations.

The economic supremacism (an ideology which holds that a particular class of people is superior to others and that it should dominate, control, and subjugate others, or is entitled to do so) is exactly what is going on.

Bigoted-like behaviors of the oligopolies should vehemently be fought against to awaken the moguls of our time that lives matter.

Global citizenry is running away from this hell we call living in search of heaven, because of the capitalist's atrocious-oriented culture that is designed to exploit people and colonize citizens for the worst, denying so many from God-endowed freedom, liberty, human rights, and the pursuit of happiness, which the good Constitution has also manifested and ratified.

When people desperately are in need of basic resources to survive, loud talks of freedom and human rights can only play an oxymoron with contrasting meaning, such as cruel compassion or living death. Oxymoron: a figure of speech by which a locution (a phrase, a clause, a sentence) produces an incongruous, seemingly self-contradictory effect, as in cruel kindness or to make haste slowly.

Human beings cannot simultaneously live and die, as they could not be free and at the same time left needy, in a system which by nature cannot sustain prolonged social and economic stability that leaves billions monetarily insecure.

Hence, the struggle for ensuring one's financial position will be the norm, and it becomes everyone's priority, with the exception that the rich elites have certainly the means to take all that they can without any remorse, and those deprived of influence and power, the destitute, the poor, end up incarcerated, if they legally malfunction to survive.

The capitalist system cunningly addresses God with the rewards and the punishments of the afterlife to prevent the victims of financial depravity from uprising and to quell resurrections. Telling billions of global hungry people that they might have a terrible situation in this life, but they will have the best of fun in the next life. This type of mental tactics will surely affect so many psychologically, believing what the hell, why bother, since we will be much better off, for our next life, in the heaven above.

With the super-rich possessing all of the resources and leaving the majority of people with almost nothing, the ruling elites would expect violent resurrection by the poverty-stricken dissidents against them. The idea of heaven and hell can to some extent calm them down, especially when people are conditioned that the rich elites must have been blessed with wealth because they are chosen to govern.

As if Jesus agreed with rich landowner Pharisees, and the affluent Sadducees, Essen, and others which in cahoots with Romans crucified him. Jesus rebuked the scribes and Pharisees so harshly in Matthew 23:13–36? In Matthew 23, Jesus pronounces woes on the scribes and Pharisees, the rich religious elite of the day. The word *woe* is an exclamation of grief, denunciation, or distress.

It is further essential to say that not all Jews were responsible for killing Jesus, where people's attitudes toward Jews, as Jewish blame for Jesus' death has long been a linchpin for anti-Semitism, that is neither humane nor right, because most Jews lacked a motive for Killing Jesus. In fact, relating to most historians, it would be most appropriate to blame the Romans for Jesus' death, since crucifixion was a customary punishment among Romans, not Jews.

At the time of Jesus's death, the Romans were imposing a harsh and brutal occupation on the Land of Israel, and the Jews were often unruly. The Romans would have had reason to want to silence Jesus, who had been called by some of his followers King of the Jews, and was known as a Jewish upstart miracle worker defending the rights of helpless, and the needy against the Roman empire. Bottom line heaven means to be one with God Confucius.

10

IGNORANCE OR INTELLIGENCE?

Which faith should one belong to?

Ignoring human intelligence, blunt in moral behavior and experiencing inferior actions will make force, fear, and uncertainty to take over, the absence of civil acts and lack of virtuosity (expert aesthetic, sensibility) can quickly tilt towards ill doings and corrupt activities.

Savagery and dark age mentality historically has left humanity with no choice, but to refuge to legal and moral imperatives, nudging inhabitants to act lawfully, and for the believers to follow spiritual maxims for acquiring a tranquil living. To endure ethical laws, mainly through religion in which most religions unanimously promise brewing punishments in the afterlife when sins are committed, and heavenly rewards when good deeds are done.

It is a no-brainer to realize that in perpetrating transgression or in avoiding sin, one's actions are relatively proportional with one's intelligence, wisdom, and by one's awakened conscience, which can sure play a decisive role in behaving good and humane.

It is relatively true that witted conducts are not born overnight, but for presentable attitudes, civil behaviors, cultured actions with pleasant human interactions also have to forgo enhanced evolutionary process, in which many religions at barbarian's era and through dark ages played viable roles.

In the meanwhile, undertaking fear tactics, denoting punishment and reward mechanism in the afterlife, which once might have been to a certain degrees effective, are no longer of much concern, since time parameter plays a huge role in implementing ideas that are dynamic in nature; or perhaps dull enough to persist on traditionally old creeds that lag behind, not in accord with new information's age. Most of the so-called traditional maxims are not able to meet today's standard since modernism demands an up-scaled paradigm shift in consciousness and civil behavior.

After all, what difference does it make which faith one belongs to when one encroaches on other people's right, infringes on other's sovereignty? Behaves self-centered and arrogant, lies, steals, is cruel, acts vengeful and unconsidered, does not believe in decency and righteous conducts, murders, rapes, and pedophiles, keeps many skeletons in one's closet, and so on?

The crux of the matter is that others should be immune from one's ills, from one's morbid behaviors, and comfortable to benefit from one's kind assistance. Regardless of what one faith is, one needs to believe in the famous maxim, as Confucius stated: "Do not Do unto others what you don't want others Do unto you."

In the meanwhile, it is informing to know what many religions say about the afterlife, which in reviewing various faith-oriented entities, I have noticed that religions have made God's concept of reward and punishment to what mankind imagine and makes it be, making God in man's image, rather than believing that man was made in God's image. the institutional religions constitute the laws of heavens like human's assessment for rewarding, punishing, right or wrong.

They present God as a worldly king that governs through his representatives, ministers, messengers, lecturers, legislative, judicial and executive branches of government, as occasionally retaliatory, or sometimes forgiving. Bottom line, it is most important that state keep away from intermingling with the religion of any kind, and for religion not to infiltrate the government. the state is a legal, earthy entity, and not a heavenly article (to bring someone to a period of service), since the state is responsible for legislative, judicial and executive branches of government to stop wrongdoings, and illegal behaviors. No state should be accountable to make mandatory moral laws, delineate virtuous conducts, and or impose any religious requirements.

No government should interfere to promote religious orientations, or encourage atheism, or dignify secularity. No pope, so the priest, no clergyman of any kind, no mullahs, no rabbi, no monk, nor any other religious head should have merit or priority over others to engage in law.

What should be respected and honored, is the individual right to worship and connect to God in which way one sees fit. An iron-clad of separation between religion and state should be implemented, that needs to be very clear in meaning.

The government cannot make laws that favor one religion over any other, it must not make laws related to the establishment of a religion or the free expression of religious beliefs. What the state should be responsible for, is to exercise contends of the Constitution, and execute the law of the land.

We ought to know that religion is a subject which lies entirely between man and his/her God, that he owes an account to none either for his faith or his homage to his/her God, considering that the legitimate powers of government reach actions only, and not opinions, thus, a wall of separation between state and religion should be built to give the man all of his natural rights, convinced that one has no natural right contrary and opposed to one's social duties.

Most religions and faith-oriented entities emphasis on the influence of divine rewards, and the punishments which stem from man's imagination. A common finding across many cultures is that such doctoring manifests pro-sociability than less or non-religious people who do not believe in an afterlife, and are not foreboding (the feeling that something is going to happen) after we expire. Implicit (implied) religious concepts, or explicit (clearly) said moral declaration and cues (signals) like God, salvation, purgatory, punishment in hell, and rewards of heaven, among many others, rise pro-sociability in religious individuals, groups, or society.

However, such promulgation (creed) and socio-cultural tendency channelized through faith-oriented concepts are mere hypotheses, since the factors underlining such findings are not clear; but it seems the empirical literature encompassing such divine rewards and the fear of punishments in the afterlife are accentuated by many religious customs and traditions that are playing a significant role in pro-sociability.

The objective should hinge on finding the best alternatives for a better living, prioritizing plans which can accommodate people with basic necessities in this life to avoid dismay (very worried, sinking feelings) and crimes, rather than relinquishing unrealistic promises, and in giving believers hope of unsubstantiated claims of afterlife rewards. To let the inhabitants of planet Earth live in peace and not prejudice against viable social welfare which if practiced can constitute good living as it is meant to be for everyone, and not just glorified living for the few, the oligopoly regime, and their gangs.

Religions need to stop belittling an infinite God since no physical, no revival (resurrection), and no being of any kind should define God, as no one has ever seen or talked to God since the Almighty has always existed, as an infinite essential, an infinite priority beyond the space, time, and motion, where no past, present, or future was ever initiated.

The limitless God is over the grasp of any mortal, is so space-less, boundless, timeless, and Omnipresent, which shouldn't be impersonated with any of mankind's attribute, as we are finite beings maneuvering within a limited domain.

Some vital issues in philosophy occur between religious and non-religious people, disclosing whether atheism can better resonate with the ethical environment and for morality to flourish, or theism is more vibrant in accomplishing such task. Theists often debate that Godless views are exhausted of fundamental objective referencing moral virtues which the end result will be immorality and hedonism believing that pleasure or happiness is the most imperative goal in life.

Many atheists and humanists have debunked the theist's view saying that what is presented by religions as moral foundations are functionaries partially rooted in self-interest, which promises divine rewards, for instant eternal euphoria (rapture, bliss, ecstasy), and forever torments promising inferno, which both heaven and hell are as recompense for heaven and acting good, and hell for ill-behaving. In the meanwhile, extensive research shows that what theologians and religious apologists say seems to be true, since many investigative reports have found that religious people behave morally prosocial than less or non-religious individuals.

The religious proclivity towards prosocial attitudes and behaviors is not the sole reason behind people's acting prosocial. Socio-cultural, socio-economic perspectives are certainly not solely influenced by religion, since millions of religious and secularly minded individuals are also influenced by education, enlightenment, the power of reasoning, compassion, civility of mind and manner, which play a pivotal role in reigning good and virtuous behaviors.

Secularity is defined as a secular religion is a communal belief system that often rejects or neglects the metaphysical aspects of the supernatural, commonly associated with traditional religions, instead of placing typical religious qualities in earthly entities. It is further doubtful if religion, per se, is the only underlying cause of the increased pro-sociality; since other factors as economy, good role model, healthy environment, and constructive upbringing also play a decisive role in one's pro-sociability; rather, religion is known to exert its effects indirectly by its appeal to simpler cognitive and effective mechanisms.

For example, Judaism concept of righteous living, and what we should expect in the afterlife.

The promulgation (doctoring) of reward and punishment is an inseparable part of every classical catalog of the primal principles of Judaism. In the Hebrew Scriptures, the creed of reward and punishment (individual, national and universal) is of this world. It is considered as self-evident that God rewards the good folks by granting them prosperity and punishes the wicked with ruins.

It should be clear this is what the American leaders had in mind when they established their Declaration of Independence, which says, "We hold these truths to be self-evident, that all men are created equal, that they are endowed by their Creator with certain unalienable Rights, that among these are Life, Liberty and the pursuit of Happiness." Finally reaching the view that in the end virtue is its own reward, and vice its own punishment.

Most worldviews must accept their belief in the afterlife on untested faith, but the Christian faith believes in the pursuits that first the resurrection of Christ and the testimony of God's Word, accepting that the Bible renders the true view of what occurs after death. Even though many Christians miscomprehend the afterlife.

Some believe that they become one of the angels, others say they go into a state of soul sleep, while some believe they will be floating on clouds playing harps. Christians can be assured that death is not something to be feared. Instead, at death, we will leave our body and are ascended to the next home in heaven.

Believers will be saved through the resurrection of Jesus our Lord. There are differing perspectives on death since the existence of mankind, humanity has wrestled with the question, what occurs after death? What we believe happens after we expire has great innuendos (implication) for our life here on Earth. Even though millions avoid the issue, we ought to sooner or later address the question.

There are many challenging answers to this inquiry. Non-believers, atheists say that at one's death, one ceases to exist. They do not believe in an afterlife or eternal soul and reject any spirit that continues in eon (eternity, the blue moon). They insist on the inevitable death of mankind and the eventual ending of the universe, where there is no meaning or any purposeful life to hope for.

Referencing the pantheistic view, it indicates that one goes through a continuous cycle of reincarnation until the cycle is broken and the person unifies with the divine. What form, what kind of quality life expectancy should endorse the person depends on how one behaved in the previous life?

Further pantheistic belief is that after unification with the divine, one ceases to exist, as the person becomes part of the divine spirit, the life force as if a drop of water reuniting with the ocean. One that believes in pantheism sees God in the entire world around one. Pantheism belief that the entire universe is in its idea of God.

The doctrine of pantheism believes that God is all around us, throughout the whole universe. Pantheism sees everything as being interconnected, as the believers see lack of separation between God, people, and things, they rather see all there is as being interconnected. Pantheism refers to a belief in all gods from all religions, insists on acceptance and tolerance for those beliefs. In Greek, *pan* means all and *Theos* means God.

Those who keep up with the animistic (the belief that natural objects, natural phenomena, and the universe itself possess souls, the belief that natural objects have souls that may exist apart from their material bodies, The understanding that natural objects such as rivers and rocks possess a soul or spirit), or tribal religions which believe that after death the person's soul stays on the Earth, or travels to approach the departed spirits of the ancestors in the underworld, also known as the realm of the shadows.

For eternity they ramble (meander, wander) in darkness, experiencing neither joy nor suffering and pain. Some of the spirits of the dead may be called upon to aid or torment (harm) those on Earth. Some of the most prominent faith do have a common denominator which they are based on, shedding light on the influences in the agendas they respectively share.

Let's start with Zoroastrianism, which is an ancient Persian faith believed to have initiated as early as 4,000 years ago. Probably the world's first monotheistic religion, it's one of the oldest religions still in existence. Zoroastrianism was the state religion of three Persian dynasties, until the Muslim conquest of Persia in the seventh century AD. Zoroastrian refugees, called Parsis, escaped Muslim persecution in Iran by migrating to India.

Zoroastrianism is still practiced today as a minority religion in parts of Iran and India. The prophet Zoroaster (Zarathustra in ancient Persian) is considered as the founder of Zoroastrianism. It's possibly the world's oldest monotheistic faith. Most of what is known about Zoroaster comes from the Avesta—a collection of Zoroastrian religious scriptures. It's ambiguous precisely when Zoroaster may have lived.

Many scholars and historians believe he was a contemporary of Cyrus the Great, a Persian king of the sixth century BC., though most linguistic and archaeological evidence points to an earlier date—sometime between 1500 and 1200 BC. Zoroaster is believed to have been born in what is now northeastern Iran or southwestern Afghanistan. He might have lived in a tribe that pursued an ancient religion with many Gods (polytheism). This religion was probably similar to early forms of Hinduism.

Based on Zoroastrian practice, Zoroaster had a divine vision of a supreme being while participating in a pagan (heathen, idolatrous) purification rite at age 30. Zoroaster started teaching followers to worship a single God called Ahura Mazda. Zoroastrianism formed one of the ancient world's largest empires—the mighty Persian Empire. It was the state religion of three major Persian dynasties.

Cyrus the Great, founder of the Achaemenid Persian Empire, was a devout Zoroastrian. By all means, Cyrus the Great was a tolerant ruler who let his non-Iranian subjects to practice their own religions.

He ruled by the Zoroastrian law of Asha (truth and righteousness) but didn't force Zoroastrianism on the people of Persia's takeover territories. In Zoroastrianism, Ahura Mazda has an adversary called Angra Mainyu (meaning destructive spirit).

Angra Mainyu is the originator of death and all that is evil in the world. Ahura Mazda, who is perfect, abides in Heaven, whereas Angra Mainyu dwells in the depths of Hell. Also within his religion, Zoroaster taught the existence of angels, demons, and saviors, ideas that can also be found in Christianity, Judaism, and Islam. Zoroastrians use the Avesta as their sacred text. The Avesta contains hymns, rituals, and spells against demons.

Some scholars say that credo (tenets, canon law, dogma) of Zoroastrianism assisted to form the major Abrahamic religions—including Judaism, Christianity, and Islam—via the influence of the Persian Empire. Zoroastrian ideas, including the concept of a single God, heaven, hell, and a day of judgment, may have been originally introduced to the Jewish community of Babylonia, where people from the Kingdom of Judea had been living in captivity for decades; hence, Judaism very much influenced with the notions of Zoroastrianism.

When Cyrus conquered Babylon in 539 BC, he freed the Babylonian Jews. Many went back home to Jerusalem, where their offspring (descendants) helped to make the Hebrew Bible. Judaism and the afterlife. Traditional Judaism staunchly (faithfully) believes that death is not the end of human existence. However, since Judaism is originally focused on life here and now rather than on the afterlife, Judaism does not have many credos (confessions, tenets, canon laws) about the afterlife, and leaves it up to individual opinion.

Comparably for an Orthodox Jew to accept that the souls of the righteous dead ends in heaven, like Christian heaven, or they are reincarnated through many lifetimes, or they wait until the arrival of the Messiah, is when they will be resurrected.

Likewise, Orthodox Jews say that the souls of the wicked are tormented by demons of their own creation, or that wicked souls are destroyed at death, simply ceasing to exist. Either way, there is explicit evidence in the Torah believing in existence after death, in which the righteous will reunite with their loved ones after death, where the evil ones will be prohibited from the reunion.

The punishment is indicated to as literally cutting off, which means cut off from his people This is normally translated as spiritual excision, believing that the soul loses its portion in the world to come. What distinguished the Pharisees (intellectual ancestors of Rabbinical Judaism) from the Sadducees is the eventual belief in the resurrection of the dead, since the Sadducees rejected the idea of the resurrection, which is a fundamental belief of traditional Judaism.

The Sadducees stated the concept of resurrection was not explicitly mentioned in the Torah, as the Pharisees claimed the notion implied in some verses as it was founded in the Torah.

The resurrection of the dead will happen in the messianic age, a time indicated to in Hebrew as the Olam Ha-Ba, the World to Come, but that term is also utilized to show the spiritual afterlife. When the Messiah arrives to originate the perfect world of peace and prosperity, the righteous dead will be sent back for the living and given the position to experience the perfected world, where the demonic dead will not be resurrected.

Reincarnation is also part of Judaism. Some sources state that reincarnation is a routine process, while others say it only occurs in abnormal circumstances, where the soul left unfinished business behind. Belief in reincarnation is also one way to describe the traditional Jewish belief that every Jewish soul in history was present at Sinai and complied to the covenant with God. (Another explanation: that the soul exists before the body, and these unborn souls were present in some form at Sinai.)

Why is Mount Sinai important? The biblical Mount Sinai is one of the most important sacred places in the Jewish, Christian, and Islamic religions. According to the Hebrew Bible, it was the mountain where God gave laws to the Israelites. Christians settled upon this mountain in the third century AD. Belief in reincarnation is normally held by many Chasidic sects, as well as some other mystically inclined Jews. The spiritual afterlife is known in Hebrew as Olam Ha-Ba (oh-LAHM hah-BAH), the World to Come, also referred to as messianic age. The Olam Ha-Ba is another, higher state of being.

However, Jews certainly believe that one's place in the Olam Ha-Ba is decided by a merit system based on one's actions, not by who you are or what religion you profess. Plus, Judaism believes that humanity has the competency of being regarded as righteous in God's eyes, or at least good enough to merit paradise after an appropriate time of purification. In Hebrew faith the place for spiritual reward and righteous people is at (Gahn, the Garden of Eden) which those with spiritual perfection end up, many compare the peace, the bliss of afterlife to the joy of sex or the warmth of a wonderful sunny day.

Eventually, the mortals can no more comprehend the nature of such promised land than the blind can realize color, since those dead will be estranged to such notion as heaven. Only the very righteous go directly to GAN EDEN. The average person descends to a place of punishment and/or purification, generally known as Gehinnom (hell). According to one mystical view, every sin one commits makes an angel of destruction (a demon), and then when we expire, we are punished by the very demons that we made. Some views decipher Gehinnom as one of severe punishment, a bit like the Christian Hell of fire and brimstone.

Other sources solely see it as a time when we can see the activities of our lives objectively, become aware of the harm that we have done and the chances we missed to do good, and render remorse for our actions. The limit of time in Gehinnom does not exceed twelve months, and then one ascends to be situated in Olam Ha-Ba.

Only the absolutely wicked do not rise at the end of this period; their souls are punished for the entire twelve months. Sources vary on what takes place at the end of those twelve months: some say that the demonic soul is completely destroyed and ceases to exist, while others say that the soul carries on to exist in a state of consciousness of contrition (regretful, remorse.) Christian views on after death.

The Bible teaches that when we take our last breath, our spirit (soul) will exit the physical body. Then we quickly receive the judgment, which decides our forever destiny. Those who have believed in Christ's being crucified for our sins will enter into eternal life in the presence of God. 2 Corinthians 5:8 states, "We are confident, I say, and would prefer to be away from the body and at home with the Lord." There will be no hesitancy in a state of unconsciousness many call soul sleep. We will instantaneously be in God's presence.

Then, the soul in heaven is made cleansed and unerring (perfect) in holiness and all of our previous sins are wiped out and eradicated. Hebrews 12:23 mentions the spirits of righteous men made perfect. The spirits of the saints are in heaven and they have been made perfect.

The battle with our sin that Paul explained and all Christians face terminating forever after death, as we enter our revered position. Those who deny this blessing will receive what they have chosen, eternity segregated from God in Hell. Hebrews 9:27 states, "Just as man is destined to die once, and after that to face judgment." There wouldn't be a second chance and there isn't any reincarnation. Our eternal fate is decided by the decision we make for Christ here on Earth.

Many presume that after receiving Jesus Christ, all that behold the believer is a blissful entrance into heaven. Scripture instructs that Jesus will reward us relating to how we have lived our life on Earth since Jesus taught us about the axiom and the essence of life in parables.

Each servant was mandated to supervise the talents the master rendered to him. Upon the return of the master, each servant had to give an account for his stewardship (leadership). The wise servants were prized doubly while the wicked servant was removed. Paul said that Christ is our substratum (foundation).

Our works are the making on this foundation. The materials of gold, silver, and precious stones refer to activities done with pure motives for the glory of God. The works of wood, hay, and straw are works done with the wrong motives to praise oneself. The unbeliever will be judged and sentenced to hell. At the end of the time, one faces the Great White Throne judgment. Here, all the unrighteous dead from the beginning of time are judged because of their denial of the Savior Jesus Christ They are then cast into the lake of fire for eternity.

In many religions and folklores (mythology), Hell is an afterlife place, often a location of pain and punishment. Religions with an additive divine background often delineate(describe) hells as eternal destinations while religions with a cyclic history often represent hell as an intermediary (mediator, a link) period between incarnations.

Typically, these traditions locate hell in another dimension or under the Earth's surface, and occasionally include the gate of entry to Hell from the land of the living. Other afterlife destinations include Heaven, Purgatory, Paradise, and Limbo. Other cultures which do not think of the afterlife as a place of punishment or reward, solely see Hell as an abode of the dead, the grave, a neutral location under the surface of Earth (for instance namely Sheol and Hades).

11

WHAT WILL WE BE LIKE IN HEAVEN?

After the soul is departed from the body, it expeditiously enters into the presence of the Lord. Noticing Paul's words in 2 Corinthians 5:8, he says, "We are confident, I say, and would prefer to be away from the body and at home with the Lord." The soul in heaven is made perfect in holiness and our old sin nature is eradicated. As discussed above, Hebrews 12:23 mentions the spirits of righteous men made perfect. The soul of the saints is in heaven and they have been made perfect.

The battle that Paul and all Christians have with sin terminates forever when we after death enter our exalted state. Christianity professes that we will not stay in heaven as a soul with nobody, but rather at God's designated time, there will be a final resurrection where the soul will unite with the body. Philippians 3:20-21 says, "And we eagerly await a savior from there, the Lord Jesus Christ, who, by the power that enables him to bring everything under his control, will transform our lowly bodies so that they will be like his glorious body." 1 John 3:2 promises, "But we know that when he appears, we shall be like him, for we shall see him as he is."

By these two passages, we realize that extolled (glorified) bodies will be akin to that of Christ. We will not be deified, but we will have the same qualities of His revival body. First, our heavenly bodies will be our eulogized (celebrate) earthly bodies. Christ's body that perished on the cross was the same one that was resurrected.

His glorified body was able to permeate through walls, appear suddenly, and ascend to heaven. 2 Corinthians 5:1 reads, "[W]e have a building from God, an eternal house in heaven, not built by human hands." The hands of God will make the resurrected body. 1 Corinthians 15:39-40, 42b-43 tells us. The further belief is that all flesh is not the same. Men have one sort of flesh, animals have another, birds another and fish another. There are also heavenly bodies and there are earthly bodies, but the grandeur (greatness) of the heavenly bodies is one kind and the splendor (grandeur) of the earthly bodies is another.

The body that is perishable, is raised imperishable; it is sown in disgrace, it is raised in honor; it is sown in weakness, it is raised in strength; it is sown a natural body, it is raised a spiritual body.

In responding to the mockers of the resurrection, Paul describes that our heavenly bodies will possess flesh that is of a different variety than our earthly ones. They will be bodies of flesh, but as different from our earthly bodies as humans are from animals. We further conclude that, like a seed, the body will be planted or buried and then one day be lifted to life. It is buried in death, decay, weakness, and disgrace.

When it is revived, it will be changed in every way. It is raised imperishable, glorious, powerful, and spiritual. We will then have eternal, permanent, and perfected bodies. We then will maintain our identities. In Luke 16:23, Lazarus, the rich man, and Abraham all retained their identity. Imagine, one day we will no longer battle with the weakness of sin, sickness, and aging. A great future is in store for those in Christ.

Some even go further and actually profess that they see themselves playing golf for eternity, while others envision the divine souls floating on clouds strumming harps of gold. Although great thoughts, they deficit the glorious future that actually becomes those that await Christ. We are told relatively little about what activities will occur in heaven. We are only given a brief view of our life to come.

Islamic view of after death.

Death in Islam is the ending of worldly living and the beginning of afterlife. Death is grasped as departing soul from the body, and its transfer from this world to the afterlife. There are several elaborate schools of thoughts approaching life after death. But it is not clear what exactly occurs after one dies, since various conclusions are derived from the Quran and other Islamic narratives manifesting life after death scenarios.

One outstanding idea is that angel of death which in the Arabic language means Malak-al-Mout shows up at the instance of death to take one's soul out. Bear in mind that the guilty soul is torturously extracted from the sinner's soul, in which the beatific (righteous, angelic, saintly) are treated with comfort and ease. Another concept is that after one's death two angels called Nakir and Munkar will interrogate the dead person and test his or her faith.

The righteous believer will live in peace and comfort with extravagant amenities if the angels are satisfied with one's answers, if not of course sever punishment pursues. Islam teaches that at the end of history, God will judge the works of all men. Those whose good deeds outweigh their bad deeds will enter into paradise. The rest will be consigned to hell. The Koran teaches that in paradise men will be drinking wine and entertained by heavenly maidens and that they may take several of these maidens for their wives.

To believe in the afterlife is one of the six apprentices of faith in the Islamic religion. Still, the home of the deceased, and where do we end up after we expire is very much questionable, since there are many suggestions in many faith-oriented schools of thought, including Islam. Islam faith believes we might go to heaven, hell, in an intermediary state, or even not become awakened until a great resurrection.

What is at stake, it seems that death is apparently not where our life ends, rather a new stage of living in another form will be the case. Islam believes that God has made us go through a testing ground, endowing humanity with the will to choose, and the responsibility to act right or wrong, giving everyone the chance to prepare oneself for the next life to approach where eventually God judges us according to our good, or bad deeds, where death is recognized as the gateway to the next life. In Islam, the precise time of an individual death is not known since only God is aware of the exact time of anyone's termination of life.

A Muslim is expected to utter their last word in this world would be the admittance of the faith by saying I testify that there is no God but Allah, and Muhammad is the messenger of Allah. Bear in mind that those near deaths are encouraged to say these words before expiring, which occasionally is whispered into the ear of the dying. Islamic faith believes that death is accepted as wholly natural. It solely signifies a transition stage from the material world to the invisible heavens or hell, to the unseen realm.

Many modern writers and believers do not adhere to the depiction of painstakingly torturous punishment after death, where traditionalists often manifest. In the Semitic view (of or relating to the language family that includes Hebrew, Arabic, and Phoenician), man is a union of body and soul/spirit. Muslims especially those predispose by Neo-Platonism, Mu'tazila, traditional Islamic theology, Shi'a and Sufis, considered Ruh unrelated human's immortal spirit.

Therefore, they discern between Nafs (*Nafs* is an Arabic word occurring in the Quran, literally meaning self, and has been translated as psyche, ego and Ruh (spirit, soul), the latter surviving death. In Semitic view (of or relating to the language family that includes Hebrew, Arabic, and Phoenician), man is a union of body and soul/spirit. The Quran itself indicates to run, later utilized as designating human's immortal self, not to the soul, but only to Nafs. Muslims especially those predispose by Neo-Platonism, Mu'tazila, traditional Islamic theology, Shi'a and Sufis, considered Ruh unrelated human's immortal spirit. Therefore, they discern between Nafs.

After being interrogated, depending on the position of the soul, the deceased will experience different journeys. The sinners or the atheists will meet the harsh angels or even the Zabaniyya to take stand in front of him. Then, they advise the soul to come out and appear to the wrath of God.

Being terrified, the soul grievously tries to conceal itself in the body, refusing to extract voluntarily, thereupon, the angels of death commence beating the soul and drag it from the body in a most excruciating way. The painful process of taking out a sinner's soul has been compared with the dragging of an iron skewer through moist wool, tearing the veins and sinews. The soul of the sinner is then wrapped in a filthy cloth which exudes a bad smell. Taking the soul, the angels head towards heaven. On the way, other angels ask about this wicked soul. They are informed this is the soul of that and that sinner person. The angels then arrive at the upper heaven, which is not opened for the evil soul. Eventually, the soul is then thrown into hell or underworld, where it is punished until the Day of Judgment.

The entire scenario alters when a righteous believer dies; glowing-faced angels descend from heaven with divine perfume and cloak (shroud.) Then the angels of death appear and instruct the soul to come out to face the goodness and mercy of God. The soul is then removed as simply as water pours out from the pitcher.

The soul is then wrapped in the perfumed shroud and is ascended to the seventh heaven where God declares: write down his name in Aala'Illiyin and take him back to Earth. I created him from the Earth, and I will raise him the second time from this very Earth. The soul is then pushed back into the body and is questioned by two angels called Munkar and Nakir.

He passes in answering the questions and is blessed with heavenly rewards. Barzakh also retains some resemblance to the Christian concept of limbo, containing some of the souls, which neither go to heaven or to hell, but remain in the grave. It is reminded that the martyrs—persons who die on the way of God—always bypasses Barzakh and the trial of the death angels and go straight to paradise without being questioned.

The Quran redundantly discusses the subject of death. Death is inevitable, no one can escape it since it will reach everyone. Those who deny resurrection and afterlife, and thus challenge God, the Quran challenges them by saying that why these people then do not put back the soul which has reached the throat (of the dying person) and is about to run-off from the body. It also states that when death nears the sinners and disbelievers, and they sense the approaching chastisement, they plead to return to life so that they can do some good deeds, but this will never happen.

The most frequently quoted verse of the Quran referencing death is: Every soul shall taste death, and only on the Day of Judgment will you be paid your full recompense. Elsewhere, the Quran urges mankind: "And die not except in a state of Islam" because "Truly, the religion in the sight of Allah is Islam" Other verses linked to this issue are: "He (Allah) who created death and life, so that He may test you as to which of you is better in deeds. And He is the All-Mighty, the Most-Forgiving" "Certainly, they see it (resurrection) as distant, but We see it as near".

Sufism is a mystical branch within Islam, also known as Tasawwuf or Faqr according to its followers. Sufism and its philosophical custom may be linked to both Sunni Islam and Shia Islam. It has been proposed that Sufism emerged from the Middle East in the eighth century, but believers are now found in many parts of the world. According to Sufism, part of the Islamic teaching deals with the purification of the inner self and is the way which wipes out all the veils between divine and man.

It was estimated 1000 CE (Common Era) and as for BCE (Before Common Era) and for BC (Before Christ) mean the same thing-previous to year 1 CE (Common Era). This is the same as the year AD 1 (Anno Domini); the latter means in the year of the lord, often translated as in the year of our Lord.

Early Sufi literature, in the form of textbooks, dissertation, discourses, and poetry, became the source of Sufi way of life, thinking patterns, and meditations. Sufi philosophy, similar to all another major philosophical modus operand (practice, habit, tradition) has several sub-branches including metaphysics and cosmology as well as other unique concepts.

History of Sufism.

The apparition (emergence) of Sufism is commonly connected to the historical developments of the Middle East in the seventh and eighth centuries subsequent to the life of Prophet Mohammad, and its expansion which took place throughout the centuries after that. Amid the tenth and twelfth centuries, Sufism became a widely spread discipline. One of the most influential early writers on Sufi philosophy was Al-Ghazali (1058–1111). He debated the concept of the self and the reasons of its misery and the causes of its happiness. By the end of the thirteenth century, Sufism had become a well-defined, well-known science of spiritual awakening throughout the Islamic World, an Islamic Golden Age.

No vital domain in the civilization of Islam remained untouched by Sufism in this period. Several tariqahs (Sufi orders) were found. In the meanwhile, a class of prominent Sufi philosophers, theologians, and jurists such as Hankari, Ibn Arabi, Abu Saeed Mubarak Makhzoomi, led this age who taught and produced the historical embodiment of philosophers and geniuses worldwide like Al-Ghazali, Avicenna, etc. An important mark made in the history of Sufi philosophy has been made by Abdul Qadir

Jilani with his jurisprudence and philosophy of Sufism that made him explain the Sufi orders.

Jilani's adopted order was Qadiriyya and the offshoot he started later became known as Sarwari Qadiri. Several other orders were also exposed in this era. Sufis were influential in spreading Islam especially to the furthest garrisons (outposts) of the Muslim world in Africa, flooded south Asia, India and the Far East. Sufism has a history in India evolving for over 1,000 years. The presence of Sufism has been under Persian influence, Sufi thought, syncretic values, literature, education. syncretic values mean Syncretism is the synthesis of various beliefs, while alloying (blending) practices of various schools of thought.

Syncretism (religious syncretism exhibits blending of two or more religious belief systems into a new system, or the incorporation into a religious tradition of beliefs from unrelated traditions), also happens commonly in idioms (expression, phrase) of arts and culture familiar as eclecticism (the practice of deriving ideas, style, or taste from a broad and diverse range of sources.

SUFI Metaphysics

The major concept in Sufi metaphysics has encompassed the notion of Vahdat or Unity with God. Two main Sufi philosophies prevail on this divisive topic. Vahdat-ul-Vojood (Unity of Being) intrinsically (inherently) says that the only truth within the universe is God and that all things exist solely within God. Vahdat-ul-Shuhud (Apparentism, or Unity of Witness), on the other hand, maintains that any participatory of unity between God and the world is only in the mind of the believer and that God and his creation are completely apart. Vahdat-ul-Vojood is the position where there is no difference between God and human being who is trying to obtain a particular state (i.e., 'No One Except God').

The concept of Sufi Metaphysics was first insightfully debated in writing by Ibn Arabi in one of his most fruitful (prolific) works known as Fusus al hikam. Ibn Arabi shows detail analysis on the subject of Oneness through the metaphor of the mirror. In this metaphor, al-Arabi compares an object being cogitated(reflected) in countless mirrors to the relationship between God and his creatures.

God's essence is witnessed (seen) in the existent human being, as God is the object and humans being the mirrors. Meaning two things, that since humans are mere reflections of God there can be no distinction or separation between the two and without God the creatures would be non-existent.

When an individual realizes that there is no segregation between human and God, they start on the path of ultimate oneness. This metaphysics of Sufi philosophy is also narrated (related) in the hadith: Whoever recognized his self, undoubtedly recognized his Rab (Allah).

Baha'i faith, the soul and the afterlife.

In Baha'i religion the soul is regarded not to be subject to natural law; rather, it is subject to spiritual law as a bond between man and God and it appears at the conception of the embryo. Heaven is within the vicinity of God, a soul being close to God, not a location, but a condition, as it ensures an eternal spiritual evolution.

Anyone who adapts and exercise virtues and guidance of God goes to heaven. Hell is being far from God, not a place, but of weakness to understand and practice virtues and guidance from God. Improvement from the worst situation is potentiated even in the next world, but one must Grass-Rooty overcome repelling (repulsive) Godly virtues. Religious labels we are known for, and theologies we are proud to be part of, are not as imperative as the reality of spiritual virtues like freedom, honor. Compassion, courage, justice, love, understanding, etc., which are the choices we make in our lives.

The Baha'i religion believes heaven is a condition more than a place, it is a realm where those who are close to God are also good to each other. It is true that the individual undergoes dramatic changes from birth and the stages of life in this life, then death and life beyond, Bahaism hold it like that the same soul will go through dramatic changes of circumstances. However, they believe life in this world and beyond are actually interwoven since womb of this life and the afterlife are interwoven. It's not like moving to a distant place; the afterlife is also here, but invisible to those living on Earth. Death is about letting go of the physical frame and its demands and has no real identity by itself.

The information about the afterlife is essentially bounded in this life. It is said that the next life is fundamentally different in many ways from this life. The parallel is made when contrasting life in the womb with this life, and the changes after birth, to the changes after death. Realities of the latter are not accessible even as ideas in the former; they are ineffable (unspeakable, unexplainable). The concept of a body in the next world is still present but it is a heavenly body. There is a realm of lights and reunion with descendants (expired) associates.

The sanctity of human nature is confirmed when free from the constraints, it reflects the light of God and the truths of existence become known and fear of death is conquered, and universal acceptance of the religions as coming from one source.

The life of the person initiates at conception when the soul relates itself with the embryo. When a death occurs, the physical body returns to the world of dust, while the soul carries on to progress in the spiritual realms. To consider that after the death of the body the spirit perishes, 'Abdu'l-Bahá has said is like imagining that a bird in a cage will be destroyed if the cage is broken, though the bird has nothing to fear from the destruction of the cage.

Our body is like the cage, and the spirit is like the bird. Once the cage becomes broken, the bird will continue and exist. Its feelings will be even more powerful, its perceptions greater, and its happiness increase. After its association with the body draws to a close, the soul will continue to progress in an eternal journey towards perfection. Bahaullah wrote, "It will manifest the signs of God and His attributes, and will reveal His loving-kindness and bounty."

An illumined spirit continues to have a predispose(influence) on progress in this world and the advancement of its peoples. It acts as "the leaven that leaveneth the world of being, and furnisheth the power through which the arts and wonders of the world are made manifest."

The world beyond, writes Baha'u'llah, is as different from this world as this world is different from that of the child while still in the womb of its mother. Just as the womb made the atmosphere for a person's beginning physical development, the phenomenal world is the arena within which we develop the spiritual characteristics and potentials. that we need for our forward journey.

Both here and in the next life, we propel with the assistance of God's bounty and grace. Also vital to the progress of our souls in the next realm are the good deeds carried out in our names here on Earth. known in this light, death is not to be feared. Bahaullah refers to it as a messenger of joy." He declared that: "Thou art My dominion and My dominion perisheth not; wherefore fearest thou thy perishing? Thou art My light and My light shall never be extinguished; why dost thou dread extinction? Thou art My glory and My glory fadeth not; thou art My robe and My robe shall never be outworn."

Mourning, the suffering and anguish of the absence of contact with family members, friends and kin for Baha'i's is, aside from cultural issues and norms in society, believed to be as another stage of life; a temporary condition that will be altered someday just as someday the infant in the womb comes into the material world through birth and into the company of family and friends. Not avoiding the sense of loss, Bahaullah accentuates the sense of mystery in death, mentioning that The Mysteries of man's physical death and of his return have not been divulged, and still remain unread.

Were they to be revealed, they would evoke such fear and sorrow that some would perish, while others would be so filled with gladness as to wish for death, and beseech (solicit, petition, conjure, request) with unceasing longing, the one true God—exalted be His Glory—to hasten (to happen more quickly) their end. Life after death in Hinduism.

Hindus religion believes that humans are in a cycle of death and rebirth known as samsara. Hinduism instructs that via enlightened knowledge the cycle can be broken. Atman means eternal self.

The atman indicates to the actual self beyond ego or false self. It is referred to as spirit or soul, and indicates our true self or essence which forms the foundation for our existence. it is (Sanskrit: self, breath) one of the most fundamental concepts in Hinduism, the universal self, identical with the eternal marrow (mainstay) of the personality that after death either transmigrates to a new life or obtain release (moksha) from the bonds of existence.

Atman alludes to the essence of each individual living thing; its soul or foremost (preeminent, principle) living energy. Each living thing—people, animals, plants—have an atman that makes each thing's eternal essence, is reborn in a different body.

Some say rebirth happens directly at death, others accept that an atman may exist in other realms. Hindus believe that an atman may enter Swarg or Narak for a period before rebirth. Hindus believe in karma or intentional action. Many believe righteous or evil actions in life leading to positive or negative merit, decides the atman's rebirth. Some Hindus believe that humans may be reborn in animal shape, and that rebirth from human to beast form solely happens if an atman has consecutively failed to learn lessons in human form.

Living life according to teachings in the scriptures will eventually lead to moksha. Some Hindu scriptures describe moksha as the atman becoming absorbed with Brahman, from where each atman is believed to originate. Other Hindu scriptures describe moksha as living in the realm of a personal God.

To know moksha, which means liberation, one must first comprehend several other significant ideas in Hinduism—especially, samsara. Samsara is a Sanskrit word that alludes to the cycle of birth, death, and rebirth, to the transformation of the soul from one life form to another. Moksha: Hindus believe that the soul passes through a cycle of successive lives (samsara) and its next incarnation is always dependent on how the previous life was lived (karma).

Moksha is the end of the death and rebirth cycle and is categorized as the fourth and final artha (goal.) Moksha: Moksha is an idea in Hinduism. Reference: Moksha in Hindu religion indicate to liberation from the cycle of births and deaths as human life is understood to be one full of pains and sufferings. Nirvana: Nirvana in Buddhism is known to be a state of mind that is achieved when one arrives at enlightenment.

The ultimate goal of Hinduism is Moksha or liberation (total liberty, total freedom). This is the personal and direct detection of one's true self, which liberates one's from the cycles of rebirth, or Samsara. This realization is termed Nirvikalpa Samadhi and is the totally transcendent zenith (apex, climax, pinnacle, top) of yoga. Atman (Sanskrit: self, breath), one of the most principle concepts in Hinduism, the universal self, identical with the eternal core of the personality that after death either passes to a new life or attains frees (moksha) from the bonds of existence, Moksha.

Hindus believe that the soul transmigrates through a cycle of consecutive lives (samsara) and its next incarnation is always relating to how the previous life was lived (karma). It is a paradox in the sense that subjugating (defeating, overcoming) desires also includes conquering the desire for moksha itself. The Maitri Upanishad states: Even as water becomes one with water, fire with fire, and air with air, so the atman becomes one with the Infinite Atman (Brahman) and thus attains final freedom. Maitri Upanishad.

What Buddhism believe happens after death.

Buddhism believe that as human beings we have a rare opportunity to try to escape the cycle of samsara. The escape from samsara is known as Nirvana or enlightenment. Once Nirvana is obtained and the enlightened individual physically dies, one will no longer be reborn. However, one's remaining in heaven is not eternal—eventually, they will use up their good karma and will undergo rebirth into another realm, as a human, animal or another being.

Heaven is temporary and part of samsara, Buddhists concentrates on escaping the cycle of rebirth and reaching enlightenment (nirvana). Relating to the Anatta doctrine of Buddhism, at the essence or core of all human beings and living creatures, there is no eternal, essential and absolute soul, self or atman. Buddhism in its main philosophical and ontological texts has denied the existence of the self, soul.

"The kingdom of heaven is like electricity. You don't see it; it is within you." Maharishi Mahesh Yogi.

12

ARTIFICIAL INTELLIGENCE, AND SINGULARITY

The industrial age, the technological progress, and any further development in Artificial intelligence (AI) is undeniably the by-products of human consciousness, which gradually will reach the pinnacle of invincibility by making miracles, not only in the field of artificial intelligence but through which humanity can peak in the unheard of scientific endeavors, where the unthinkable become the norms, assuming that such harbinger of hope does not stray from fundamental human morality and ethics since we are touching on very sensitive agendas, as we should act conscientiously in prioritizing mental wellness, where human behavioral dynamics need to be prioritized, and not to operate as mechanically robotics.

What we might be missing is that human consciousness is an inseparable part of cosmic energy which is the driving force behind all tangible matters and the motivating force in concept-oriented phenomenons, where thoughts and the infinite potentiality for new discoveries originate.

Artificial Intelligence, in fact, is obviously an intelligence transmitted by conscious subject, an intelligence placed in equipment. It has a clear origin, in fact, in the intelligence of human creators of such equipment. Pope Benedict XVI.

The universe decisive interactivities, and the entire nature's mechanism is without a doubt purposefully designed to relentlessly capture new ideas and propel forward for reaching parallel universes, where magical realms will further witness human's ingenious maneuverability and might.

As for the artificial intelligence, the reality is far less dramatic for now, since advancements in AI is certainly linked to progress in human intelligence, which needs to Grass-Rooty be dealt with for further accomplishments in robotics and affiliated fields. In the meanwhile, directing artificial intelligence towards lessening violent criminal activities, where digital gadgets can sure be enhanced further to report crimes instantaneously since time is of the essence to protect victims by informing legal authorities, as soon as possible to prevent tragic situations.

I am afraid Hollywood mentality, and similar media entities where money-oriented culture carelessly encourage violence has taken over the constructive thoughts and humane behaviors, where dystopias (an imagined state or society in which there is great suffering or injustice, typically one that is totalitarian or post-apocalyptic) is wrongly finger-pointed. the actual causes of people's misery are not correctly identified giving millions the wrong impression for their misfortunes. We further explore the possibilities and challenges revealed by this game-changing technology linking to AI.

Artificial intelligence is the concept of expanding intelligent machines—for instance, computer algorithms which function and react like humans. Applications that exhibit speech recognition, natural language processing and interpretation, visual perception, teaching, learning, reasoning, inference, tactical maneuverability, logic-based strategizing, planning, intuition, and decision-making, etc.

It is an undeniable fact that AI is presently very resourceful from saving lives in medical diagnosis, and in dealing with economics, finance, real estates and for processing of loans and mortgage applications, in the legal system, in complex military industrial services, in aerospace, even in our ordinary living like driving fully automated vehicles, and so on. the AI awesome benefits have motivated many multinational corporations, public and private's companies, governmental entities and states to further invest in developing artificial intelligence for better efficiencies and maximizing productivity.

So far, we are witnessing the expansion of much more efficient and smarter machines, that with no doubt are helping us learn new ways to enhance our living which truly gives meaning to the culture of innovation and modernism. Artificial intelligence is also coherent with algorism through which programmers write computer programs, by telling the computer exactly what the programmer wants. The computer then executes the program, following each step mechanically, to complete the end goal. That's where computer algorithms come in.

The algorithm is the basic technique used to get the job done. An algorithm generates the same output information given with the same input information, where several short algorithms can alloy (synthesize, fuse, blend) to exhibit complex tasks like writing a computer program for simple to complex problem solving through which AI systems ameliorate (make better, revamp) their intelligence.

Also, through AI computer hardware processing power and notable speed have increased, where cloud computing empowers so many to share and incorporate data by developing power all over the world; through which billions of dollars are made by multinational companies giving global businesses a tremendous boost in everyday voice recognition communications.

Artificial intelligence is specially very promising in Robotic and automation processes for handling high demands in various industries like aviation, insurance, surveying, statistics, civil and architectural design, accounting, bookkeeping, speech and facial recognition at sensitive places like the airport and many legal, financial, trade and commerce centers, in political arenas, and many other crucial entities that can be targeted by terrorism, where safety and security extremely matters.

Since automated decision makings with precise calculation and accuracy are raising the reliability and scientific bar to the next level for intricate planning, scheduling, optimization, and even more efficiencies. human based decision making and perhaps erroneous judgment will further diminish the risk of inaccuracies.

Currently, robotics is prevalent in wholesale warehouses, retail management, and in many other diversified arenas; where neural-like networks for artificial intelligence in machinery aims at learning capabilities, matching human brain for customers' interactions via speech production and natural language development making it user friendly and as practical as possible for enhancing communications, and thriving more for the pursuit of excellence in technically oriented environment.

Scientific communities expect future evolution in artificial intelligence in which clarity on the probable progression can create miracle like agendas in sensitive fields like space, auto-piloting, auto vehicle driving, medical and other decisive endeavors to even save more lives, and perhaps discover other inhibitory planets. The AI systems are potentiated to expand expertise in a particular domain that extends beyond the capability of humans because of the sheer volume of information they can access to make each decision.

Some of the key issues are how future machines can be designed with having the mind of their own, where they would possess the mental states to sensibly dialogue with humans and other machines, give advice. For example, having a sense of understandings, beliefs, intentions, knowledge, and how their own logic functions. With having the capacity to reason, negotiate, and perhaps help with a global hunger problem, global warming dilemma, finding a better economic system, and how to better cure challenging diseases.

New governing can be employed to avoid nuclear holocaust in which millions can perish, also conveyed with invigorated (energize) new ideas that experts believe such algorithms (a set of steps that are followed to solve a mathematical problem, or to complete a computer process) are present at the development stage, but we can expect to experience them in the near future.

The notion of superhuman is using bio-engineering and artificial intelligence to upgrade human abilities. If they use the power to change themselves, to change their own minds, their own desires, then we have no idea what they will want to do. Yuval Noah Harari.

In the meanwhile, I am not worried about the machinery outsmarting humans, since no matter how artificial intelligence and automation develops, they still would be the byproducts of the ingenious human brain with advancing mind. It might be a race, but a race which humanity never loses, they simply will not exceed the human mind since intelligence, curiosity, motivation, drive, my, mine and I factor rewards, and other decisive variables fuel our spirit.

We should also be reminded that no sophisticated machinery of any kind is linked to universal energy, where the human mind is an integrated part of. Many worries are lurking that at some point may artificial intelligence and dominance in machinery automation supersede human intelligence, where technology might outsmart us. Not realizing that the human brain is an inseparable part of cosmic energy with infinite opportunity in innovation and progress.

Humans are the only beings with the out of body experience, as they are also self-aware creatures, with conscious, will, curiosity, drive, emotions and feelings, creativity, seeking beauty, are in search of excellence, with purpose and setting goals, with spirit, with soul and thousands of other innate means designated as the only source to lead the life's evolutionary concept.

That we will never be able to capture and digitize human consciousness. Despite the fact that many fervently believe that we can one day reach Singularity and Transcendence—this is the idea that the exponential expansion in technology path can lead to a massive expansion in human capability.

We might in the near future, one day be augmented and improved such that could connect our brains to each other and to a future successor of the current internet. collective mind would let us share ideas, solve problems and render others access to our dreams as observers or participants giving true meaning to hive mind which in (science fiction) means a unified consciousness or intelligence formed by a number of alien individuals, the resulting consciousness typically exerting control over its constituent members.

Further, we might also upscale the limits of the human body and connect to other forms of intelligence on the planet—animals, plants, weather systems, and the natural environment. Even to an extent, where telepathy way of communication can become the norm. There are already plenty of envisioning concepts for a smarter world as many scientists and physicists are working hard to develop them in the arena of quantum life and the subatomic particles which it seems the mysteries of our world lay, that I am certain the artificial intelligence will be of huge scientific leverage for more outstanding inventions.

Despite the recent emergence of artificial intelligence AI, several businesses have already developed numerous applications that can replicate human thoughts, performing superior cognitive and creative tasks. Artificial intelligence has quickly grown from being a distant hope to a casual part of the present reality.

Computer programs capable of performing human-like cognitive and computational tasks without human intervention are rapidly growing in capability as well as ubiquity. Every new AI application that emerges expands the limits of what the technology can achieve, leaving us in awe and excitement for what the future holds. Following are a few mind-blowing applications of AI that will definitely make you reconsider the limits of what's possible:

Identifying Criminal Threats, Machine learning-enabled AI applications are being generated and utilized by law legal authorities in some part of the world to foresee and prevent crimes. Japan is considering the use of AI and big data to anticipate criminal activities, which will enable the law enforcement authorities in Japan to prevent crimes by proactively dispatching patrols to high-risk areas. The application also developed in the USA, France, UK, and China.

Providing Personal Assistance, the most commonplace, and hence the most underrated application of AI, are the Personal AI assistants. Personal AI assistants like Siri and Cortana can not only enable you to operate your phones using your voice but can communicate with you like a human and can even engage in banter (joke, jest, pun, quip) in some cases.

The assistant programs use machine learning to relentlessly gather information on users through interaction and provide them with highly effective results and exclusive responses. AI can be programmed to read people's minds. Scientists have researched and made AI programs that can scan one's brain's blood flow to trace mental activities and detect the thoughts associated with brain activity.

The AI system can detect the picture produced in the subject's mind while looking at actual images. In addition to performing cognitive tasks, AI can also be trained to perform creative tasks. Artificial intelligence that can read people's minds but also their hearts! New AI applications powered by machine learning algorithms and trained utilizes historical data on patients with heart problems can often anticipate the risk of heart attacks better than doctors do, that can save so many lives.

The prominent issue is the position of singularity defined as a point at which a function takes an infinite value, especially in space-time when the matter is infinitely dense, as at the center of a black hole. An imaginary point in time when artificial intelligence and other technologies have become so improved that humanity experiences a noticeable and irrevocable situation.

Furthermore, the singularity is described as the hypothetical future creation of super-intelligent machines. Superintelligence is explained as a technologically created cognitive capacity far beyond that possible for humans. The technological singularity, also simply called the singularity is the hypothesis that the discovery of artificial superintelligence (ASI) will unexpectedly actuate (trigger) level technological progress ending in unfathomable alteration to human civilization as technically manifested cognitive potentiality can go far beyond what is currently foreseen by humans.

As far as existence is a concern, it seems that singularity plays a very decisive role in creation. Kurzweil describes his law of accelerating returns, which anticipates an exponential appreciation in technologies like computers, genetics, nanotechnology, robotics, and artificial intelligence. Once the Singularity has been reached, Kurzweil says that machine intelligence will be infinitely more powerful than all human intelligence combined.

Then, Kurzweil foresees intelligence will radiate outward from the planet until it saturates the universe. The Singularity is also the point at which machines intelligence and humans would merge. As far as a singularity and the existence, it seems that singularity has a lot to do with creation since the explosion of the infinitely focused mass in very tiny point can expand astronomically large as physicists tell us have occurred in the big bang, where life has originated from.

The big bang is an event-like singularity; a black hole is like an object. A catastrophic collapse, such as a massive star imploding in a matter of seconds, will produce an event-like naked singularity. When a naked singularity is event-like, it looks like an explosion. If so, the very fundamental life born energy must have been originated, because of the explosive employment in singularity creating the fertile ground for existence to happen, which if not certainly impregnated with required ingredients for life to incept, no Darwinism evolutionary theory, or any other kind of theory could ever have been possible.

According to general relativity, the modern theory of gravity a puzzling issue is known as a singularity, a region with infinite density is situated at the heart of each black hole where space and time as we know it ceases to exist there.

Scientists believe that in the center of a black hole is a gravitational singularity, a one-dimensional point which conveys tremendous mass in a significantly small space with density and gravitational force becoming infinite as space-time curves limitlessly, where the laws of physics as we know them to cease to function. Also known to physicists that (greater mass in a smaller volume = greater gravitational force exerted).

The theory of general relativity anticipates that a sufficiently intense mass can deform space-time to form a black hole. Singularities are predicted to occur in black holes by Einstein theory of general relativity. The boundary of the region from which no escape is possible is by physicists known as the event horizon.

A wormhole is a theoretical passage through space-time that could create shortcuts for long journeys across the universe. Wormholes are predicted by the theory of general relativity, wormholes bring with them the risk of sudden collapse, high radiation and perilous contact with exotic matters. In the vicinity of the singularity, particles and materials are so squeezed. as matter fall apart into a black hole, its density becomes infinitely large as it must fit into a point which relating to equations, is so small that it has no dimensions.

Stellar-mass black holes are basically in the range of 10 to 100 solar masses, while the supermassive black holes at the centers of galaxies are estimated about millions or billions of solar masses. The supermassive black hole at the center of the Milky Way, Sagittarius A*, is 4.3 million solar masses. The event horizon is where the runaway speed passes the speed of light: one has to be going faster than light (which is impossible for any bit of matter) to get away from the black hole's gravity.

A singularity is what all the matter in a black hole gets crushed into. In general relativity, a white hole is a hypothetical arena of space-time that cannot be entered from the outside, which matter and light can escape from it. The white hole is the reverse of a black hole that can only be entered from the outside, and from which matter and light cannot escape.

13

ECONOMIC MISDEEDS

Western societies are heightening consumer-oriented culture, where the exchange of goods and services are done through capital transactions for maintaining a fair balance between supply and demand. It is extremely essential that investors avoid glut since they unnecessarily can flood the market with a certain product. In the meanwhile, scarcity of an item, and not having enough of something to satisfy demand can create a shortage of certain products. The capitalist's system if not monopolized, then must indulge in creativity and innovation, making it possible to survive in a very competitive environment

Some economists believe that the invisible hand of the market or the laissez-faire economy is best since very little interference of the government is required; which can eventually balance supply and demand, where glut or scarcity could barely occur. Many economists forget the element of greed, as so many investors, and so-called businessmen play devil's advocate to disturb the equilibrium of supply and demand, or the absence of a state to allocate proper resources to designated markets were most required, since so many surreptitiously plan to withhold certain products by hoarding them, to be delivered at later times when most requisite (required) for higher profit, and to maximize wealth.

Let's not forget that human beings by nature can become addicted to what feeds them through force of habit. The issue becomes challenging when the force of habit drives so many people to addiction often to the point of no return. As the atmosphere effects are sure decisive in our upbringing and overall behaviors as we are to a large extent the products of our environment. In a culture where so much emphasis is put on money, I am afraid that becomes a serious problem since eventual addiction leads to greed and hoarding wealth which inevitably takes over, driving all sorts off ills and inhumane conducts, certainly resulting in manufacturing evils because of the hell created. It is a no-brainer to conclude that humanity has to put up with countless violence ending in rampant crimes globally leaving billions to suffer the ugly consequences of a system that has gone mad.

In the midst of such anxiety-driven market some economists act like a frightened mouse which closes his eyes, thinking the cat which is about to devour him is not there. They forget that we live in an environment where self-interest, self-preservation, aggressive behaviors, greed, betrayal, misconducts, and wrongful competition has replaced honesty, ethics, righteousness, and good faith, turning business-oriented markets into the cut-throat atmosphere rather than pursuing the fair and justified monetary transactions.

Obviously, the capitalist's market is not mission-driven, as it is not aiming for serving the fundamental needs of the people, but is to maximize profit at the sufferings of others, it is clear that unless citizens are collectively inoculated to Grass-Rooty pull people's power to harness constructive changes, no positive happenings can ever occur to stop the few global financial monsters, making them to unleash their iron-clad hold on global resources where more than eight billion are supposed to live on.

An unregulated market also has something to with the chaotic outcome which will eventually run so many investors out of presumably competitive position destroying their business, their livelihood, and only for a few to reach the pinnacle of financial invincibility by monopolizing the global market. leaving others behind and with no choice but for millions of businesses to quit this shenanigan of the so-called free enterprise notion that can cause irreparable financial damages, and in making a social disaster, since so many become bankrupt as they lose hope of recovery as they perish, because of multinational corporation's take over.

When the market is left unchecked, unregulated, and exhausted from proper state supervision. Concentration of wealth becomes inevitable by the few since they so irrationally handle the market by hoarding, via market manipulation, through outsourcing jobs, where they can seek cheap raw material, dirt cheap labor resources, dodge taxes, and not playing by the rule of the trade demoralizing (disheartening) the rest to vacate, forcing them into bankruptcy, leaving so many to deal with perilously irreparable criterion and with terrifying consequences.

The culprits are influenced enough to cut through the red tapes, and by kicking one's way up through the hustle and bustle of the market to reach the top. the expression of it is not who you are, but who you know can play in one's favor; or simply because of availability of more funds to afford better technology and skilled labors, compounded with having savvy information.

A decisively dynamic means of production can robustly maneuver to distinguish the winner from the losers; and since failure can often occur because of unanimated strategy, dull planning, and not competent enough to intelligently compete in a radicalized market beyond many entrepreneur's capacities, and many business men's potentials. We live in an era where global economy operated by multi-national corporations directly effects local economies all over the globe.

Natives and even the most primitive tribal communities can financially be deranged by a corporate takeover, and since the living dynamics that the natives are accustomed to become quite challenging, as they are not somehow compensated in any way to adjust to the new criteria. One might think that modern life and integrated groups are always better than tribal communities. But put a human face into a socio-cultural, socio-economic situation since the inhabitants are forced to migrate often to nowhere lands, where families become polarized, not because they want to, but because they have to.

Then, perhaps compassion should kick in to call for some type of Grass-Rooty remedy, where constructive social welfare and reliable monetary programs can be implemented to save human lives before forcing locals out of their ancestral homelands, and confiscate their resources through local governments which often play poppets in the hands of the foreign exploiters, as they mostly are in cahoots with multinational corporations.

The problem does not stop there since many of these natives are called xenophobic, which should alarmingly raise the question that wouldn't anyone behave toxic and acting hateful towards those who destroy their lives, as locals passionately disagree with what happens to them as their tribal identity is denied, and their way of making a living is lost forever without any chance for financial compensation, but to expect imprisonment and torture by the bullying state that governs them. The issue sadly remains that when thousands of local business are-driven out of the market, millions tragically lose their jobs, and their means of livelihood, since they are not able to survive the ugly consequence of wrong political, and economic policies, often wreaking havoc on the entire nation.

The point is that even with the absence of the state-regulatory market, any competitive environment can eventually make some businesses to rapidly thrive, where trade and capitalism can expeditiously expand. The greater the demand, the greater the surplus value (surplus value is a central concept in Karl Marx's critique of political economy. According to Marx's theory, surplus value is equal to the new value created by workers in excess of their own labor-cost, which is appropriated by the capitalist as profit when products are sold). Business productivity peaks, creating immense wealth, leaving the market vulnerable to monopoly.

"In an effort to eliminate the possibility of any rival growing up, some monopolists would sacrifice democracy itself."

— Henry Wallace

Material based societies encourage dreaming big, manufactures perceptual anomalies, dramatic (theatrical) episodes, and maddening temptation, but at whose expenses other than the victims, when millions lose everything by taking the uncalculated risk, as so many do not act diffidence (modest) but emboldened with a trap like a mentality to reach an unrealistic goal. One should acquire leading information through correct competitive market analysis, dynamic strategies, robust planning, devoted experienced crew, knowledgeable personals, reliable partners, professional management, expert book-keeping, and adept accountant.

Dreaming big, glamorizing hype, irrational exuberance and pursuing what is beyond one's means become the very elements of destruction for millions. Capitalist's system is fundamentally designed to have differentiated class. Building up few tycoons, creating an oligopolistic class, where they live opulent living, beyond anyone's imagination, and leaving so many with economic depravity, as billions globally cannot even afford to live beneath the poverty line.

The stratified socio-economic system so unjustly maneuvers that the class system nonetheless bothers to shed light on how global social layers are faring. Let's start with the aristocrats who live by hereditary wealth as they enjoy the high social station. They behave as the common man is indebted to them as ordinary people should pay their dues to the privileged elites, and the gentry class. According to dictionary, aristocracy is defined as a form of government that places power in hands of a small, privileged ruling class, like for example Saudi Arabia, England, Spain, Belgium, Norway, Sweden, Brunei.

Further, the capitalist's society is classified as the upper class, the middle class, the working class, the working poor, the poverty level, and of course billions who live beneath the poverty line. The upper class, which makes up about one percent of the world population, generally consists of those with vast inherited wealth (sometimes called old money). Members of the upper class are such as Rockefeller, DuPont, Walton's, Forbes family, Kennedy, and others. The newcomers with new money are people like Jeff Bezos. Bill Gates, Warren Buffet, Bernard Arnault and family, Mark Zuckerberg, Amancio Ortega, Carlos Slim Helu and family, Charles Koch, also others with new money are people like Oprah Winfrey, Michael Jordan, and other celebrities.

The category known as new money is a relatively new grade on the social ladder and comprises about twelve to fourteen percent of the population. New money includes people whose wealth has been with them only for a generation or two. Also indicated as the nouveaux riches (French for newly rich), they have made their money rather than inheriting it. Unlike the traditional upper class, they do not have a family link with old money. The newly rich do not have every day financially stressful concerns that often plague the rest of society.

"There is nothing noble in being superior to your fellow men. True nobility lies in being superior to your former self."

Ernest Hemingway

I am afraid extreme inequality results in bleak outcomes for so many poverty-driven people; that is pitiful, since there are no reliable social programs, and financial safety nets to save those needy, and the destitute that are struggling to survive. We should realize that capitalist's society is confluence with symbolism, since in every field of endeavor only symbolic few can and are apt to reach the pinnacle of success, and leaving others behind, which in some cases most victims have thrived their entire life to objectify dreams, but to no avail.

They are gullible enough to fall into the trap, as they become tempted, and lured into what is beyond their means to accomplish. Typically, the capitalists socio-cultural, and socio-economic agendas destabilize people mentally, pushing them to behave unrealistically. It puts people on the edge of a high-rise and encourages them to jump as if the standpoint is right, and one can land safely without any parachute training, or with no flying equipment's. Unfortunately, so many flies to their death, landing on a concrete and hard floor without any protection. only is a miracle, if one in thousands can occasionally land on a soft material, cushioned and elastic enough to bounce back to safety.

For thousands of years, profits of God, creeds, sages, and the scholarly minded people have relentlessly advised practicing modesty, and against desiring the impractical; they have insisted on equilibrium and in safeguarding balance; they have persisted on compassion and kindness, and they have preached against the obsession with the material world. But then, when looking at the mechanism of monetary, and fiscal policies, and the way the entire capitalist's system operates.

It encourages the exact opposite, and of course for so many to pay the dire price with ill-consequences, often paying with their very own lives, and sometimes so senselessly taking other people's life. Regrettably, so many apparently do not learn any valuable lesson from the misconducts of such wrongful, and morally dysfunctional system. The psychotic behaviors further happen when corporations, the big boys and their goons label those who dare to talk about redistribution of wealth as socialists and radicals.

They are adamant to subsist regardless of harms done to citizens, as they tempt consumers via calculated schemes and relentless advertising tactics which lures people into buying spree as if there is no tomorrow. They utilize extremely effective techniques in commercialism where buyers subconsciously are cornered into acting by instinct, behaving as their will to make sensible decisions become hostage as the consumers become the victims of their own dull decision makings, and in acting like zombies (someone who moves around as if unconscious and being controlled by someone else), ill-responding to crucially decisive matters in their lives.

They become conditioned to behave on impulse since they purchase what they often do not need, making them unable to prioritize, not competent enough to allocate funds adequately. leaving millions with no money available to pay for what they might urgently need because they have already hoarded what they did not need. Regrettably, so many repeatedly pay a dire price, since they must sell what they need for the mistake of buying what they did not need; but avails the businessman a great deal of profit, and of course with luxurious living. "If a free society cannot help the many who are poor, it cannot save the few who are rich." ~ John F. Kennedy.

The problems of the world that we live in, not only include extreme income inequality, and astronomical wealth accumulation. But also immigration, populism, sustainability, peacekeeping, the formation of bubbles in financial markets, or with the global warming, the threats of atomic bombs, wars of aggression, genocide, fascism and dictatorial behaviors, unbearable violence with extreme criminal activities, etc.

Malaise as such need to be watched, it has to be measured, and they should be predicated in terms of ill-consequences. requires an international body, a super-national entity, to watchdog for decisive issues that are out of balance, to prevent lopsided behaviors. we have reached the age of maturity since technology has broken and made the boundaries collapse, making it easy to notice cries of the victims from all over the world, by which many are vigilant, making it a blessing for noticing injustice and in fighting back against it.

14

HUMAN BRAIN AND MIND

Is the brain the cause for our mind, or vice-versa? The fact is that the brain as matter does not exist, what exists as the substantive brain is energy-driven, and for sure not a dull entity with low-frequency rate. It is quite obvious that the human brain by far the most sophisticated product, is dynamic in nature, resourcefully animated, notably energy oriented, and in line with the spirit of the universe, and the immaterial mind.

Traditionally, scientists referred to mind as the consequence of our brain activity, regarding it as a physical substance, saying that the mind is the result of brain firing cells (neurons), but contemporary arguments are that our mind goes far beyond physical activities of the brain. in comparison, most animals are with lower frequency rate brain, and not as robustly as the human brain that is extremely versatile, a consciously based entity, potentiated with a great deal of plasticity.

Yes, the brain is a tangible organ that controls all imperative human functions, but unless it was also energy oriented, it would not be able to accord within the energy-related atmosphere, to vigorously dialogue with our senses, as the brain is an inseparable part of our entire nervous system. In retrospect, our mind percolates (pervade, impregnate) every cell in our body and coordinates with every part to produce action and for what we must do to survive, empowered by the brain which has dominion over our lives.

We know that our senses literally interact with the environment that we live in, as our five senses of seeing, hearing, smelling, tasting, and touching collect information, and data less than a blink of an eye, since they communicate messages back and forth to our brain, and for the brain telling us what to do, making living possible. If so, it seems that without our immaterial senses, our brain will be in vain and of no use. Imagine that we are exhausted of our human senses, utterly without any of our five senses of sight, hearing, smell, taste or touch, then no dynamic brain activity could ever be experienced, except being left with a dull entity, an obsolete organ practically of no use.

It becomes more complicated when we believe that the brain through our senses instructs the ghost within to run the daily chores, commanding us what to do to get by in our lives; but the concern should be which us? To whom are the instructions addressed? When our senses register messages and communicate with the nervous system mainly the brain, telling us to do this or to do that, who are the brain, the mind, and the senses collectively referring to? To whom are they pointing at for executing orders?

The reality is that we are an inseparable part of the universal energy that is fueling the entire existence since all animated beings, the birds and the bees, flowers and the trees, the beasts, the invertebrates, mammals, amphibians, reptiles, fish, and so on, are either instinctually activated by the awesome designer God, or like humans consciously awakened and partially instinctual.

Since being consciously awakened should indicate that human senses, our entire nervous system, our brain is absolutely energy-driven telling us that we are here because of an infinitely insightful creator, because of a boundlessly magnificent mind, in which even the human brain need to subordinate to, for functioning efficiently? Human brain and mind are uniformly active; they are consciously based, as they are linked to the ever-present cosmic energy as both functions with much higher rate frequencies in comparison with other less animated low-frequency beings. The brain assuages (mollify, propitiate, placate, calm) propellant (stimuli) which through our five senses observes the external world and responds accordingly.

The thalamus is the clearinghouse for all sensory information other than the smell. Once sensory information is sorted in the thalamus it is sent to the hippocampus and the amygdala. The smell, however, goes directly to the hippocampus and amygdala. The hippocampus is the place of learning and contrast, the sensory knowledge from the external world perceives how the world should operate as if making quality control for expecting feasible standards.

The hippocampus is the seat of learning and memory and compares the sensory information from the outside world with its perception of how the world should be, like a quality controller checks products to ensure they meet industry standards. The hippocampus indicates any discrepancy or problem to the amygdala which dispatches and accepts information from every part of the brain and body. For instance, bodily hormones are set of very complicated networks which would be fair to link them to literal brain activity, but as dynamic as they are it would be wacky to analyze their superbly intricate activities without a magnificent designer creating them.

With all the brain activities received, we can often be deceived by the fake information through our mind. Five centuries years ago, Michel de Montaigne said: "My life has been filled with terrible misfortune; most of which never happened." Now there's a study that proves it. The study checks into how many of our imagined calamities never substantiate. many subjects were asked to write down their worries over an extended period of time and then clarify which of their imagined trouble did not occur.

Consequently, it turns out that 85 percent of what subjects worried about never initiated and with the 15 percent that did happen, 79 percent of subjects discovered either they could handle the difficulty better than expected, or the difficulty taught them a lesson worth learning. This means that 97 percent of what you worry about is not much more than a fearful mind punishing you with wrong perceptions. The stress it produces makes huge health problems.

The distress hormones dump into one's brain have been linked to shrinking brain mass, lowering your IQ, being prone to heart disease, cancer, and premature aging, predicting marital problems, family dysfunction and clinical depression, and making seniors more likely to develop dementia and Alzheimer's, and other ill health related problems.

Another instance of mind cheating us happens when watching a horror movie as we jump out of our seat thinking that killing, rape or other frightening situations are literally happening, or when some people engage in cybersex, and for the brain to believe the imaginary sex partner is an actual participant, and so on. There is no doubt that our brain, our mind can frequently misinform us, and where are we when imagining things, a feeling that we are not in the real world.

The brain often does not distinguish between reality and fiction, it is accustoming to certain movements, the brain is familiarized with habituated routines making it very difficult to discern another movement than repeatedly perceived. For an instant, it is easy for the brain to detect human-like running by a robot, or any other animal since our brain is aware of the concept of running.

In the meanwhile, it is extremely difficult for the brain to detect plants movement or perceive animal interactions, where it seems cognitive behaviors are surreptitiously designed in which may be and only may be an expert botanist or an experienced ecologist or zoologist can point out certain meaningful maneuvers by the plants and animals since many become acquainted within the uncharted territories where it is beyond human nervous system to extrapolate theoretical precision since creative ability of our mind where great scientific endeavors raises from audacity of imagination, assumption, feelings, emotions, intuition, and dreams which they come out quite handy.

Telling us that the mind of the universe is very much alive with an infinite variety of blueprint for all that exists not excluding human mind, informing us it is wise to pay attention to the cosmic mind where no entity can live without.

Biological intelligence expert Monica Gagliano from the University of Sydney believes it is possible to direct plants in the same way as a dog. Dr. Gagliano quoted her most disturbing find involved a fast-growing and climbing pea plant that developed a Pavlovian response. Ivan Pavlov (1849–1936) was a Russian physiologist who conditioned dogs to salivate every time a bell was rung.

The bell anticipated the arrival of dinner, and yet eventually he rang the bell without bringing dinner and the dogs would continue salivating, Dr. Gagliano said. She stated, "Instead of the bell, we used a little fan, which I knew plants didn't care about. And instead of dinner, I used a little blue light, which I know plants care about very much for growth. The fact many plants grow towards blue light is very well accepted."

The scientific investigators had the fan directed onto the pea plant from a particular direction before they change it with blue light, repeating the fan-light combination from random angles for several days.

Eventually, the fan was blown onto the trained plant from a certain direction.

When the researchers came back the next day to turn on the blue light, they found the plant had bent towards it in anticipation.

"The fan had no meaning whatsoever to start with, but it acquired meaning to the plant through its own experience, the same as the bell did for the dog," Dr. Gagliano said. "The plants don't have brains. They don't have neurons and yet they're still performing the exact same task as the dog. How did they do that? We don't know."

Another experiment with growing pea plants in a maze and running water via one of the pipes shown the plants tilted towards it.

Plants are competent to locate nearby water by sensing its humidity gradient. "But then I recorded the sound of water and substituted the real presence of water inside a pipe with just the sound," Dr. Gagliano said. "Even if the actual water isn't there and it's just the mere sound of it, they will grow towards it." She also tried playing random sounds like white noise but the sound of water managed the greatest effect.

"The experiment showed there is a selectivity in response to sounds around them, and water, of course, is ecologically relevant," Dr. Gagliano said.

She said, "It suggested there was another system of cognition beyond neurons and brains that humans had not yet considered."

Hormones and Neurotransmitters

The endocrine system utilizes hormones and the nervous system uses neurotransmitters to transit between the body and the brain. The endocrine system is the collection of glands that generate hormones that regulate growth, metabolism and development, tissue function, sexual function, reproduction, sleep, and mood, among other things. Hormones are the body's chemical messengers.

They take information and instructions from one set of cells to another. The endocrine system permeates nearly every cell and the function of our body. Hormones are released by endocrine glands into the bloodstream and carry information to and from different parts of the body and communicate with the brain by working on neurons through receptors. Neurotransmitters are chemicals that allow nerve cells to dialogue with each other.

In this case, the nervous system communication between the brain and the body, by hormonal activities and neurotransmitters, report interceptive (relating to stimuli produced within an organism, especially in the gut and other internal organs).

The point is that so many neuroscientists, biologists, psychologists, psychoanalysts, psychiatrists, anthropologists (anthropology is the study of humans, early hominids and primates, such as chimpanzees, anthropologists study human language, culture, societies, biological and material remains, the biology and behavior of primates, and even our own buying habit), and those involved with human anatomy and mind, draw their conclusions based on mechanical activities of hormonal organs as instinctual, as if these apparatus (a complex structure within an organism or system) are self-propelling without a competent fomenter, without an expert programmer.

As sophisticated as this biological maneuverability's are, they seem to see these complex hormonal activities without deliberate and awesome management; where obviously any meddling on the homeostasis or balance of the organism is stressful enough to cause malfunction of the organs engaged in a particular task.

The brain's responsibility is to regulate all stress and return stability to the internal milieu (surrounding), ensue protective actions like increases in blood pressure and serum glucose levels that make us ready for the situation of fight-or-flight; break down health affects the quality of our lives, the same way bad tools and an unreliable situation manifests a hostile work environment. When hormones and neurotransmitters are overworked, they transmit into hypertension, cardiac disease and diabetes, and a host of other ills.

Chronic over-usage results in allostatic the duration by which a state of internal, physiological balance is kept intact by an organism in response to actual or perceived environmental and psychological stressors. Hence, allostasis is the projection that keeps the organism alive and working (i.e., maintaining homeostasis or maintaining stability the cumulative adverse effect on the body).

Homeostasis is the ability or tendency to maintain internal stability in an organism to compensate for environmental changes. An example of homeostasis is the human body keeping an average temperature of 98.6 degrees.

For instance, the nervous system helps keep homeostasis in breathing patterns, because breathing is involuntary, the nervous system ensures that the body is getting much-needed oxygen through breathing the appropriate amount of oxygen. When toxins get into one's blood, they disrupt one's body's homeostasis, this ongoing process continually works to restore and maintain homeostasis. For example, during body temperature regulation, temperature receptors in the skin communicate information to the brain (the control center) which signals the effectors: blood vessels and sweat glands in the skin.

When allostasis happens too frequently (as when the body is subjected to repeated stressors) or is wanting (insufficient, inadequate) over weeks, months, or years, exposure to increased secretion of stress hormones can end in allostatic load and its pathophysiologic (physiopathology is a convergence of pathology with physiology, it can also mean the functional changes associated with or resulting from disease or injury, another definition is the functional changes that accompany a particular disease outcome).

Allostatic load refers to the long-term effects of continued exposure to chronic stress on the body. Colloquially, it is often indicated as wear and tear. Long-term exposure to allostatic load can lead to disease and bodily destruction. Bear in mind that because of today's stressful lifestyle, millions suffer memory loss which, without, life is not worth living.

One should try to dodge distressful living and try to boost one's memory and mind through balanced diet by taking multivitamins, vitamin d, vitamin c, high doses of omega3, fish oil. Whether you suffer from Alzheimer's disease or you simply have memory problems, certain vitamins and fatty acids have been said to slow or prevent memory loss. Know that low blood flow in the hippocampus is the reason for memory loss.

Try to meditate, sleep well, listen to soothing music, eat well, exercise, avoid attention deficit disorder, stay alert, read, and most of all, avoid loneliness. Laugh and enjoy the moment. Avoid lead and mercury and mold exposure, try to learn new things, like a new language, music, solving puzzles, playing chess. Work your memory. Good memory is the most important part of a smarter and faster brain. Make association, make goals, eat food that boosts brain power, think positive, and stay delightful, be happy, play brain games, do mental math.

The long list of potential solutions includes vitamins like vitamin B-12, herbal supplements such as ginkgo biloba, and omega-3 fatty acids. Salmon, gingko, beet, hot peppers, red bell peppers, green vegetables, green tea, blueberry, and should consume lots of leafy green. One needs to drink lots of water, eat as much as organic food as possible, consume fiber, eat spinach, cauliflower, broccoli, cabbage, dark chocolate, nuts, pumpkin seeds, turmeric, ginger, cinnamon, avocado, garlic, onion, mushroom, sweet potato, zucchini.

When people talk about brain foods, fatty fish is often at the top of the list. Coffee, if coffee is the highlight of your morning, you'll be glad to hear that it's good for you, but should be taken within the limit, like one or two cups max a day. Try to lose weight, since being overweight is directly related to memory loss, diabetes, sleep apnea, snoring, stopping breathing, and a host of other troubling diseases.

Memory is all we are; without it, one's living is not worth it. Try to rest, sleep, at least eight hours a day. Avoid caffeine, try to keep your room as dark as possible while sleeping, keep your room rather cool, take magnesium and melatonin for a restful sleep. Know that sleep apnea, snoring, and stopping breathing is directly linked to being overweight.

For the anti-inflammatory diet.

Tomatoes, olive oil, eat green leafy vegetables, such as spinach, kale, and collards. Eat nuts like almonds and walnuts, fatty fish like salmon, mackerel, tuna, and sardines, fruits such as strawberries, blueberries, cherries, and oranges. Curcumin, the active compound in turmeric, is a strong anti-inflammatory agent. It's been found to be more effective than aspirin and ibuprofen at reducing inflammation without the health risks the over-the-counter medicines.

Foods that cause inflammation

The main foods that people following an anti-inflammatory diet should avoid include processed meats, sugary drinks, trans fats, found in fried foods. White bread, white pasta, potato chips, gluten, soybean oil, and vegetable oil, processed snack foods, avoid processed food such as chips and crackers, junk food, avoid MSG and chemically oriented food, food with preservatives and artificial coloring.

Avoiding inflammation.

The fastest way of reducing inflammation in your body: Load up on anti-inflammatory foods, cut back or eliminate inflammatory foods, control blood sugar, make time to exercise. Lose weight, manage stress, do not eat sugar, avoid gum disease.

The actual power of the mind, its influence on our future, our well-being, our health outlook, and self-concept, is an enigma sparking much discussion and arguments for centuries. As food for thought, here's what some of the world's most prominent figures of the past had to offer on this intriguing subject.

The energy of the mind is the essence of life. – Aristotle

"Physical concepts are free creations of the human mind, and are not, however it may seem, uniquely determined by the external world." Albert Einstein.

15

THE WAR ON TERROR, AND THE RHETORIC OF COUNTERTERRORISM

It's not right to respond to terrorism by terrorizing other people. And furthermore, it's not going to help. Then you might say, "Yes, it's terrorizing people, but it's worth doing because it will end terrorism." But how much common sense does it take to know that you cannot end terrorism by indiscriminately dropping bombs?

HOWARD ZINN,

The rhetoric of the war on terror is a series of institutional exercise along with a set of political anecdotes (story) which they acquire the methodology of dying discussion analysis. The discourse states that the language of the war on terrorism is not simply a nonaligned or objectified dispersion(reflection) of policy arguments and the actualities of terrorism and counter-terrorism; rather, it is a very precise and deliberately build-up public powwows (seminar)that are particularly orchestrated to make the image of the war appear justified, responsible, and basically good.

The real problem with this whole show is that the talk and practice of the war on terrorism construe radical disputes to the democratic state, not to exclude jeopardizing the legal and moral imperatives of the community, where nation's trust is at stake. The organized terror often is financially fed via umbilical cord attached to many powerful and resourceful entities, in which frequently the head of state from specific developing countries are the actual culprits as they play double standard, exhibiting tolerance as they show apparent concern when terrorism strikes, but in reality they are tied to extremists ideologies and stern radicalism philosophy that are alarmingly dangerous; aiming to destroy animated concepts where progressively faith-oriented credos (ideology, set of beliefs) interpret holy books different than what they approve of, which ironically supposed to worship the same God, and not to follow satanic rituals shedding innocent blood through horrific act of violence and terrorism.

This holocaust view of resolving terrorism must stop which is manufactured through perpetrating wars of aggression, and sanctions, where genocide like extermination is exercised; since millions of innocent people perish, either being slaughtered, via sanctioned therefore hungered to death, a famine like punishment, or banished, being forced to leave their country pushing them into refugee status. They don't leave their countries voluntarily, as they are forced to flee or face ill-consequences, as so many lose their lives while in horrific transitions the midst of this inhumane persecutions. No civil society should ever be dragged down to agree with such barbaric behaviors, since it can entrap a nation of goodwill, making their decency in mind and manner questionable.

But their surreptitious activities do not stop there, since they are also adamant to discredit nations that are the sworn enemy of medieval mentality, and the defenders of freedom, democracy, human rights, liberty and the pursuit of happiness. They camouflage their demonic intention for weakening popular values and civic culture, undermining the legitimacy of democratic institutions and forestalling the enunciation (talk, utterance) of potentially more effective counter-terrorism advances.

It seems that some menacing governments from developing countries are dictating to the west that either turn a blind eye to our inhumane behaviors and atrocious conducts, or else. That is if you want to enjoy billions of dollars' trades in arms deal along with other financially based projects, and for flexible pricing on the oil and gas purchases, also known as the black gold.

Frighteningly enough, we should see the huge ambiguity in the war against terrorism when already the real source of terror is several times identified, but the corporates dynasty convolute people's perception and redirect the culture of thoughts to nowhere land, where facts are somehow misconstrued and eventually denied.

The corporate elites work in cahoots with autocratic regimes to cover up heinous crimes done by the head of states under the banner of national security, which should rather be called for corporate security. This analysis is particularly relevant in the context of the current political climate in the United States, and Europe where the War on terror rhetoric carries on to normalize the logic of Islamophobia aimed at utterly irrelevant places and groups It should remind one of when rubbers plan to rob a bank, and deliberately set fire elsewhere in the vicinity of the susceptible bank in question to distract by standards and the guards, to execute the unethical deed. "Wanton (capricious, arbitrary) killing of innocent civilians is terrorism, not a war against terrorism." NOAM CHOMSKY

The corporate elites operate beyond the constitution, beyond the government, and act above the will of the people, since they have the entire media to pounce on the incredulous (dubious) images that are meant to be imprinted into people's mind making the victims agrees with their entire ill-natured agendas. It is not so wacky (loony) to believe that like colonialism, fascism, slavery, and piracy, terrorism also has no place or any position in the modern world. But unless those in charge are willing to identify the head of the snake and avoid sleeping with the enemy, as the pythons of terrorism walk the red carpets in the very states that are attacked, but are seen as allies, we are actually just playing with the python's tail.

Look, let's be frank; not a few barefooted Bedouins can create sophisticated plans, facilitate expensive training and equipment's, produce intelligent documents which even the most up to date passenger scanners, and x-ray system with very competent security personals cannot detect the culprits until is too late. They frequently make an extremely effective attack on a foreign soil in which many of those nations are so technologically advanced and brilliantly guarded that even a fly should have a difficult time to infiltrate and pass through, but it happens. Yes, it is true that terrorism has become the systematic weapon of a war that knows no limit or any boundary, and so anonymous which rarely has a face. But there is more to it than meets the eye.

There are powerful people and even governments that play as a wolf in sheep's clothing which they are the financiers and the actual troublemakers defending radical ideologies to protect Islam. Islamophobias shouldn't be of any treatment as so many God-fearing innocent people are either erroneously targeted, or deliberately dealt with as scapegoats, while they throw shindig (big party) to celebrate the big business deals with the perpetrators of the terror, and the actual malefactors against humanity. Either way, it is wrong for great nations to descend to uncivilized mentality, since answering terrorism with terrorism is an impractical idea which should be condemned.

The big threat to America is the way we react to terrorism by throwing away what everybody values about our country—a commitment to human rights. America is a great nation because we are a good nation. When we stop being a good nation, we stop being great. BOBBY KENNEDY, *O Magazine*, February 2007.

The war being fought against terrorism is more than a military discord which needs to be ideologically detoxified from the dark ages mentality, not by coercion and force, or by engaging the military industrial complex, but by practicing what the free world has so much to be proud of against ruthless often religious-based tyranny. It is the decisive ideological struggle of the twenty-first century. On one side are those who believe in the values of freedom and moderation, the right of all people to speak, and worship, freedom of religion, freedom of the press, freedom of assembly and live in liberty with the pursuit of happiness, to even bear arms against despotic and unruly state practices, which dignifies and upholds What does land of the free and home of the brave means.

On the other side, facing those-driven by the images of cruelty and fanaticism, forcing their way in by a self-appointed few which impose their radicalism views on the rest of inhabitants. As veterans, you have seen this kind of enemy before. Comparatively speaking they should remind one of the successors to Fascists, to Nazis, and other totalitarians of the twentieth century. History shows what the result will be, a victory for the cause of freedom, liberty and exercising utter human rights. The object of terrorism is terrorism. The object of oppression is oppression. The object of torture is torture. The object of murder is murder. The object of power is power. Now, do you begin to understand me? GEORGE ORWELL, 1984

It is not far from reason to see that terrorism is the war of the poor, and war is terrorism of the rich imposed on the poor, since the poverty plays a big role into this whole equation as the nasty aristocrats and the rich elites control the seemingly infinite oil and gas, and other valuable minerals as they play evil in their everyday demonic rituals. Recruiting the financially destitute and naively minded characters, mostly young breeds that easily fall trap into the ludicrous idea of being summoned by God to resurrect against the Kofar (the unbelievers), basically the west, so is the rhetoric of Armageddon which means the final confrontation between good and evil, which by evil it means Satan, but metaphorically implies to other faith, specially Islam.

The impact of fear and anxiety can disorient many people and affect their lives for the worst. Fear is a human emotion that is triggered by a perceived threat. However, when people live in constant fear, whether from physical dangers in their environment or threats they behold, they can become debilitating. Yes, terrorism is no exception and must be dealt with as a prevalent virus. Terrorism is prevalent like a bacterium. There is a global entanglement with terrorism, which follows any system of primacy (supremacy) as though it were its shadow, ready to activate itself like a double agent. Contrary to the violence we watch on movies and allow ourselves to believe it, the objectives of terror are not to perish people but to kill though, to prove a point, to demoralize a nation that it is about to implode (collapse) from within.

Terrorism does not engage in conventional warfare, where two or more military industrial complex becomes involve in a frequently prolonged war. The essence of terrorist's strategy is to camouflage and attack places and people when expected the least, just like a shark or a crocodile, or any other predator with no conscious, as if instinctually programmed to kill. Most crime-oriented activities aim at causing fear to incapacitate the victims. Human beings do vicious, and despicable things to each other. Homicide, betrayal, conspiracy, genocide, torture, mutilation, rape, pedophile at times done while loved ones are forced to watch or public hanging before a crowd, and done intentionally, brutally without conscious and with abusive words and verbal assault to amplify the suffering exerting excruciating pain often to innocent people.

Then, the plagues of poverty, prostitution, homelessness, child abuse, humiliation and hopelessness, racism, sexual exploitation, and other forms of distributed violence; and these are fused by the neglect and carelessness and condescension and insensible rationalizations that add insult to injury, without any remedy for millions entangled in a web of uncertainty and despair.

The troubling issue is that many nations have to deal with their own dictatorial governments that are the actual cause of terrorism, as they are supported by super-powers and are considered as our allies, and if so, then many progressive countries which brag about upholding human rights and democracy, but do not hear the victims outcry and horrific position they are in, are surely behaving double standards. It makes one believe that equity comes with a price, millions are doomed to perish because apparently, they are not able to afford justice, literal hypocrisy in action.

Yes, progressive nations have the very rich lexicon to expose injustice and wrongdoings not to exclude evil, transgression, acting insane, cruelty, savage, sadistic, degrading, inhumane, horrific, ungodly, demonic, atrocious, and the list goes on. But such consensus in words to actually bring any remedy is either futile, skipped or impractical. When millions of victims are experiencing genocide by a racist state, or tortured and incarcerated by their own ominous governments without the world paying any attention.

It brings the worst out of the innocent victims, those who so unjustly lost everything, even their loved ones, that they are left with nothing to live for. Justice is meant to be relevant everywhere and for everyone, it is a sacred word that is rooted in humanity's moral as it is very conscious-driven, it simply must not have toyed with. When fair play is deliberately ignored, and the culprits are not even warned for their wicket crimes because they are in the position of power and influence, not even a slap on the hand. It leaves a ripple effect of deep mental and physical injuries which leaves the victims with no choice but to do the unthinkable terrorist actions, exterminating innocent people which of course is diabolical, but to them, terrorists seem justifiable.

That terrorism is a crime against humanity. One problem is that the attribution is so arbitrary. Hence, the evil needs to be located in those regimes who practice state terrorism, because unless we get rid of the root causes of such ills, it is going to exponentially grow nationally and globally. Terrorism is a crime against humanity, it should warn us not to behave prejudicially in favoring certain so-called ally's terrorists over others denoting us as hypocrites and in denial of the truth, and certainly against our values. It is not so puzzling to know that the root causes of evil are greed and astronomical profits that the arm industries secure from selling a variety of high tech weaponry to globally troubled areas as peace is pre-meditatively disturbed, where fear is literally manufactured to make sure for the high demand of horrific armaments and inhumane weaponry.

In his final speech from the White House, President Dwight D. Eisenhower warned that an arms race would take resources from other areas; such as building schools and hospitals. On Jan. 17, 1961, President Dwight Eisenhower gave the nation a dire warning about what he described as a threat to democratic government.

He called it the military-industrial complex, a formidable union of defense contractors and the armed forces. As NPR's Tom Bowman tells *Morning Edition* co-host Renee Montagne, Eisenhower used the speech to warn about "the immense military establishment" here is an excerpt. "In the councils of government, we must guard against the acquisition of unwarranted influence, whether sought or unsought, by the military-industrial complex. The potential for the disastrous rise of misplaced power exists, and will persist."

When such terminology as the access of evil or the evil empire denote certain states that probably are at fault and not certain others that are truly at fault, then it solely discredits us as a great nation and puts our leadership in questionable position taking their words as not au+3thenticated but as demagoguery. Phrases as such are contorted to represent and appeal to unwitting and hubris (conceited, arrogance) in order to elaborate the speaker's political potency while lessening public liability (accountability.)

Shrouded in secrecy, executive powers redundantly declare that evil must be fought, which should not give anyone a second thought in wiping evil out, but it must be done without recourse to nefarious activities, if not, what would make a civilized people with progressive government different than the barbarian mentality since they try to bring out the worst in us. We are way past the Machiavellian era, in which he believed that evil exploits goodness governments must be prepared to be not good, so. Machiavelli, states that any means can be used if it is necessary to maintain power.

The word comes from the Italian Renaissance diplomat and writer

Niccolò Machiavelli, born in 1469, who wrote *Il Principe* (The Prince.) In today world it is difficult to discern who and what is the actual evil, since many advanced states are also lured into doing the unspeakable crimes beyond anyone's comprehension since they use force exhausted of civil discourse, and without concentrating on the economy of violence.

The heads of many governments maneuver idly by playing to cognitive bigotry (bias) utilizing mass media in which many are in cahoots with the state to easily keep the public at bay which the people are saintly unaware of the often troubling networks of friendship with the fascist regimes and the informal relationships that make the foreign affairs. often the declaration is: You're either with us or against us; you're either evil because you are not as resourceful as we need you to be, or you're good with plenty of valuable resources that you should willingly render if you want to stay in power and as an ally.

One should ask what does the ordinary person that works hard 24/7 trying to make a basic living has to do with taking the side in a military industrial complex confrontation between two oligopolistic governments; which for some odd reason cannot come to term in taking people's resources, since the commoners have to indeed pay a grave price either through war of aggression calling it the good war, or by crippling sanction imposed on them, which only is going to affect the poor and financially deprived, since the rich can afford food and housing at any rate, or take off to dreamland places where they can enjoy their unending wealth. "The number of people killed by the sanctions in Iraq is greater than the total number of people killed by all weapons of mass destruction in all of history." NOAM CHOMSKY.

What is the solution?

Before endorsing for a solution people need to realize that extreme wealth concentrated in the hands of a tiny portion of the society is the real problem empowering them with the enormous political influence which has frankly put democracy at grave risk where negative consequences are already visible. We ought to know that class mobility is no longer the case since fiscal tax policies and deregulations and other lopsided programs are designed by the super-rich to protect the opulent and their properties against the commoners which will eventually resurrect the deprived to restructure the entire economic system since the welfare agendas that was originally introduced by Aristotle which meant to avoid extreme income inequality, a safe- haven for the rich against the poverty-stricken masses for not confiscating the properties of the super-rich is not available; which leads for widening the gap between the rich and the poor proportionally related to the health of the society. The wider the gap, the unhealthier the republic.The fight against the few for a global egalitarian society should happen via voting rights and democratization to further stop economic terrorism which has so sadly resulted in radicalism and encouraging terrorism which I am afraid has given the culprits the excuse to kill innocent people all over the world. The multinational corporations, the banks, the insurance companies, and the international investment firms and their political lackeys are relentless in keeping the workers and the poor insecure as they yank and obliterate laws that are democratically instituted to safeguard the majority of the population against the outrages behaviors of the financial moguls of our time.No materially based system where the few elites can be in charge of the entire nation is of remedy, especially when God is the absence making socialism, the communism or any other ideological, economic and political entity not promising since the revisionists will always be a threat unless a truly spiritual system with God-fearing representatives elected vastly by the majority of educated people structurally from bottom-up voting to take place, making an educated society decisively imperative, and the essence of real success. We should bear in mind that any hyper machoism culture and the bullying way of dealing with the world does not comply with the democratic perspectives and justice for all scenarios where male chauvinism and the patriarchic attitudes need to balance out with the collectivism conducts where democracy, freedom, and prosperity can be experienced by everyone and not only by the few who can afford to live as kings and queens do at the expense of enslaving others leaving out the majority to regret they were ever born. We need to introduce more females into the decisive roles of the state and into meaningful socio-cultural, socio-political, and socio-economic decision makings to advocate soft and more humane approach into the system to reflect moral and due process legal values where the basic needs of the population are met, since easy access to education, medical, housing and transportation are the keys to any successfully triumphed nation, for example, the Scandinavian "social democrat governments" are doing much better in attending to the needs of their people. There is nothing wrong to emulate the good work of others, for what is practical and to discard what is in vain which perhaps can help us to once and for all get rid of the cosmetic views of a tough and rough male-oriented attitudes , and push to neglect being indoctrinated into the belligerent business of wars that can bring humanity at the brink of destruction.

16

SPECULATION ON CONSCIOUSNESS

All matter originates and exists only by virtue of a force
which brings the particle of an atom to vibration and
holds this most minute solar system of the atom together.
Max Planck

The hard problem of explaining the conscious experience is not rooted in
the complexity of whichever kind. The troubling issue is much deeper:
It is permeated in the failure to connect describing the gap between any
level of structure in our neuronal networks and conscious experience. The
conscious experience has its own unique dynamic properties—properties
that do not seem to be 'emerge able' from the complicated buildup of any
kind. This sets it apart from any developing properties. Every incipient
(emergent) property can be elaborated on as an epiphenomenon of the
implicit (implied) procedure in terms of the specific pattern of these
methods (mechanism.)

These arrangements are complex and sometimes stochastic (randomly
determine) or self-regulating so we cannot always foresee or quantify
what is going to take place, but principally we can learn how the property
appears. For every developing property, we have something to say that
convincingly describes in principle how the emergent property arrives
from underlying mechanisms—underlying patterns that are eventually
embedded in the basic laws of physics as we are familiar with today, but for
the conscious experience it looks like being fundamentally unemergeable.

This has made some scientists believe that we must be ignoring a fundamental aspect in our current comprehension of physics—or we have not yet reached the pinnacle laws of physics. Other scientists simply disregard the unemergeability of consciousness by positing that consciousness must be magically emerging somehow from a complex pattern of neuronal networks. Physicists often denote dynamic patterns as fields, and similar ideas are acquired in brain science.

They talk about gravitational fields, temperature fields, electromagnetic fields, quantum fields, information fields, communication fields, and much more. For instance, a temperature field shows that temperature depends on both location and time. In equivalent cases, brain fields might represent patterns of action potentials in individual neurons, synaptic activity, oxygen levels, and so forth in brain tissue with masses of various sizes.

When one exhibits some mental tasks. Certain parts of the brain may be noticed to light up some measure of brain activity, typically electroencephalography (EEG) or functional magnetic resonance imaging (fMRI), will respond as the particular mental task is exercised, while this approach designates important information, but it does not mean a high level of mental activities should relate to more lights burning brighter.

The dynamic aspects of consciousness apparently demand certain kinds of brain activities that insist on for at least a half second or so, furthermore, consciousness is closely linked to special kinds of brain rhythms, registered as electric field (EEG) oscillations. Apparently, brains must be appropriately tuned to be conscious. Finally, there is the matter of the multiscale nature of brain fields, thus, brain fields include dynamic sub patterns within sub patterns within patterns calculated at different organizational levels. In truth, consciousness apparently requires special maneuverability types within high levels of perplexity in brain fields.

It is the shortcoming of such events for a conscious experience that makes the hard problem hard, conscious experience appears to be fundamentally unemergeable. This has convinced some scientists to believe that our physics does not seem to be complete yet, perhaps there are missing links that the physicists are not aware of.

The answer is yes; what is missing is that some physicists do not want to accept that universal consciousness is the cause to what exists, including a human brain that is certainly energy based and able to maneuver with infinite diversity, since there is no limit to the human mind, neither is our heart. Our heart does limitlessly desire and will be in wanting mode to the day we die, so is our mind which possesses the infinite ability to progress in which, if let live.

The collective mind of humanity will one day see God. Implying that conscious awareness must somehow magically emerge from the complex patterns of neurons networks and activities might be true; but it cannot tangibly be located in our brain since it correlates (agree, tally, harmonize, dovetail) with the cosmic energy permeated in the entire existence. It is what the sages have for so long indicated that what is not seen manages what is seen.

In conclusion, the important thing is for humanity to be reminded that we possess two sacred and extremely valuable entity, which they both are coherent with the infinite nature of our creator, and nature itself. One is our heart and the other is our mind, since our heart will not stop craving, and will desire to the day we are alive. Our human mind is potentiated with infinite intelligence that will not stop, and further continues to one day conquer the universe and beyond.

Our heart is correlated with what we know as feelings and emotions, our mind is the spirit which needs to be kept cleansed, and not pollutes with toxic thoughts and desires. Good conscious (thinking), good words, and good deeds become prevalent regardless of race, color. authenticity, ideology, creed, gender or any other factor encompassing humanity.

The key to growth is the introduction of higher dimensions of consciousness into our awareness. Lao Tzu

17

MAKE SENSE DIALOGUE

The flawed, misleading, and false debates are these days prevalent. A logical argument is intellectual self-defense against imposing assault on reason and avoiding irrational behaviors on logic and what makes sense. Logic, as well as a methodology for quality control, keeps the validity of one's views in check. From the tiniest essentiality to the peak of religious abstraction, from the most primitive man's invention to the modern macro discoveries, everything we are, everything we possess comes from one attribute of man-the function of his deduction and reasoning mind. "Man is the only animal capable of reasoning, through many others possess the faculty of memory and instruction in common with him." Aristotle.

Formal logic is the gateway to a fascinating and elegant branch of dialogue and adequate communication and the very key to philosophy, mathematics, and science since issues as rationality and inference are agendas attached at the hips which without, probing into any viable matter can prove us futile. As no true evaluation and correct assessments can be rendered, as the essence of philosophy is the power of reasoning which demands enlightenment to often contemplate intricate subject and insightful matters beyond the ordinary.

Philosophy gives us the opportunity to ponder and dig into the deepest questions about the world, about our universe, and God. Is there a God? Does life have an ultimate purpose? Do I have a purpose? What am I? Why am I here? What do I want? How can I serve? What should I be grateful for? How can we be sure that we're not dreaming or in the Matrix? What does it mean to be human—contrary to being an animal or a robot? Does free will exist?

What sort of life is the happiest? What is knowledge? Can we depend on our senses to know what's real? What makes an action right or wrong? Who are we? Where did we come from? Where are we heading? What happens after we expire? How should we live and treat others? Derived from the Greek words, philosophy or love of wisdom is the subject that can come closest to these imperative and intriguing issues.

Making sense dialogues should relate to rationality as wisdom can be applied to complex oriented subjects as their discernibility's can often be difficult, like for instance knowing if our brain or mind, call it spirit or soul if you wish, is playing the decisive role in our lives.

It nudges one toward critical thinking, cultivating logic and ethics, aesthetics, searching for the whys of the world, and much more. The other relatively make sense concern would be: if our brain is the cause for our human mind, or vice-versa? The brain as matter does not exist, what exists as the substantive brain is also energy based, and for sure not a dull entity with low-frequency rate.

It is quite obvious that the human brain by far the most sophisticated product, dynamically animated, which is extremely competent to communicate with energy based thoughts and our senses, traditionally scientists denoted that mind is the consequence of our brain activity, regarding it as a physical substance, saying that the mind is the result of brain firing cells(neurons). But contemporary arguments are that the brain goes far beyond physical activities of the brain.

In comparison, most animals have a lower-frequency-rate, energy-based brain, and not as dynamically oriented human brain extremely versatile, and conscious based entity, the same as our mind. Yes, the brain is a tangible organ that controls all imperative human function, but unless it was also energy oriented, it would not be able to accord and dialogue within the energy-related atmosphere, and with our senses which the brain is an inseparable part of our entire nervous system.

In retrospect, our mind percolates (pervade, impregnate) every cell of our body and coordinates with every part to produce action and in what we must do to survive, which has dominion the brain. Human brain and mind are interchangeably active as they are both consciously based linked to prevalently cosmic energy as they both function with much higher rate frequencies in comparison with other less animated low-frequency objects.

The brain assuages (relieve, alleviate, palliate, abate, soothe) propellant (projectile, stimuli) which through our five senses observes to the external world and responds accordingly. The thalamus is the clearinghouse for all sensory information other than the smell. Once sensory information is sorted in the thalamus it is sent to the hippocampus and the amygdala. The smell, however, goes directly to the hippocampus and amygdala. The hippocampus is the place of learning and contrasts the sensory knowledge from the external world perceiving how the world should operate as if making quality control for expecting feasible standards.

The hippocampus is the seat of learning and memory and compares the sensory information from the outside world with its perception of how the world should be. Like a great manager, the hippocampus indicates any discrepancy or problem to the amygdala which dispatches and accepts information from every part of the brain and body.

For instance, bodily hormones are set of very complicated networks which would be fair to link them to literal brain activity, but as dynamic as they are it would be wacky to analyze their superbly intricate position without a magnificent designer creatively programming them to activate in thousands of different occasions, if not in millions of scenarios.

"The question of science, the authority of a thousand is not worth the humble reasoning of a single individual." Galileo Galilei

18

ARE WE MADE OF STARDUST?

Nothing is as it appears; what seems to be solid, physical reality is, in fact, a complex system of vibrating energies. What our eyes actually see are dancing patterns that we recognize as objects or living creatures. We are connected with what we see by pulsating waves of light-energy. Karen Wise.

Scientists believe a star exploded, then a big bang someplace in our galaxy happened, which did spread the mass of dust and gas. This supernova (a star that suddenly increases greatly in brightness because of a catastrophic explosion that ejects most of its mass.) which they believe occurred about five billion years ago.

The remnants from the explosion then collided into the near vicinity cloud of gas, together they build up the elements necessary for our solar system. This highly energy-oriented explosion made the dust mixture extremely hot and things began to muster. In the meanwhile, bits of dust started to cluster, constructing bigger and bigger lumps, and the synthesis (alloy, blend) began to pull together under its own gravity.

Later on, the central lump became so hot and tight that it started to produce its own energy, igniting nuclear fires. This is how the sun was born. What remained of dusty mixture whirlpooled around the star, creating a disc. As the sun gradually grew bigger, and the dusty disc cooled off. Then, over millions of years the constellation was made into grains, then lumps, boulders and eventually planetesimal, (is an object formed from dust, rock and other minerals.) chunks of rock big enough to have their own gravitational field. Some of these planetesimals became the emergent forms of the planets in our solar system today.

Gradually, but surely, these rocky planets initiated to organize sitting at a well-off distance from the sun and making their own orbit. Earth detected its path as the third planet from the sun. In the early day's rocky pileups were still common, leaving craters on the surface of all of the planets.

They believe that about 4.5 billion years ago a large planetesimal, about the size of Mars, gave Earth a glancing blow, taking a chunk of Earth's crust out into space. Some of the planetesimals merged with Earth, while the ejected lump began its own orbit encircling the Earth and became the moon. Proof for this theory arrives from samples of moon dust, exhibiting that the moon is made of fairly similar rocks to those detected in the upper layers of the Earth's mantle and crust. The moon formation impact pushed the Earth sideways, altering its angle of tilt to the sun from 0 degrees to 23.5 degrees.

Therefore, the Earth began to have seasons: winter for the hemisphere lifted away from the sun, and summer for the hemisphere inclined towards the sun. Originally the planet didn't have a crust, mantle, and core, and instead, all the ingredients were evenly combined. There were no oceans nor continents and no atmosphere. A meteorite crashed, radioactive dilapidation (decay) and planetary contraction forced the Earth to become hotter and hotter. After a few hundred million years the temperature of Earth arrived at 2,000C—the melting point of iron—and Earth's core was shaped.

Geologists believe there may have been lava (hot liquid rock) ocean at the surface which gradually cooled and the planet made into a mainstay (core), mantle (something that covers) and the hard outer surface, the (crust.) This layering of the planet helped to change the structure of the Earth surface and the Earth began to shape a bit similar to what it is now. Geologists assess that the Earth oceans and atmosphere are because of multiple volcanic explosions that occurred approximately four billion years ago which may have generated mostly from the debris of comets, sometimes debris of asteroids.

The part of a meteoroid or asteroid which survived the passage through our atmosphere and collided with the Earth then released water and gas at the surface. Comets are smaller celestial bodies mainly made of ice and dust. However, scientists say the Earth's situation in the solar system was fortuitous (happened accidentally) Mercury and Venus are too close to the sun, so too hot for oceans to form since they just evaporate, while Mars is too far away because if any liquid it just freezes. Only on Earth, they were just positioned right.

Geologists believe the first single-celled organisms evolved about 4 billion years ago. Gradually the composition of Earth's atmosphere altered chewing their way via carbon dioxide and water and releasing oxygen. By approximately 2.5 billion years ago, significant amounts of oxygen had accumulated the Earth's atmosphere. The site was set for intricate life to emit.

"The atoms of our bodies are traceable to stars that manufactured them in their cores and exploded these enriched ingredients across our galaxy, billions of years ago. For this reason, we are biologically connected to every other living thing in the world. We are chemically connected to all molecules on Earth. And we are atomically connected to all atoms in the universe. We are not figuratively, but literally stardust." Neil DE Grasse Tyson

One scientific analogy is that originally, hydrogen and a little helium existed, and not much of anything else. Our bodies do not convey Helium. Hydrogen is, but that's not the immensity of our weight. Stars are similar to nuclear reactors. They take fuel and change it to something else. Hydrogen is molded into helium, and helium is made into carbon, nitrogen, and oxygen, iron and sulfur—everything that we're building off. As the stars are about to die, they inflate and expand as they fall together, the stars throw off their outside layers.

If a star is a tubby (heavy) enough, it will explode in a supernova (the explosion of the star that causes the star to become extremely bright). Scientists believe that most of the material that we are made of arrives from dying stars, or some stars that expired in explosions. Those stellar explosions carry on. We have stuff in us as old as the universe itself, even some stuff as old as maybe only a hundred years ago. all of that amalgamates (mixes, combine) in our bodies.

> "There's a flame of magic inside every stone & every
> flower, every bird that sings & every frog that croaks.

There's magic in the trees & the hills & the river & the rocks, in the sea & the stars & the wind, deep, wild magic that's as old as the world itself. It's in you too, my darling girl, and in me, and in every living creature, be it ever so small. Even the dirt I'm sweeping up now is stardust. In fact, all of us are made from the stuff of stars."

— Kate Forsyth, The Puzzle Ring

Many theories of the genesis of life have been suggested but since it's hard to prove or disprove them, no fully depended theory exists. Today, there are several competing theories for how life arose on Earth. Some doubt whether life started on Earth at all, acknowledging instead that life came from a distant world or because of a fallen comet or asteroid. Others believe that life probably has arisen here more than once.

Most scientists accept that life went through a period when RNA was the head-honcho molecule, leading life through its earliest stages. Relating to this RNA World hypothesis, RNA was the nitty-gritty molecule for primitive life and only relaxed when DNA and proteins—which exhibits their jobs much more efficiently than RNA—fostered.

RNA is very similar to DNA, and carries out numerous vital functions in every cell, also acting as a transitional-molecule between DNA and protein synthesis, and functioning as an on-and-off switch for certain genes. But the RNA hypothesis doesn't say how RNA itself first showed up. Like DNA, RNA is a complicated molecule made of repeating units of thousands of smaller molecules known as nucleotides that connect together in very exclusive, patterned ways. While there are those scientists who think RNA could have arisen spontaneously on early Earth, others believe the odds of such a thing taking place are astronomical.

What are the geneses of life on Earth? How did things arrive from non-living to living, from something that could not regenerate to something that could? How can a sum of inanimate atoms become animate? How did organic molecules obtain a high enough level of complicacy to be considered as living? The proper reply is that we do not really understand how life created on planet Earth.

The study of the inception of life on Earth or, more directly, how life on Earth started from inanimate matter, is scientifically familiar as abiogenesis (as opposed to biogenesis, which is the process of lifeforms generating other lifeforms, and as contrary to evolution, which is the study of how living things have altered over time since life first began). The contemporary explanation of abiogenesis is the original evolution of life or living organisms from inorganic or inanimate substances.

It regards the buildup of the simplest forms of life from primordial chemicals. It then becomes the search for some kind of molecule (along the lines of RNA or DNA) which is simple enough that it can be made by physical processes on the young Earth, yet complex enough that it can take charge of constructing more of itself, which most people would detect as constituting life.

Biologist scientists believe that the first living things on Earth, single-celled micro-organisms or microbes without a cell nucleus or cell membrane familiar as prokaryotes, seem to have initially shown on Earth almost four billion years ago, just a few hundred million years after the formation of the Earth itself. By far the longest portion of the history of life on Earth, hence, has contained the biochemical evolution of these single-celled micro-organisms, bacteria, and archaea: we can locate individual fossilized microbes in rocks 3.4 billion years old, yet geologists can only conclusively detect multi-celled fossils in certain rocks younger than 1 billion years.

It is assumed that over a few hundred million years of evolution, pre-biotic molecules gradually evolved into self-replicating molecules by natural selection. While some impression of the subject is well known, others remain puzzling and are the source of much debate among scientists. However, much progress has been made, there is still no single sure theory.

Life for all of its complexity is braided out of about 30 or so different molecules, made from some of the most available elements in the universe: oxygen, hydrogen, carbon, nitrogen, sulfur, and phosphorus. However, no one has yet succeeded in synthesizing a protocell (protocell is a self-organized, endogenously ordered, a spherical collection of lipids suggested as a stepping-stone toward the origin of life) utilizing basic components which would have the required properties of life. The beginnings of life are, strictly speaking, a matter of biology, not physics, which modern science suggests we are. After all, are we made of stardust?

QUOTES BY RUMI JALAL AD'DIN

I died as a mineral and became a plant,
I died as plant and rose to animal,
I died as animal and I was human,
Why should I fear? When was I less by dying?
Yet once more I shall die human,
To soar with angels blessed above.
when I sacrifice my angel soul
I shall become what no mind ever conceived.
As a human, I will die once more,
Reborn, I will with the angel's soar.
when I let my angel body go,
I shall be more than the mortal mind can know.
— Rumi Jalal ad 'Din

He says, There's nothing left of me.
I'm like a ruby held up to the sunrise.
Is it still a stone, or a world?
made of redness? It has no resistance
to sunlight.
This is how Hallaj said, I am God,
and told the truth!
The ruby and the sunrise are one.
Be courageous and discipline yourself.
Completely become hearing and ear, and wear this sun-
ruby as an earring.

If science should be a reliable gauge to depend on, then most scientists acknowledge that approximately sixty tons of cosmic dust fall to Earth every day. Researchers hypothesize that anywhere between 0.4 and 110 tons of the star stuff come into our atmosphere every day. If so, and for billions of years, then why should it be of any doubt that we are an inseparable part of these extremely rich and very valuable mineral soil and the brilliant atmosphere that energizes it with oxygen since without surely not an animated being can ever survive.

The stardust, the cosmos, is within us. We are made of star-stuff. You couldn't be here if stars hadn't exploded, because the elements—the carbon, nitrogen, oxygen, iron, all the things that matter for evolution— weren't created at the beginning of time.

The assay (estimate) is that about 36 and 166 meteorites larger than 10 grams drop to Earth per million square kilometers each year. Over the entire surface area of the Earth, that translates to 18,000 to 84,000 meteorites bigger than 10 grams per year. But most meteorites are too small to fall all the way to the surface. "You are the universe expressing itself as a human for a little while." Karen Wise

Many scientists believe, yes, we are made of atoms which perhaps were made up in millions of stars, saying that one's right leg atom might be from an entirely different star than the atoms in one's left leg. In truth our body—and everything in the world around us—is possibly made of atoms from innumerable (incalculable) different stars, originally estranged from each other by millions or even billions of light-years.

Those atoms rambled through space for millions or even billions of years, before eventually summing up in our primeval (prehistorical, primordial) solar system and coalesced (converged) because of gravity, to form the Earth and everything on it; including, ultimately, you and I. Not only are we made of stardust, but the atoms in our bodies are amazingly antiquated (surely billions of years old—at least as old as the solar system itself), and they have traveled an extremely long way, over a very long time, in order to build themselves into us. You are truly a child of God within the cosmic realm.

It doesn't deactivate there, because when living organisms expire, their atoms are reused by the processes of ruination (decay) and pass back into the air, water, soil, and rocks. over millions of years, many of these atoms will gradually become absorbed as food, water or air by ensuing generations of living organisms, and incorporated into their bodies in turn, and fluctuate in the food chain for centuries or millennia, until they are eventually digested into our body as the food, the air we breathe or the water we drink for survival.

So it is entirely probable that we carry atoms in our bodies that once were in the bodies of the first living organisms on planet Earth, and then in the bodies of prehistoric mammals, and in the bodies of apes, and then in the bodies of Neanderthals or homo sapiens and so on, up and up, until they reached you . to here. So as well as being a child of the cosmos, our body is also an atomic microcosm of all the life that has ever lived on planet Earth.

And, assuming the exponentially number of atoms in our bodies, and how they get widespread and mixed up over many centuries and millennia, our physical bodies will certainly have atoms from a considerable proportion of all the human beings who ever lived—as well as a few famous characters or not popular ones; maybe there's a carbon atom in your left pinky that once belonged to Cyrus the great, Plato the Greece philosopher, your eye may once belong to Jesus Christ, or your ear belonged to profit Moses, maybe Buddha, or perhaps one's rear end had belonged to nasty Hitler, may be Mussolini, or a hydrogen or Sulphur atom in your right hand that once belonged to Rumi the Persian philosopher and poet, may the great Shakespeare, or Lenin.

In truth, pick any random person from history, and you've possibly contained a bit of them in you! We know that water and electricity together make a dangerous pair. Mixing water and electricity, either from a lightning bolt or electrical socket in the house, is an extremely dangerous thing to do. Bear in mind that pure water is actually an excellent insulator and does not conduct electricity.

Water that would be considered pure would be distilled water (water condensed from steam) and deionized water (used in laboratories.) Water is an excellent solvent. No matter if the water comes out of your kitchen faucet, comes out of the ground or falls from the sky, the water will contain significant amounts of dissolved substances, minerals, and chemicals.

These things are the solutes dissolved in water. Free ions in water conduct electricity and Water is no longer an insulator once it begins dissolving substances. Even a small amount of ions in a water solution makes it able to conduct electricity. Once water contains these ions it will conduct electricity, such as from a lightning bolt or a wire from the wall socket, as the electricity from the source will seek out oppositely charged ions in the water.

The point is that 97 percent of the human body consists of stardust, claim scientists who have measured the distribution of essential elements of life in over 150,000 stars in the Milky Way galaxy. Body fluid contains electrolytes, chemicals which, when they dissolve in water, produce charged ions.

These ions enable the flow of electrical signals through the body. Electrolytes play a vital role in our body electrolytes that generate ions and enables the body to function. The principal electrolytes convey sodium, chloride, potassium, calcium, and magnesium. These five nutritional elements are minerals, and when minerals dissolve in water they separate into a positive and negative ion. Just like vitamins, minerals help our body grow, develop, and stay healthy.

The body utilizes minerals to perform many different functions—from making strong bones to send (information, sound, etc.) in the form of electrical signals to nerve impulses. Some minerals are even used to make hormones or create a normal heartbeat. The human body conducts electricity, because of minerals and conveying chemicals in our bodies. If any part of the body receives an electric shock, the electricity will go through the tissues with little obstruction. Then, the internal tissues start burning. Electrical current can damage the heart, which could cause the heart to either stop or beat erratically.

The electron current is what causes harm to tissue or nervous system damage, causing death or serious injury. Effects from electrocution can include burns or interference to our body's electric signals. A small current can actually kill you by entering the body, going through the heart, and exiting through the other side. The conductibility of the human body is due to the fact that chemicals and stardust minerals are the building blocks in making what we are, the very elements identified in stars.

Nature is endlessly resourceful, with the advent of new technology, and with the bigger and more powerful scientific equipment we are rapidly improving Earth's view of the universe. It will be at least 50 times more powerful than any telescope on Earth.

NASA is building the biggest telescope the world has ever witnessed and it will render scientists the opportunity to observe cosmic events that occurred about13.5 billion years ago—just 220 million years following the big bang. It is known as the James Webb Space Telescope (JWST), it will be 100 times more powerful than the Hubble Space Telescope, and is estimated to be fully operational within the next three years. It seems that no matter how advanced we become in new technologies, there are continuously recent things in nature that will never quit exhibiting amazing entities and fresh wonders.

Humanity will not see an end to the adventure of our universe since there will not exist blank pages not showing exciting ideas and miracle like resources, they will gradually be invented and explored. The human mind and heart resemble nature and are extremely important and the undeniable extension of this progressively oriented agendas.

Both our heart and mind simulate nature, and the cosmic events, since there is no ending in what our heart carves and desires, and our mind seeks. because the architect of the human brain and heart is born from the same energy-oriented principle that is the literal cause of the entire universe. It is the same precise mathematics that is rooted in plants, the birds, the bees, the flowers, the trees, the stars the galaxies, and the Higgs particles. That is why the view of human aesthetic is as demanding as the aesthetic nature itself. We are not outside observers; we are an inseparable part of this whole magical world anchored inside this magnificent universe.

In the beginning, they thought cells are the tiniest unit, then learned cells are structures that are made up billions of molecules, and figured out that each molecule is composed of atoms (in turn, atoms are made up subatomic particles called protons, electrons, and neutrons, and those are comprised of even smaller particles called quarks). Quarks, like electrons, are fundamentally particles which for now they can't be broken into tinier parts. Scientists believe that the first fount (source) was the big bang that made the universe 14 billion years ago.

When the big bang happened, the elementary particles originally were too hot to make any stable atoms. But after a few thousand years later, when things cooled down a lot, hydrogen and helium got made. Protons, neutrons, and electrons can then form to build atoms. Atoms are then used to create the molecules in our atmosphere. There are about 120 elements that can be sought in the molecules we recognize so far. Smaller molecules can manage together and construct macromolecules.

Then the question which crosses an inquisitive mind is that what comes after quarks and leptons. Quarks are the smallest units or building blocks of the Standard Model of particle physics and therefore cannot be split up into further constituents. On the other hand, if one chooses to believe in string theory, basically everything is made up of tiny vibrating strings, including quarks. Strings or points?

In experiments, tiny particles like quarks and electrons seem to behave like single points of matter with no spatial (having extension in space relating to the position, area, and the size of objects distribution). Quarks represent the smallest known subatomic particles. These building blocks of matter are considered the new elementary particles, replacing protons, neutrons, and electrons as the fundamental particles of the universe. Up and down quarks are the most common and least massive.

Singularity.

If you go back in time as far as you can, you'll find a universe that was hotter, denser, and more energetic. If you were to extrapolate back to an arbitrarily hot, dense state, the laws of physics that describe space, time, matter and energy break down; you'll arrive at a singularity.

Yet a singularity is also exactly what you find if you were to fly inside a black hole, to the final destination where all in-falling matter and energy winds up. These are the only instances in the entire universe's history—past, present, and future—where a singularity occurs. Perhaps the two of them are connected? It's not as crazy an idea as you might think.

General relativity and quantum mechanics, together, do an excellent job of describing the physics of the universe outside of a black hole, like of a gas cloud being torn apart outside the event horizon. But to understand the physics at or near a singularity, a successor theory, like quantum gravity, is needed. Normally, the universe is governed by two sets of rules: quantum mechanics, for particles and their electromagnetic and nuclear interactions, and general relativity, for masses, gravity and the curvature of space-time.

Quantum mechanics tells us that all particles exhibit wave-like properties and have some level of intrinsic uncertainty between position/momentum and energy/time. In particular, every massive particle has a wavelength associated with it: A Compton wavelength, which explains how it scatters in collisions. If you were to take a photon's wavelength and convert it into a mass, via Einstein's $E = mc2$ you'd get a massive particle's Compton wavelength.

A singularity is where conventional physics breaks down, whether you're talking about the very beginning of the universe and the birth of space and time or the very central point of a black hole. However, we can calculate what happens to space-time inside the event horizon all the way up to (but not including) the central singularity.

Surprisingly, with just a coordinate transformation, the space inside a black hole can be mapped, one-to-one, onto the space outside a black hole. What happens when the universe stops expanding? In a loosed universe, gravity eventually stops the expansion of the universe, after which it starts to contract until all matter in the universe collapses to a point, a final singularity termed the Big Crunch, the opposite of the big bang.

19

THE ANTHROPIC PRINCIPLE

The anthropic principle is a philosophical consideration that by looking at the universe, it must be in harmony with the conscious and sapient life (referring to homo-sapiens, wise) that observes it.

The fundamental laws of nature carry utterly imperative constants, like the gravitational constant, the electric charge, the mass of the electron, the speed of light, plank's constant from quantum mechanics.

For example, gravitational constant: decides the power of gravity, if the strength is lower than stars, the pressure would not suffice to quell(overcome) Coulomb barrier which will result in the stars not shinning, since no thermonuclear composite (alloy, synthesis, mixture) is possible. If higher, stars burn too fast, consume fuel before life has a chance to develop.

Arno Penzias (Nobel prize in physics): Astronomy leads us to a unique event, a universe which was created out of nothing, one with the very delicate balance needed to provide exactly the conditions required to permit life, and one which has an underlying (one might say supernatural) plan.

The Coulomb barrier is the energy barrier due to electrostatic interaction that two nuclei need to overcome so they can get close enough to undergo a nuclear reaction. Electrostatic: relates to stationary electric charges or fields as opposed to electric currents. powerful force coupling constant: keeps particles attached in the nucleus of the atom. If weaker than multi-proton, then, particles couldn't have fastened together, hydrogen would be the sole element in the universe. If stronger, all elements lighter than iron would be scarce. Also, radioactive decay would be less, which heat melts the core of planet Earth.

The electromagnetic coupling constant: Decides the power of the electromagnetic force that joint electrons to the nucleus. If less, no electrons can be held in orbit. If stronger, electrons will not bond with other atoms, if so, then resulting in no molecules. All the above constants are critical for the arrangement of the basic building blocks of life. And, the range of possible values for these constants is with extremely narrow margin only approximately 1 to 5% for the amalgamation (fusion, synthesis) of constants.

Outside this range, and life (specifically intelligent life) could not be possible. what science is not able to answer is that why is there any structure at all to our universe? Why this universal or planetary structure guide to the ability for life to exist? Why does life create intelligence to relatively fathom life's intricacies?

Scientists, the physicists, tell us a universe with a lower gravitational constant would have a weaker force of gravity, where stars and planets cannot form. Or a universe with a highly powerful force would inhibit thermonuclear synthesis, which would lessen the luminosity of stars, then, a darker universe, leaving life without sunlight. Why don't those universes exist? Why does our universe, with its exclusive value exist rather than not, and why not another?

Did you know that not only space but the time itself is distorted by heavy objects since matter, energy, motion, space, and time are intertwined as Einstein's theory of general relativity predicted that the space-time around Earth would be not only warped but also twisted by the planet's rotation? In it, he determined that massive objects cause a distortion in space-time, which is felt as gravity. Since matter carries energy (via Einstein's famous relation that energy is mass times the speed of light squared), such objects will have a gravitational field and so they will distort space-time. So one way in which a charge or a magnet will distort space-time is by virtue of its matter.

The general belief by physics is that the universe is expanding, which is due to the geometry of the universe, at least on an extremely large scale, elliptic. In a closed universe, gravity eventually stops the expansion of the universe, after which it starts to contract until all matter in the universe collapses to a point, a final singularity termed the Big Crunch, the opposite of the big bang. Edwin Hubble space telescope indicated the definitive evidence that the universe was expanding. The idea was that the universe received all the energy required for its expansion in the first few moments after the big bang.

Scientists believe that the curve changes noticeably about 7.5 billion years ago when objects in the universe began flying apart as a faster rate. Astronomers theorize that the faster expansion rate is due to a mysterious, dark force that is pulling galaxies apart. One explanation for dark energy is that it is a property of space. In the 1920s, astronomer Edwin Hubble learned that the universe was not static, rather, it was expanding; a find that exhibited the universe was apparently born in a big bang. After that, it was thought the gravity of the matter in the universe was sure to slow the expansion of the universe.

But what should be clear is that the universal expansion, the gravitational forces, the wonders of millions and millions of black holes, the magic of electromagnetic forces, the atomic forces, the effects of entropy, the subatomic world of particles, the quantum world, the string theory, and the probabilities of some parallel universes, the magical maneuverability's of trillions galaxies, billions of universes, and millions of other perhaps magnificently unknown phenomenon's are breathtakingly operating without the slightest flaw, making the fine-tuning of the universe possible as quoted by the prominent George Ellis (British astrophysicist): "Amazing fine tuning occurs in the laws that make this [complexity] possible. Realization of the complexity of what is accomplished makes it very difficult not to use the word 'miraculous' without taking a stand as to the ontological status of the word.

Further, why should the constants even be present to help with the stability of the universe and lead to the evolution of human consciousness, as they are known as the anthropic principle or the fine-tuning of the universe? This should activate neurons, and raise eyebrows to ask if the anthropic principle has the properties which substantiate intelligent life, then, there must exist a graceful designer beyond human imagination that planned to sustain our universe for reaching specific purpose with having a definite goal, or goals in mind.

Declaring the position of the fine-tuned universe states that a slight alteration in several of the dimensionless physical constants would force radical changes in the universe. Stephen Hawking said, "The laws of science, as we know them at present, contain many fundamental numbers, like the size of the electric charge of the electron and the ratio of the masses of the proton and the electron. The remarkable fact is that the value of these numbers seems to have been very finely adjusted to make possible the development of life."

For instance, if the strong nuclear forces were 2 percent more powerful than it is, indicating its strength was 2 percent larger, leaving the other constants unaltered, diprotons would be secure; stated by physicist Paul Davies, hydrogen would fuse into them instead of deuterium and helium. This would extremely alter the physics of stars, and doubtlessly preclude the existence of life similar to what we know on Earth.

The fine-tuned universe is the proposition that the conditions that permit life in the universe can occur only when certain universal dimensionless physical constants lie within a very narrow range of values, so that if any of several fundamental constants were only slightly different, the universe would be unlikely to be conducive to the establishment and development of matter, astronomical structures, elemental diversity, or life as it is comprehended.

Either the entire cosmos, not excluding our universe is a stroke of luck, a lucky accident, a random object that appeared out of nowhere, and we all are the felicitous (fortunate) products. But as experienced for billions of years we should admit that life is robust, and the universe is fined tuned, well-orchestrated and managed, otherwise it certainly would have not lasted as long as it has where scientists do predicate for billions even trillions of years to go; which should imply there can be other forms of life beside the carbon-oriented life that we know.

An ensemble of other different universes is necessary for the existence of our universe (multiple universes.) There are two sorts of anthropic principle issues weak and strong. The weak anthropic principle simply believes that the current universe is of the matrix (form) that allows intelligent spectators. In other words, there is the right amount of complexity and time for intelligent observers to vent (emit, evolve).

Then, is the strong anthropic principle which states that the universe must have these requirements in order to sustain intelligence life (us). Our existence is then the end result of a plan. The strong form seems extreme and the weak form appear not gratifying. The key point here is that a naturalistic view for science requires that the universe is causally closed. That science is whole (full-blown, complete) and the forces of physics are the sole forces in the universe and everything can be described by those forces.

The anthropic principle is observed as a challenge to the naturalistic view and demands an outside an omnipotent force or guiding deity. The philosophical quandary (dilemma) is that the constants of the universe on both microscopic (atomic constants), and macroscopic (electromagnetic forces) and cosmological levels in their entirety appear to be extremely finely adjusted-tuned, in order for life and intelligence to emit.

We should seriously question linking the natural-selection doctrine, and the survival of the fittest theory behind the reason for creating even the simplest living organism which has not only proven futile but the evidence of an omnipotent designer is found in nature and the higher realms that Darwin couldn't have dreamed of.

Darwin argued that the emergence of design could be simplified as the product of a purely unguided mechanism, referencing natural selection and random variation. Modern Neo-Darwinists have likewise indicated that the undirected process of natural selection and random mutation generated the complex designed-like build up in living systems. They state that natural selection can emulate (simulate) the powers of a designing intelligence without itself being directed by an intelligent agent.

As Darwin himself insisted, "There seems to be no more design in the variability of organic beings and in the action of natural selection, than in the course in which the wind blows." Or as the renowned evolutionary biologist Francisco Ayala has debated, Darwin is chronicled for "design without a designer" and showed "that the directive organization of living beings can be explained as the result of a natural process, natural selection, without any need to resort to a Creator or other external agent."

But did Darwin describe all evidence of patent (apparent, obvious) design in biology? Darwin tried to explain the origin of new living forms initiating from simpler pre-existing forms of life, but his theory of evolution by natural selection did not even attempt to fathom the origin of life, the simplest living cell in existence.

Yet, there is now absorbing proof of the intelligent design in the inner recesses of the simplest living one-celled organisms. Furthermore, there is a key component of living cells that convey the intelligent design of life detectable which Darwin was not aware of, and that modern evolutionary theorists have not explained away.

20

HUMAN BEINGS RESEMBLE TREES

Trees and plants create the food they need for living and to grow through photosynthesis, a process that happens in their leaves. To produce food (in the form of glucose and other sugars), a tree, or a plant needs energy from sunlight, carbon dioxide from the air, and water. They make their own food from these imperative elements, like sunlight, water, carbon dioxide and nutrients from the soil.

During the process of photosynthesis, plants use carbon dioxide to make food and release oxygen, as a result. Roots carry water and nutrients to the plant. Trees and Plants absorb nutrients and water through their roots, but photosynthesis—the process by which plants create their fuel—occurs in the leaves.

Therefore, plants need to get fluids and nutrients from the ground up through their stems to their parts that are above ground level. One of the mysteries of nature is how despite the force of gravity water and nutrient go up to reach the branches and feed the leaves, and the entire plant, or the whole tree.

As those trees and plants must have the essential elements to bear fruits, flowers, shade, beauty and release oxygen, the human beings also need clean air, clean water, sunlight, nutrients, rest and productivity which are definitely essential for their existence. these very required elements are absorbed through our digestive system as the sun is via skin to rejuvenate every cell in the human body.

The similarity is that as trees and plants produce astonishing colors, wonderful fruit with great taste, as often exotic flowers do with divine smell; good human beings are meant to bear amazingly fruits like thoughts, and beautiful flower-like minds, with compassionate and kind hearts to make a difference for a better world, creating good thought, with good words, and good deeds; since it is through our mind, heart, and soul that we can cultivate the awesome drive and the impetus to do good, to make it a purposeful living.

A tree requires the four vital elements for survival—soil, water, air, and fire (sun). Human beings also need the same imperative elements.

The soil provides nourishment for the tree, also allows the roots through which the food is absorbed to grow and expand. A person with a great deal of wisdom, but not doing many good deeds is like a tree with numerous branches but with few roots. A brief storm can uproot and destroys it. In comparison, a person whose good deeds exceed his wisdom is like a tree with few branches but whose roots are numerous. It is deeply and firmly planted, and even if many strong windy storms below against it, will not fall apart.

When one belongs, irrespective of his wealth and position, then, there is a strong connection with one's community and people around him which signifies strong roots. But when one does not belong and is behaving like a remote island, even though one might appear wealthy and successful, it denotes much like fancy branches of a tree, but with few roots.

It can easily fall when faced with hardship and lose the challenges that life can unexpectedly throw that are often impossible to overcome. Human beings are group animals they need to collectively thrive to conquer over nature's challenges. Zest, vitality, encouragement, hope, the power of intention, perseverance, blossoming, success, serving others in the name of God and humanity, constructive attitudes, challenging nature, and collectively reaching prosperity, is without a doubt most beneficial to everyone, rather than acting isolated and single-handedly.

WATER

Rainwater is sucked into the ground and through a complex system of roots—it is then carried throughout the trunk, branches, and leaves.

Without water, the tree will wither and die. Comparatively, when deprived of water, a person will end up dehydrated and eventually disoriented, even to the point where the victims can lose one's memory.

Air

Trees and plants need air to survive since the air carries oxygen that trees and plants must have for respiration, also carbon dioxide for photosynthesis. Comparatively, humans also must have oxygen to live, even a couple of minutes with no air to breath, we will expire.

Sunlight

A tree also needs sunlight to survive. The absorption of energy from the light activates the process of photosynthesis, a chemical reaction that is necessary for the growth and health of the tree. Humans also need fire and warmth to survive, the warmth of mankind and community, through which family, friends, and associates can be very helpful and supportive in the times of need. Caring people can boost one's energy and channel that into positive actions. Today's lifestyle has cast us all into the bleak vicinities of fear and anonymity.

The urban culture has pushed so many into cyberspace mentalities. It seems there is no scape, but to behave robotically like, exhausted of nourishing the human soul through caring and warmth, which has I afraid created millions with a psychological problem which has manifested a breeding ground for violence and criminal behaviors, which should demand rationally decisive change if humanity is to pull through.

21

WHAT GOES AROUND, COMES AROUND

Experiencing life is basically channeled through our senses, materially based evidence is executed via our nervous system and through what we see, hear, taste, smell, and touch. When we notice so much injustice, suffering, cruelty, misery, ordeal, and pain on one side in an extremely troubling world, and the absence of God on the other side, it gives the impression that God does not hear our cry for help, then, what most feel is despair, which discords and disorients them from the reality of a living that meant to be good; making it apropos (suitable) and conducive for so many not to realize the infinite traces of God and the consequences of the divine justice.

We ought to know that nothing occurs by chance since everything happens within the universal law of cause and effect, we reap what we saw. It is clearly understood that for every action, there is an equal and opposite reaction. The invisible hand of this divine mechanism is relentlessly at work to make sure that not a single manifestation takes place without being noticed. Yes, so many of man's deed might appear to have no immediate result but concealed. Until eventually all catch up and forms a complex but justified web of cause and effect. As humanity advances in technology, what we presently might consider as miracles, will one day be taken for granted as common.

The endowed human drive will relentlessly push forward for new inventions and magic like concepts to materialize what once was thought as miracle become a contemporary fact. The response often is difficult for millions to link the magnificent design, discipline, and intricacy of this enchanting universe to our Creator.

Traces of God should be quite obvious in God's superb planning, and the ultra-competency of a designer that incredibly manages the cosmos and beyond, which without chaos and definitely perdition (damnation, doom) days should be expected. But the question which most atheists ask is that if God created the cosmos, and if God overseas the divine justice, then, who created God?

Many dilettantes (dabbler, layman, not expert) states that the cosmos is so complicated, it must have been created by a creator, but if that's correct, then, it must alert us that God is even more Byzantine (complicated) than the cosmos. So if the cosmos needed a maker, surely this higher God also needed a creator! Therefore, if it is improbable that the cosmos exists without a beginning, it is even more unlikely that God exists without a beginning. So, why believe in this notably dubious God? Cynic (doubter) and believers both agree that out of nothing, nothing comes. But clearly, if nothing had ever existed, there would be nothing now and nothing endlessly.

Those concerns hence accept that since something exists, something had to exist from all of eternity. In retrospect, the atheists say the cosmos existed from all of eternity, believers say God existed from all of eternity. The famous debate which many creationists have redundantly set forth is that every event has a cause. A universe is obviously an event. Hence, the universe has a cause, and that cause is God. In response, the non-believers have argued that if so, then God must have a cause. But then there is a missing link and a huge discrepancy in the position which the atheists take.

The atheist forgets that the cause and effect events are only authenticated in the observable world, where materially based living can empirically be manifested, and do not make sense in the unseen world since they do not apply to the invisible spiritual realms. They cannot fathom that the physical laws belong to the material world, and are not applicable in the spiritual and the hidden domain.

Edgar Andrews, of the University of London England, an international expert on the science of large molecules, writes this in defense of God's existence: "Because cause and effect are only proven for the physical world, we can no longer insist that cause and effect are relevant when it comes to the origin of a spiritual entity like God. Therefore, God doesn't have to have a cause—he can be the ultimate uncaused cause, a being whom no one has made."

Creationists believe that God is the infinite and perfect spirit in whom all things have their source, support, and end. As mysterious as God is, but certainly not contradictory, when we are faced with the choice of the cosmos existing from all eternity, or the Divine Spirit existing from all eternity, the believers answer is God. The startling discipline, and the mindboggling complexity in the universe and what it holds, is just beyond chance and random maneuverability which should put any inquisitively intelligent mind at awe. Things have to operate the way they originally have, otherwise, we would not be here to question them.

For instance, if the power of the electromagnetic force were just a bit different, atoms would not be secured. Scientists believe that Just a 4 percent alteration would stop all nuclear amalgam (mixture, fusion) in stars. the arrangement which builds the carbon atoms that our bodies are significantly made of. Likewise, there is a sensitive balance between gravity that pulls matter towards itself, and the dark energy, which acts in reverse making the universe grow ever faster, that is required to make the existence of stars possible, while not collapsing the universe on itself.

There is a reason that the neutrons are just a tad heavier than protons, if it were the reverse, atoms would not exist, because all the protons in the universe would have dilapidated (ruination, decay) into neutrons after the big bang. No protons, which then, no atomic nuclei and no atoms. Without atoms, no chemistry, no life.

Adding to the controversy is an unanswered question lurking at the very heart of science -the origin of the laws of physics. do they come from? The wonders of mathematics that correlated with the laws of physics as they comfortably corroborate with the laws of nature. Why do they have the form they do?

We ought to bear in mind that crucial universal functionings are concept oriented which without no decisive living is ever possible, so is the concept of good and evil, as they will be met with divine justice, as they are due in a timely manner.

22

IN GOD, WE SHOULD BELIEVE

Innumerous tragedy and harms behold humanity because of not knowing and lack of information. It is a no-brainer that once one realizes the infinite intricacy of the world we live in and the awesome universe which our galaxy the Milky Way is part of, forth with thousands of other mind-boggling phenomena already discovered, and millions more waiting, if not billions to be contrived. Then, it should nudge intelligent minds to wonder about the magnanimity (magnificent, generosity) of a great designer's footprint in all there is, and all there ever will be.

We should know that our solar system consists of our star, the Sun, and its orbiting planets (including Earth), along with numerous moons, asteroids, comet material, rocks, and dust. Our Sun is just one star among the hundreds of billions of stars in our Milky Way Galaxy. The universe is all of the galaxies—billions of them.

Hence leaving humanity with no choice but to meditate on the enormity of cosmic with limitless universes and infinite galaxies that operate with extreme discipline and accuracy, which ought to leave no doubt that we must be living a purposeful life, since we are an inseparable part of this extremely colossal existence; which should relentlessly spur humanity to delve into the unknown, and to further become competent in discovering the magic that awaits us, to pinnacle the wisdom in searching for God, to tirelessly progress, and for living a life with virtuous intent.

We can communicate through our senses, via our mind, in which our thoughts interact, making it able for limitless messages to get across, they become substantiated because the atmosphere we live in is fundamentally conductive. The environment is an active conductor, where there are no barriers to halt the fluidity of what we think, conducive to our feelings, emotions, and imaginations. The same life force that allows seeds to grow, trees to bear fruits, potentiates embryos to mature, and basically allows any animated activity to take place; it is the entity that deals with the entire universal maneuverability.

The cosmic forces not to exclude electromagnetic forces, gravity force, the strong and weak atomic forces that are engaged in making it a fertile ground for prolific mind and ideas to function and revolutionize the world we know. The same life force that makes it possible to invent x-rays machines, MRI, SCANS of many sorts, EKG/ECG machines, which renders an extremely measured atmosphere so disciplinary that makes it possible to materialize all kinds of scientific inventions, and so reliable making our life easier, not to exclude the internet, satellites, GPS, and other media feats.

A life that we can resonate with and function through our everyday living, since the atmosphere that we operate in, is not insulated, but a great conductor for mandating infinite possibilities in the near and far future, where kneeling next to the gates where God resides becomes an option.

The reason for our brain which apparently is energy based that can produce thoughts, and for our mind to communicate and interact is because of the conductibility of the surroundings which makes it possible. It is because our brain also is a fabulous conductor compatible with the environment in which we operate. Our thoughts, feelings, desires, and emotion can interact just because the fertile ground already providing the means absolutely necessary to produce such tasks, and relate to employing science, manifest philosophy, constitute arts, music, creativity, imagination, and host of modern socio-cultural, socioeconomic activities conveying wonderful ideas, and innovations.

Our mind and hearts ought to act as awakened agents to simultaneously accord with the extremely alert environment that we live in since we are an is an inseparable part of nature, nature so robustly impregnated with magic and never-ending surprises which has amazed the most talented and magnificent minds of our times.

Gradual brain neuroplasticity is directly proportional to the brain producing more brain cells, and in creating billions of neurons firing at trillions of synopsis (junctures) to produce millions of thoughts every day to make magic, that is because of the fluidity of mind and its congruency with the universally exuding energy that is prevalent in our world, in our universe, and billions of other universes having their own solar systems.

our solar system consists of an average star we call the Sun, the planets Mercury, Venus, Earth, Mars, Jupiter, Saturn, Uranus, Neptune, and Pluto. It includes the satellites of the planets; numerous comets, asteroids, and meteoroids; and the interplanetary medium.

It seems promising that one-day people are able to communicate thoughts by means other than known senses known as telepathy. Telepathy falls into two parts: Telepathic communication, that is the ability to delegate information from one mind to another, and telepathic perception, which is the power to receive messages, information from another mind that sounds colossally exciting, since reading minds can encourage good thoughts, good words and good deeds, perhaps a wonderfully effective way to lessen wrongdoings and violence behaviors.

It is a blessing knowing that the human mind and soul, our heart and imagination is so coherent with the energy-driven universe that is infinite in nature, so is our mind and our heart. There is no limit to our heart desiring and our mind imagining to the day we take our last breath, which should excitingly get ready for our next step up adventure in the next runner up living. Otherwise, transparency of human communication and any other activity for that matter would have been insulated and absolutely futile.

What we see and feel as solid matter is made of nuclei and electrons, and when we get down to investigate the really small things like atoms and nuclei and the distinction between matter and empty space, we confront a much different meaning. We face solid matter as what we cannot penetrate and walk through it, because what we know as mysterious forces connect the nuclei and the atoms so tight to each other, making it into the solid position that is impermeable.

Liquids, the life force, or if you like the mysterious fields and forces hold the atoms less tightly over each other, and more loosely than the position of atoms in solids, making it possible to wall through water, and of course not as fast as one can walk through air than the water. Walking through the gas is easy, since the atoms in the gas are not tied together, but rather whizzing freely.

Let's look at a few things out of thousands of wonders taking place in our own body. If we pay attention to so many things happening in our own body, it should put anyone at awe since amazing mechanisms occur in human anatomy which we take for granted. For example, if the tongue gets caught between two layers of sharp teeth every time we eat, or when talk, it would be extremely painful. But the tongue by instinct maneuvers so magically, moving side to side, bouncing food up and down without getting caught and becoming injured by our sharp teeth.

The miracle of saliva, and other wonderful digestive hormones; and no matter how much food and drink a healthy digestive system can take in, until one is full, one does not feel any discomfort as food gradually travels through the digestive system. What we experience is feeling full, and quenching our thirst, enjoying the ride. Many frequently question how can human spirit experience the joy of lovemaking, playfulness, experience fear, or any other human feat, as there is no live physical body after we expire?

What I can say is, one should think about one's dream in which our mind, the spirit, or the soul, call it what you wish, often does the unthinkable as we are very well alive in our dreams, without our body lifting a finger when deep in its sleep.

Obviously, billions of phenomena, if not trillions of cases are so precisely calculated that is utterly infallible, making life possible; which should put any intelligent mind at awe and reverence for the infinite mind of a creator with such incredible fist beyond imagination. A magnificent designer beyond space and time, that is over the human mind to assess its infinite abilities and greatness.

In the end, we should pound on science, philosophy, and seek poetry and art as they all play great roles in our lives, as for science it is enormously important since scientists relentlessly delve into nature to discover the infinite resourcefulness of the world we live in. They insist on looking into the root-causes of all things as their findings will never face any unwritten page, as the infinite universe would constantly expose new ideas to inquisitive minds, surprising them with fresh concepts to the end of times.

A society without philosophical endeavors is empty of wisdom, where a society without poets has no soul, and a nation without artists has no beauty, and gatherings without music can seldom be happy, as music can excite the body, and thrill the soul, as these entities and the like bring us closer to God.

23

TESTOSTERONE AND AGGRESSIVE BEHAVIORS

Lack of information, and for some not even willing to talk on the subject of sex, and evaluate why for example some men are more aggressive, and to some extent violent than other sexually timid ones. So many are irrelevant to correctly evaluate this rather decisive subject as millions carelessly are inclined to harsh and often inhumane punishment as they are for sexual predators to forgo life imprisonment and even death in many developing nations, and third world countries, reminding one of the dark age mentality where cruel and savage retaliations often the case.

To act incredulous (cynical, dubious) referencing men's motive for sex as many females say or believe that men's brain is between their legs can biologically be better described as men's brain being located directly in the testes the male's testosterone factory. What undeniably is medically known aside from any baffling (confusing, mix up) psychological factors which initially been decided on that men's sexual craving is solely related to the amount of testosterone in a male's system.

If male's testosterone, also called T-level, is high, then more tendencies should be expected towards the opposite sex. That is how sex drive, also known as libido, is described by how much (T) one produces. Apparently this is correct for both male and females, knowing that on average basis males produce about ten to twelve times as much of this sex hormone as do females which should explain why men commonly have more irrepressible sex drive urges than women.

Stressful positions, such as trauma and the like, inflict significant inhibition on testosterone secretion. High testosterone levels or an increase in basal (relating to bottom layers) concentrations are associated with aggressive manifestations, whereas high cortisol concentrations are linked to submissive behaviors. Aggression has been differently described and it is shown with a broad spectrum from the tendency to verbal abuse and physical violence.

It is a primitive and common social behavior that the media report with covert gratification as if it is something to hurray about using it as a leverage for describing exciting news, in which the people of civilized nations accept its manifestation with horror and a subconscious disturbance, because such declaration yanks (uproot) the comfortable belief of the difference of human conduct from that of animals.

Violent and aggressive behavior is a natural and physiological element that rules beastly living, driven as it is by the instincts of survival and the preservation of species through reproduction. Attenuated (diluted, weak) remains of these instincts stay in humans, albeit (although) repressed by homey and social inhibitions, but it still patents (manifest) in transformed and various forms in accordance with the idiosyncrasy (mannerism, eccentricity), temperament (individuality, makeup, disposition) and the psychological state of each person.

Atavistic ancestor residues of belligerent behavior victorious (prevailing) in animal life, ruled by testosterone, stay diluted in man and choked via domestic and social reticence (inhibition.) Thus, it still manifests itself in different intensities, shape, and forms including thoughts, verbal aggressiveness, anger, frustration, offensiveness, competition, dominance behavior, physical aggression and violence conduct.

Testosterone plays a decisive role in the arousal of aggressive behavior in the brain centers involved in offensive conducts and on the growth of the muscular system that help with their findings. There is proof that testosterone levels are higher in people with aggressive behavior, those who have committed violent crimes.

Also, there is evidence that testosterone levels increase during the highly intensified sports games and other radical situations, where the victor's testosterone rises. Just like the fight or flight situation the sympathetic nervous system sends out impulses to glands and smooth muscles and instruct the adrenal medulla to relinquish epinephrine (adrenaline) and norepinephrine (noradrenaline) into the bloodstream.

These stress hormones make several changes in the body, including an increase in heart rate and blood pressure. In response to extreme stress, the body's sympathetic nervous system is invigorated (activated, quickened) because of the sudden rush of hormones. The hormone is known as the catecholamine, which includes adrenaline and noradrenaline.

The autonomic nervous system has two elements, the sympathetic nervous system, and the parasympathetic nervous system. The sympathetic nervous system works like a gas pedal in a car. It triggers the fight-or-flight response, providing the body with a burst of energy so that one can count to received dangers.

Many studies have shown that offensive behavior appreciates in the brain via interaction between subcortical structures in the amygdala and the hypothalamus in which emotions are generated and the prefrontal cognitive centers where emotions are perceived and controlled. Subcortical structures. The subcortical structures of the nervous system have a complex motor and non-motor functions.

The subcortical structures include the limbic system, the diencephalon, and the ventricles. The activities of testosterone on the brain initiates in the embryonic stage. It seems that in the beginning development of the DNA level, the number of CAG repeats in the androgen receptor gene seems to play a role in the expression of aggressive behavior. A (DNA) segment known as a CAG trinucleotide repeat.

This part is a buildup of a series of three DNA building blocks (cytosine, adenine, and guanine) that appear multiple times in a row. Neuroimaging testing's in adult males have shown that testosterone motivates the amygdala ameliorating (improving, enhancing) its emotional activity and its resistance to prefrontal curbing (restraining) control. This maneuverability is countered by the action of cortisol which simplifies prefrontal area cognitive control on impulsive inclinations (tendency) awakened in the subcortical structures.

The degree of impulsivity is regulated by serotonin inhibiting receptors, and with the meddling of this neurotransmitter, the major agents of the neuroendocrine influence on the brain process of aggression form a triad. Testosterone activates the subcortical areas of the brain to cause aggression, while cortisol and serotonin act antagonistically with testosterone to lower its consequences.

Inducing testosterone is biologically demanded as it is urged to literally guaranty the survival of the species. So it must be seen positively, and it should not be lightly. Still, given the constraints of civilization, and the nature of the human psyche, it also guarantees colossal frustration and sorrow—and possibly as much for men as for women. When a male's T-levels rise beyond a certain degree he can barely help but have sex on his mind virtually (practically, almost) all the time.

That's why it's not at all uncommon to hear a male's behavior described as testosterone-driven. Undeniably for males in their later teens and early twenties (when their T-levels rush), their thoughts and feelings are permeated hugely by what really is going on between their legs. They experience an almost continual thrilling in their genitals—sensations that howl (scream) for attention but that society does not permit being fully signified.

Knowing that, regardless of such austerity (inhibition, self-control), the very sight of a female can't be helped, but fan this not-to-be-denied and burst of libidinous flame. Generally speaking, many adolescent girls and women correctly criticize that they feel de-valued and less worthy when men look at or treat them, as sex objects. But obviously, this criterion shouldn't be loggerhead (state of strong disagreement) situation, since it is debatable that so many adolescent boys and men, tempted, and seduced from within by elevated T-levels, can't much help but be lured into very difficult position.

Like animals in heat, males under the influence since the beastly part of human being acting by instinct, will kick in harder when no sex education is ever presented to them as millions if not billions are exhausted from having the opportunity to become enlightened. so many are hardly alerted not to perceive females other than one-dimensionally—as objects for sexual pleasure.

These hormonal activities should remind one of not having a choice to either being born in ghetto, any other Godforsaken place and so many condescending hoods, or to be born in an upgraded, affluent family that are highly luxurious with money, influence, and prestige in which the difference would be like growing up in hell or heaven. Without having the slightest choice or say so, referencing where and whom one should be born to, or to what nationality, religion, race, clan and so on. They are mandatory, and thanks to God there is no prejudice to whom these hormonal activities should belong to since everyone is unanimously born with them without any exception.

Expect those with having good opportunities and decisive means which are able to better control aggressive behaviors, since they can identify with good education, and equate to constructively respond for great upbringings, and can accord with reliable role models, which most indigenous and poor are exhausted from having such prominent variables for making a better difference in their lives.

The harsh reality is that so many poor people will face stringent punishments, without having the knowledge or opportunities to be aware of the reason behind their anger and frustration which has a compounding effect when they are born into poverty and within desolate condition not being aware of the trouble inside which certainly would be mitigated and healed with education and through professional therapeutic procedures that they are denied of since they cannot afford such bonuses available to the rich.

What I mean is that we are part animal and part human, as there is not much we can do to stop instinctual mechanism which they make us partly beast, since our physical body must breath, must be nourished, must sleep and have rest, need to keep up with good hygiene, must have intercourse to produce life, must work to survive, and so on, which they are also blessings since they keep us afloat to survive for reaching our objectives which by having conscious, being mindful, and through our will, also for being free to choose we can reach our goal in life, as we are potentiated to reach stars.

Hence, we need good education and professional training to constructively manage human instinctual apparatus that are probable for civil and cultured nations in which they realize the human malaise (anxiety, heebie-jeebies), feeling of distress brought by uncertainties early in life, as they ought to prioritize devoting time, allocate more funds, with plenty of accessible expertise and sincere intention to capitalize on improving people's mind and behaviors.

To mold and better condition people from the early ages, so that the overall society can live in tranquility and peace, where aggression and violence can alleviate. It a fact that environment plays a huge catalyst in shaping people's mind and conducts, either a product of a constructive atmosphere which should relatively result in fruitful personality or born to the destructive and toxic environment which can introduce menacing characters to the society.

Bottom line, a curse should be upon those deprived victims if they are overflowed with testosterone since hormones as such cause aggression, belligerency and apparently forces one to act violence; also, because proper education, training, financial empowerment, social recognition, and prestige are available to the elites as they can buy the most prominent attorneys, if they ever face any legal trouble, as obviously the poor are exhausted from having them.

No wonder so many poor and financially deprived are incarcerated, as they globally have saturated prisons with some facing inhumane retaliations from the so-called law authorities. Just like when a heroin addict chases a substance-induced high, sex addicts are bingeing on chemicals which is their own hormones. as heroin addicts need professional medical therapeutic, sex addicts must also be treated medically and professionally attended to, and not by forceful means.

Many advance God-fearing nations slogan that in God we trust where liberty, human rights, democracy and pursuit of happiness should mean something, as millions know that some behavioral malfunction in human beings is due to hormonal abnormality such as testosterone-driven personalities that are much more inclined to act belligerent and have anger issues.

Making them much more vulnerable to do wrong, since this should be detected early in people's lives to avoid disaster, and stop tragic events. millions end up in overcrowded jails and prisons, causing the taxpayers billions, and society is ridden with violence and crimes which many innocent victims pay with their lives for heinous crimes committed by offenders that could have been avoided.

I gather you have heard of the yin and yang, which believes that the principle of Yin and Yang in all things exist as inseparable and contradictory opposites, for example, female-male, hot-cold, dark-light and old-young. The principle, dating from the third century BCE or even earlier, is a fundamental concept in Chinese philosophy and culture in general. (in Chinese philosophy and religion) two principles, one negative, dark, and feminine (yin), and one positive, bright, and masculine (yang), whose interaction influences the destinies of creatures and things.

Testosterone brain hormones natured for aggressive behaviors originates in brain centers that instigate metabolic stimulation of the neuroendocrine system, this guides the feeling of aggressiveness via the mobilization of the body's muscles. The neurons of the prefrontal area, the hypothalamus, and amygdala that are regarded with aggression show significant quantities of androgen and estradiol receptors, along with the enzymes imperative for the steroidogenesis of these hormones.

The local production of testosterone in neuroendocrine neurons introduces a new factor into the interpretation of the interaction of this hormone with offensive, bright manifestations as yang, and cortisol's hormones can play the role of ying. Thus, it makes sense that the hormonal axes that regulate testosterone levels and cortisol levels are antagonistic. According to research, chronically elevated cortisol levels can produce impotence and loss of libido by inhibiting testosterone production in men.

The effect of testosterone maneuverability on the brain initiates in embryonic life. Testosterone receptors are shown in the fetus earlier than the biosynthesis (the production of complex molecules within living organisms or cells of testosterone) which happens in the seventh to eighth week of pregnancy. In the fifth month, the testosterone values in male fetuses reach a max with levels approaching those of adult men. This secretory surge lasting for a few weeks inundates the brain with testosterone, prompting anatomical and organizational alteration that mark the sex disparity (separation, polarity) of the male brain in adulthood.

The first study in prisoners was initiated in 1972, soon after the accessibility to testosterone estimation, by Kreutz and Rosel, who captured that prisoners who had committed violent crimes when adolescence had higher testosterone levels (13). In a single sample size of free testosterone in the saliva of 89 prison inmates, it was revealed that at the extremes of the testosterone distribution, the relationship between testosterone to aggressive behaviors was more striking (14).

Ten out of eleven prisoners with the highest testosterone concentrations had committed violent crimes, whereas nine out of eleven who had committed non-violent crimes had the lowest testosterone activity levels.

The question of fairness does not apply in the above situation, when the administration of hyper physiological doses of testosterone does increase aggression and violent behavior, compounded with lack of opportunity to escalate wisdom and intelligence that is also depleted in some people, because of deficiencies in funds, which sure in capitalist system money is so decisive for good and manageable upbringings that would make one much prone to luck for making it.

It is a fact that environment plays a huge catalyst in shaping people's mind and character, as we are either a product of a constructive atmosphere which should relatively result in fruitful personality, or born into a destructive and toxic environment which can introduce menacing personality to the society. Often in the dark ages, castration is also known as gonadectomy was performed on slaves, prisoners of war, violent criminals and so on. is a surgical procedure (excision of both testes), also chemical castration that utility pharmaceutical drugs to incapacitate the testes, and by other cruel means of removing one's testicle to ensure sterilization (preventing the victim from reproducing).

It is meant to significantly lower the production of specific hormones like testosterone, treating humans just like animals that were neutered that is the surgical castration for animals to prevent reproducing. Castration was also applicable for females in which they removed the ovaries, also known as oophorectomy. If so, the estrogen levels lower precipitously (hastily, hurriedly), and long term effect of drastic lowering of sex hormone should be expected.

The term castration may occasionally be used to indicate emasculation where both the testicles and the penis together are taken out, since in certain cultures, and in some translations, no distinction is made between the two. It was sometimes utilized to prevent overpopulation.

Castration was often performed for religious or social reasons in some cultures in Europe, South Asia, Middle East, Africa, and East Asia, and many other places. After battles in some cases, winners castrated their captives or the corpses of the defeated to represent their victory and seize their power.

Castrated men known as eunuchs were frequently accepted to special social classes and were used especially to staff bureaucracies and palace households, in designated harems. Religions, such as Judaism, were strongly opposed to the practice. The Leviticus Holiness code, for instance particularly denies eunuchs or any males with defective genitals from the priesthood, just as castrated animals are removed from being gambit (sacrificed.)

In antiquity era castration frequently involved the utter removal of all the male genitalia. This made the victims much more inclined to death because of profuse bleeding or infection and, in some states, like for example the Byzantine Empire, it was seen similar to the death sentence. Removal of only the testicles had a much lower risk. Either surgical removal of both testicles or chemical castration may occur in the case of prostate cancer.

Testosterone-depletion treatment (either surgical removal of both testicles or chemical castration) is done to slow down cancer which greatly reduces sex drive or interest in those with sexual drives, obsessions, or behaviors, or any combination of those that may be considered as deviant. Castration has also been performed in the United States for sex offenders. Involuntary castration appears in the history of warfare, often used by one side to torture or demoralize their rival enemies. It was exercised to exterminate opposing male lineages and thus let the victor to sexually own the defeated group's females.

Historically, because of ignorance, lack of education and because of not having skillful training to implement corrective means, and for non-availability to learn and accentuate on good habits; that, compounded with instinctual necessities for humanity to survive which often has gone way overboard also because of self-interest and greed, which these shortcomings have affected so many for the worst, causing heartbreaking pain and suffering beyond belief.

It is an undeniable fact that testosterone and other forceful hormones as such can either be a blessing if one is enlightened to leash them and a demon like if unleashed and not intelligently enabling one to reign them.

When in the qualm (stabbing pain, pang) of starvation, our senses are without a doubt emphatic on food. Wretchedly (unpleasant state of emotion) exhausted of an essential requirement, the dire (critical) quest for sustenance overpower and determine any other concern, which at the moment must feel absolutely immaterial, inorganic, and impertinent. The state of hunger has no conscience.

Ethical regards become secondary bearing no impact in situations where the excruciating ache of starvation must overcome any other thought.

It's easy enough to criticize a testosterone-driven man for his one-track mindedness. As Darwin say? After all, is it not part of "evolutionary wisdom" to make sure that the virile sperm carrier is distracted with spreading that sperm? A male's conscious reasons may not be to procreate his seed. Experiencing an almost overwhelming sexual tension—which is inseparable from carnal (bodily) desire—he may simply feel coerced to alleviate (soothe) it.

Besides, his beastly physical (and unconscious mind) has evolved exactly to make him concentrate on attaining this natural act. Therefore, how much can one be blamed for approaching his genital prime many years prior to his capturing maturity in wisdom, emotional intelligence, and ethical progression to adequately deal with his sexual needs, wants, and feelings of the objects he desires for?

After all, it sure is a blessing that biological imperative is extremely resilient since it surely gifts us the most potent imaginable defense mechanism contrary to extinction. Yet, I am afraid it seems what needs to be celebrated, is predominantly looked upon as a curse in many naïve and backward cultures, often leaving behind many socio-cultural ills, and psychological ailments, mental gridlocks where millions of men and women literally are infected which some are negatively impacted for life.

It is a no-brainer to know that the primitive message which a male perceives by his amoral (not moral) sex hormone is to pursue females not for their selves but for their bodies. The same so-called testosterone culprit which without no life is possible, go figure. yes, societal hindrance can wrongfully inhibit what nature has endowed humanity to pursue life, but it sure wouldn't be without its dire and irreparable damages often reflecting the entire society for the worse. It is not a lie that everyone rich or poor, young or old, pretty or not, wise or dull, intelligent or not and so on can indiscriminately become gloomy and sad, occasionally get depressed with much anxiety.

They say is all about behaving positively and not acting pessimistic. Yes, true to some extent, but we should not forget that we cannot help it when certain stressful and sad hormones force their way in because of the ugly circumstances which one is faced with, or when one is so mal-nutrition beyond grasp and born into broken family and a violent atmosphere which the ends justifies the means just to survive.

The hormonal brain is activated by the occasions and the atmosphere which we are engaged in and is part of. But it seems we just do not care to deal with the reality of what is happening. Planting oak seeds in a pot will certainly affect the ability of the oak tree to grow and reach its full potential since the tree is inhibited with the circumstances that are not suitable for its true nature to expand which demands different criterions.

Our brain dialogues with itself by delegating chemicals from one neuron, or nerve, to the other, which this natural rapid-fire messaging enacts a big role in how one feels and function every day. There are two categories of neurotransmitter that are known as excitatory, meaning they arouse brain activity, and inhibitory, meaning they have a more relaxing effect.

For an instant, serotonin plays a huge role in sleep and in depression, but this inhibitory agent also plays a major role in many of your body's imperative functions, not to exclude appetite, mood arousal. Etc. Many antidepressants aim at serotonin receptors to better one's mood and mitigate depressive symptoms. Bear in mind that serotonin is also accumulated in our intestine which helps with the digestive work mechanism too.

Dopamine controls many activities, including emotion, conduct, and cognition. This chemical also interacts with the front part of our brain, that is linked with pleasure and reward, it helps motivate you to work toward reaching one's goal and a reward. because dopamine is linked to the movement as well, low levels of dopamine have also been connected to Parkinson's disease.

Glutamate, this is the most common excitatory neurotransmitter, located throughout one's brain and spinal cord. Glutamate has many vital functions, for example, brain development, cognition, learning, and memory.

Norepinephrine

Its original role is part of your body's stress response, it assists with the hormone adrenaline to make the fight-or-flight feeling. Norepinephrine which is as well utilized as a drug to elevate or maintain blood pressure in some illnesses. Norepinephrine and other related hormones, like adrenalin, melatonin, adrenaline, and other neurotransmitters affect our moods, even can change the health of our brain.

Cortisol is exuded when one is stressed. It's often helpful, but for too long, and too much of it can cause memory loss as we get older. Hormonal imbalances in neurotransmitters can potentiate many ill-conditions, including schizophrenia, depression, bipolar disorder, autism, Parkinson's disease, and host of other incurable diseases. Keeping a balance in the hormonal brain, and chemicals are the essence of a savvy mood which tightly depends on having balanced nutrition, good rest, exercise, avoiding stressful lifestyle, meditation, listening to relaxing music, enjoying family, friends and all of which can uplift one's spirit.

The point is that human behaviors are not all discretionary (optional) for example, we simply cannot help it when frightened and scared, or when become excited and the adrenaline hormone is secreted by the adrenal glands, especially in conditions of stress, increasing rates of blood circulation, breathing, and carbohydrate metabolism and preparing muscles for exertion. In fact, hundreds of brain and bodily hormones are mandatory since they are activated when they see it fit.

We need to realize that there is a beast within all of us that needs to be balanced and tamed, but when a rogue system realizes that and feeds the animal within us, tempting us in a clandestine manner, rather than educate and train people to wisely harness the animal inside by capitalizing on the enormously potentiated human intelligence.

Then, living can eventually be more peaceful and tranquility of mind and manner can become the norms. You might inquire that is it our genes, or is the environment and upbringings responsible for our ill-behaving or good conduct?

The answer is that we all are affected by our genes and of course the relative products the environment that we live in, which must be paid attention to.

In the meanwhile, also keep in mind that most poverty-stricken neighborhoods, atmospheres, and cultures are the embodiment of cruel and unjustified criterions where millions live way under the poverty line devoid of good nutrients, proper rest with good hygiene, with lack of proper education or proper medical coverage, as they live an extremely stressful life, and most with no hope for either recovery, or upper mobility exponentially impacts so many when not wise enough to think twice in the verge of doing wrong, and not potentiated to correctly discern they are the victims of the circumstances which they must overcome that is extremely difficult.

All of the resources are congealed and taken by the rich elites that literally play the devil's advocates and are not willing to constructively invest and are refusing to believe in human spirit and productivity, where nations would not go to devastating wars, leaving behind horrific consequence just because the rich elites must add a dollar more to their already humongous concentration of wealth. Come to think of it, all ills return to malnutrition, stressful living, with lack compassion, lack of love, being born in a broken family exhausted from any financial remedy and living in toxic environments, which no doubt can affect our genes for the worse, wherein the long run abnormal living can make genes to go berserk and haywire, leaving one vulnerable to irreparable damages.

Why shouldn't we believe that genes can be ill effected because of toxic food, wrong upbringings and poisonous atmosphere potentiating one to wrongfully coexist with the beast inside, and often paying the price with their lives. After all, balance is the virtue, where wisdom and the impetus to gain conclusive information and knowledge can sure help with breaking the vicious cycle of greed, lust, and temptations to avoid ill desires, where good judgments can detour one from doing wrong.

24

GOD AND SCIENCE

Science does not need God to explain the universe, as Einstein said, "Only two things are infinite, the universe and human stupidity, and I'm not sure about the former," which signifies those with callous minds that expect God to explain the universe, which has unnecessarily become a human dilemma.

What should be of concern is that when science is unquestionably the product of human consciousness which without no experience of any kind either scientific or not would ever is ever possible, as it cannot be identified and be located anywhere in the human brain should not be considered a fact and a priority not only over science, but the entire existence, and is the cause behind all there is, and all there ever will be. should hold true to the day science can examine and test it in scientific laboratories as it should remind any savvy and intelligent mind that would be to the day which hell freezes since it is utterly beyond the scope of scientific endeavors to deal with locating God or even consciousness.

It is hilarious that the subject of science which is the byproduct of human consciousness and intelligence, somehow for certain people is naively refused to see, not grasping the fact that what we do not see, manages and controls what we see. Stephen Hawking said in his book *The Grand Design* that God did not create the universe. He then, says that our universe followed inevitably from the laws of nature, and people like Hawking capitalize on such shallow rhetoric. The point is if so? Where did these irrefutably disciplined laws of nature come from?

Then he said that the search for this particular Holy Grail is over, now that scientists have come up with a type of theory, known as M-theory, that may describe the behavior of all the fundamental particles and force, and even account for the very birth of the universe. If this theory is backed up by experiment, it might perhaps replace all religious accounts of creation.

Mr. Hawking got excited about something that cannot be authenticated, which is not true since it cannot be tested. Here is what the scientists are saying on M theory: M-theory is a new idea in small-particle physics that is part of superstring theory that was initially proposed by Edward Witten.

The idea, or theory, often causes arguments among scientists, because there is no way to test it to see if it is true, which I am afraid is already taken place in Mr. Hawking's capricious mind. It seems Mr. Hawking is saying that accepting God-made the universe can be replaced with a belief in M-theory, a good candidate for a Grass-Rooty theory of nature at its finest level, as its potentiality which can be promising, as we should believe in human intelligence that might one day be as competent to conquer galaxies and perhaps the universe, since it is the human intelligence which gradually exploits the mysteries of nature arrow headed by further human awakenings.

But the shortcoming with the theory is that it looks as though it will be exorbitantly (excessively) difficult to test unless scientists can build a particle accelerator the size of a galaxy. Even if that hypothetically becomes probable, and the M-theory succeeds in all related tests, the cause behind mathematical order at the heart of the orderly universe order would remain an irresolvable mystery What prominent physicist are saying is that one notable feature of string theories is that these theories, not hypotheses coming about not from just any layman, but from precious scientific evaluators, which they say it requires extra dimensions of space-time for their mathematical consistency. In bosonic string theory, space-time is 26-dimensional, while in superstring theory it is 10-dimensional, and in M-theory it is 11-dimensional.

The point is that for string theory, M theory, superlative theory and theories alike the scientists are searching for higher dimensions, since obviously we do not live in a 10, 11, or 26 dimensions since they all need extra dimensions of space and time; but oddly enough when believers say the almighty God is beyond the existing space and time, the atheists are reluctant to accept it. perhaps we should attach the word science to God as the scientific God for them to comply.

As Hawking justly stresses, it is clear that Einstein did not think of God as a white-bearded benefactor capable of interfering with the functioning of the universe. Rather, Einstein followed closely the views of the philosopher Spinoza, for whom the concept of God is an expression of the underlying unity of the universe, something so wondrous that it can command a spiritual awe. Something as potent as mathematics which patterns in the basic fabric of reality—the mathematical laws that rule the workings of nature at its finest level.

There is plenty of evidence that these laws hold good all the way back to the origin of time, that is how scientists have put together an exorbitant detailed and well-tested theory of the big bang. "the remarkable fact is that the values of these numbers seem to have been very finely adjusted." Stephen Hawking

What we should pay attention to is that human mind and heart are potentiated with infinite urges in which both seek wants to the day we expire. furthermore, if brought up in a constructively dignified the environment which humanity inclusively deserves, then, rest assure that human heart is filled with good intentions and infinite compassion, and our mind with infinite intelligence craving wisdom and persisting on progress, manifesting the God within.

If endowed with such blessings then when one hears of, or sees a misdeed, a crime or a tragedy about to happen, one most probably will go to an extent sacrificing one's life to stop it, yes, because the infinite compassion and the infinite intelligence are an inseparable part of what God is all about substantiating the fact that we are made in God's image.

Now science which by the way is a product of human conscious ironically cannot be dragged into any laboratory and is absolutely not found anywhere in our brain. science advances over the wreckage of its theories by relentlessly placing theoretical ideas to empirical testing; which does not matter how impressive a theoretical concept might be, it must be discarded if not coherent, or at odds with experiment. This indicates that like any other human endeavor or activity, science also has flaws which often do not always comply or go smoothly as scientists expect.

We should appreciate science, because science assist humanity to understand the world, and underpin technology which is the vehicle that without we would have still been in the dark ages territory, which should also inform us not to expect science to divulge whys of the world, since this inquiry encompasses millions of mysterious unanswered questions beyond scientific capabilities to shed lights on. Bear in mind that Newtonian theory is the nervous system of the material world, which without its magnificent scientific reality has already proven deficient in non-material realms that has become identified literally because of advancement in human intelligence which constantly deals with the idea of Pragmatism.

Pragmatism is a philosophical movement that includes those who claim that an ideology or assertion is true if it works satisfactorily, that the meaning of an assertion (proposition) is to be found in the practical consequences of accepting or rejecting it. Does pragmatism also deal with an educational philosophy that says that education should be about life and growth?

Two important elements of pragmatism include practical learning, which focuses on the real-world applications of lessons, and experiential learning, which complies with learning through experience, contrary to idealistic is pragmatic, a word that explains the philosophy of doing what works best. From Greek pragma deed, the word has historically described philosophers and politicians who were concerned more with real-world application of ideas than with abstract notions, knowing that it is through the idea of real-world applications which scientists gradually divulge the abstract notions which initially seem beyond our reach.

Einstein's views were predominantly shared by his friend Paul Dirac, the great English theoretician since Newton. For Dirac, the biggest mystery of the universe was that its most fundamental laws can be stated in terms of beautiful mathematical equations. At the end of his life, in the 1970s and early 1980s, Dirac often uttered that mathematical beauty "is almost a religion to me."

Earlier in his life, Dirac was an outspoken atheist, attracting his colleague Wolfgang Pauli to say that There is no God and Dirac is his prophet. Decades later, in 1963, Dirac was eager to use theological imagery: God is a mathematician of a very high order. He was talking metaphorically, but we know what he meant. perhaps reminded him of the infinite disciplinary precision in mathematics that is the kernel of any scientific endeavor, which without no scientific manifestation should be possible.

An entity imbued with logic and reason that cannot be seen or touched, but so prevalently real in our lives helping scientific empirical come alive.

Then when theists ask the non-believers what has caused life to come about? What is the cause of existence? They respond to nature is the cause. By the way, do they mean matter? As any savvy mind would perhaps hastily say that matter has no intelligence, and is not imbued with any common sense, and since I am afraid we cannot think beyond what our mental capacity is, and over the grasp of our nervous system, then we need to accept an infinitely intelligent designer behind this miraculously oriented universe, as we should refuse a senseless matter exhausted of any intelligence to have caused a magnificently intelligently life bearing criterions.

Furthermore, when believers inquire that if the nature you atheists talk about, or matter in which you believe in has any motion? They say everything has motion, nature has motion. When we ask does this motion which evidently is incorporated in the tiniest to the most grandeur demands time and space? The non-believers say yes, again the right answer. But when we ask any motion must have an origin and a final destiny to serve a purpose.

They so illogically refute the fact of having a beginning, an end as they do not budge to a purposeful life. The further inquiry that no perishable matter can be the cause of an infinitely durable life beyond anyone's imagination, as no matter is stable enough since matter can appear in the form of Solids. In a solid, particles are packed tightly together so they are unable to move about very much.

Liquids.
Gases.
Plasma.
Bose-Einstein condensates.
Melting and freezing
Sublimation.
Vaporization.

Then, we have those who pull their hair and insist on the laws of physics, and the world of science like Newton's laws and other affiliated scientific methods, as they say, it runs the real world as no God is necessary.

That might be true, but it absolutely should not mean that the almighty creator is not the real cause to all that exists. as is the nature of science to discover new things, as it historically has, then science found out that in general, the behavior of the subatomic particles cannot be explained by Newton's laws.

Here are how the Newtonian's laws of motion can be explained. There exist particles with a peculiar position and velocity interacting with each other via means of force. There are several kinds of forces in Nature, in which they can act between two particles, and their strength and direction are based on the position and the velocities of those particles.

Newton's first law states that every object will remain at rest or in uniform motion in a straight line unless compelled to change its state by the action of an external force. Newton's second law of motion describes the relationship between an object's mass and the amount of force needed to accelerate it. Newton's second law is often stated as F=ma, which means the force (F) acting on an object is equal to the mass (m) of an object times its acceleration (a) Newton's second law of motion pertains to the behavior of objects for which all existing forces are not balanced.

The second law states that the acceleration of an object is dependent upon two variables -the net force acting upon the object and the mass of the object. The third law states that for every action (force) in nature there is an equal and opposite reaction.

As many sages and philosophers of past and present indicated, there is more to life than we grasp out of our limited human sense, as we should not be hasty and finalize that science and the laws of physics are what the universal magic is all about, which then the quantum world appeared.

Saying that the laws which rule the action of the subatomic particles are entirely different since it is not possible to commit a particular position and velocity to a specific particle. Each particle can be in a superposition of various states, which means it is found simultaneously in a whole region of space conveying a whole range of velocities.

When one measures the position or the velocity of the particle, one obtains certain values from that range, randomly so, possibly with various probabilities for each value. Yet, this is not because the particle truly had secured that position, not knowing the particle in actuality had a whole range of positions just before the moment of measurement. many physicists admit it is very strange and in the meanwhile beautiful. Einstein was the first physicist to say that Planck's discovery of the quantum (h) would require a rewriting of the laws of physics.

The ability of the particle to be in several different states simultaneously results in a well-known wave-particle duality: the subatomic particles (electrons, neutrons and other) can behave like waves and show interference. Suppose we have a particle source aimed towards a wall with two slits where the particles can pass and a detecting screen beyond this wall. First, we allow the particles to pass only through one of the slits, and then only through the second one.

In a third experiment, the particles can pass through both the slits. When looking at the results, the results of the last experiment seem to be completely unrelated to the results of the first two. This happens because when particles are allowed to pass through both slits it's not that some of them pass through the first slit and some of them through the second one, but in some sense, each particle passes through both of them. On the detecting screen, we see a picture identical to the one which is obtained from the interference of waves.

The faculty (ability, competency) of the particle to be in many different states at the same time indicates a wave-particle duality: the subatomic particles (electrons, neutrons and other) can act like waves and exhibit interference.

The theory which is able to describe the subatomic particles is quantum mechanics. In quantum mechanics, a system (sometimes a single particle) can be explained by a wave function (or by a vector in a multi-dimensional space). The information conveyed in the wave function is just the weight of each possible state in the current state of the system.

Therefore, we should notice that there is much more to the reality of life than what we as human beings decipher through our five basic senses of sight, hearing, smell, taste, and touch which in association with our brain can understand and perceive the world around us. Knowing that it is the invisible realm that manages the visible materially based world.

Furthermore, many believe that we are the products of our environment, that is fundamentally a materially based atmosphere which we have to deal with where no spiritual laws are applicable, and since it has nothing to do with innate variables that might lightly or heavily affect the outcomes of our lives. Mostly encouraged by Marx and Angles proponents which dictate Dialectical materialism, a philosophical approach to reality derived from the teachings of Karl Marx and Friedrich Engels.

For Marx and Engels, materialism meant that the material world, perceptible to the senses, has an objective reality independent of mind or spirit. Dialectical materialism looks at the process of change and how the physical world and individuals move from one state to another, basically through historical class struggle.

Marx proposed that this evolution occurs through conflict and opposition in contrary to Hegel's materialist history in which Hegel claimed that history occurs through a dialectic, or clash, of opposing forces. Hegel was a philosophical idealist who believed that we live in a world of appearances, and true reality is ideal. However, so many inquisitively minded individual, philosopher, scientists, and scholarly mind people objected and elaborated on the fact that genes and other prominently innate factors also were decisive of who we are.

Either way, this was dubiously dealt with until the birth of quantum mechanics, or better known as quantum physics which completely altered the concept of materially oriented nature since physicists unanimously agreed that no substance or entity of any kind is-driven or is exhausted of energy, since solid, liquid and gas are all energy-driven and of course made of atoms through which subatomic particles play I huge role.

The external world is energy-driven human mind is capable to correlate and accordingly respond to the outside world, because our mind, conscious and human spirit are energy-driven as well making the environmental conductibility and human intelligence to actively interact to accomplish our daily tasks and substantiate what needs to be done for further progress.

The Einstein theory of relativity of $E=MC^2$ basically states that mass is another form which energy can be altered too. For instance, if you collide particles with a very high kinetic energy in a particle accelerator, one can make that kinetic energy to convert into a mass, and thus create particles with much higher mass than the particles one collided. $E=mc2$ explains nuclear fusion, how matter can be annihilated and converted to energy and energy can flip-flop back to mass.

It describes the atomic energy generated by nuclear power plants and the atomic energy relinquished by atomic bombs. Neither would be possible without Einstein's equation. Energy equals mass times the speed of light squared. On the most fundamental level, the equation states that energy and mass (matter) are interchangeable; they are various forms of the same thing.

Under the right conditions, energy can become mass, and vice versa, as if an androgynous with (having both male and female characteristics or qualities.) then when the theists related to the non-believers that things can appear and disappear out of nowhere, they said that is superstitious magic, that cannot be, as many blatantly rejected the idea.

At the quantum level, matter and antimatter particles are constantly popping into existence and popping back out, with an electron-positron pair here and a top quark-antiquark pair there. This is what the physicists are saying quote, between the plates, only waves (particles) with wavelengths smaller than the separation between the plates can exist.

They further say that quote, the quantum effects are probabilistic, not deterministic. Therefore, a quantum fluctuation has no cause. Quantum fluctuations are a point change in the energy of a volume of space due to the Heisenberg Uncertainty Principle. Zero point zero is extremely precise, and in quantum mechanics, unstable. According to quantum mechanics, a vacuum isn't empty at all. It's actually filled with quantum energy and particles that blink in and out of existence for a fleeting moment—strange signals that are known as quantum fluctuations.

There are no particles there, and nothing to interfere with pure physics. In fact, old explanation of gravitation is not capable to resolve quantum vacuum problem. Relating to Heisenberg uncertainty principle a vacuum isn't empty and filled with particles-antiparticles that appear and disappear randomly fashion.

Mr. Hawking believes that gravity is the cause for existence, gravity with having no intelligence, weaker than other forces, depends on mass, which without its existence is very much questionable is the cause to exist. let's elaborate a bit on the forces of our universe.

Gravity is relatively simple to understand: any two things that have mass (atoms, rocks, people, planets, stars) are pulled towards each other. The bigger the mass, the stronger the pull.

Electromagnetism? It's electricity and magnetism squashed. The electromagnetic force describes how things that are electrically charged (positively or negatively) they interact with each other, a magnetic charge can create an electric charge, and vice versa. Those interactions are responsible for electric power production that is vital.

Electromagnetism and the way it pushes and pulls objects are responsible for the energy in things such as batteries and magnets, but it also includes light, which is about waves of electromagnetic radiation.

for the weak and the strong nuclear forces since they're both stronger than gravity they only act in diminutive (tiny) spaces between atoms when even smaller spaces where quantum physics makes everything really strange.

The strong nuclear force is indeed the strongest of the four known forces and fundamentally the glue that binds everything together. It is responsible for keeping protons and neutrons (which along with electrons make up atoms) stable and then lets those to cinch (bind) into atomic nuclei. In the meanwhile, the weak force o is liable for radioactive decay, the opposite of the strong force, it controls how things on a nuclear level fall apart, also it's accountable for fusion, and keeps our sun bright, nice and warm.

Surprisingly enough now the physicists talk about the fifth force, which they say we need to realize what makes other forces of the universe do their tasks. They believe since one body with mass does not just magically start moving towards another massive thing, scientist anticipates that this moving mechanism possibly happens by force carrier particles.

Force carriers are the particles that carry information between things and alert them on how to maneuver and forces them to behave by the rules, which should remind one belief in a committed and purposeful life. The force carriers for gravity are hypothetical things called gravitons, for electromagnetism they're the photons. For the weak nuclear force, the carriers are called W and Z particles, and for the strong nuclear force, gluons. These force carries are all known as examples of bosons.

But he adds, "There are many experimental groups working in small labs around the world that can follow up the initial claims, now that they know where to look." We should bear in mind that without mass no gravity is possible. The Moon's surface gravity is weaker because it is far less massive than Earth. A body's surface gravity is proportional to its mass but inversely proportional to the square of its radius. The Moon's surface gravity is about one-sixth as powerful, or about 1.6 meters per second.

Gravity in our universe. Gravity is what keeps the planets in orbit around the sun and what holds the moon in orbit around Earth. The gravitational pull of the moon fancies the seas towards it, producing the ocean tides. Gravity not only pulls on mass but also on the light. Gravity from Earth keeps the Moon and human-made satellites in orbit.

It is true that gravity lessens with distance, so it is possible to be far away from a planet or star and feel less gravity, or perhaps in some state no gravity. Earth's gravity arrives from all its mass. All its mass generates a combined gravitational pull on all the mass in your body, which you weight. if you were on a planet with less mass than Earth, you would weigh less than you do here. Therefore, there is no question that gravity depends on mass, which without it wouldn't exist.

Mr. Hawking believes that a force without intelligence, weaker than other forces in our universe, which must depend on mass to exist, as it alters with distance and weight, an unseen force should replace the omnipotent omnipresent creator, which its magnificent traces should be seen and felt. As the traces of Gravity can only be felt, as it cannot be seen, and in some states, it does not even exist.

Then, oddly enough gravity is the God known to Mr. Hawking and alike and the cause for our existence. Gravity is most accurately described by the general theory of relativity (proposed by Albert Einstein in 1915) which describes gravity not as a force, but as a consequence of the curvature of space-time caused by the uneven distribution of mass.

Albert Einstein's general theory of relativity is one of the towering accomplishments of twentieth-century physics. Published in 1916, it says that what we know as the force of gravity in true sense arises from the curvature of space and time. Einstein suggested that objects like the sun and the Earth alter this geometry.

In the presence of matter and energy, it can evolve, stretch and warp, forming ridges, mountains, and valleys that make bodies moving through it to zigzag and curve. So although Earth appears to be pulled towards the sun by gravity, there is no such force. It is simply the geometry of space-time around the sun telling Earth how to move. The general theory of relativity has far-reaching outcomes. It not only describes the motion of the planets; it can also elaborate on the history and development of the universe, the physics of black holes and the bending of light from distant stars and galaxies. Bear in mind that as you move faster in space, time goes slower.

However, it is the undertaking of science which teaches us about the magnanimity (generosity) of nature since science delves into the unknown and discovers the wonders of our universe to progress and for a better living. In the meanwhile, we should give credit where credit is due, as we should not believe that science can replace our creator, as science has not to exhibit why the universe came into existence nor what preceded its inception in the big bang.

Furthermore, biological evolution has not shown humanity how the first living organisms arrived from inanimate, unintelligent matter, and how progressive eukaryotic cells-highly structured building blocks of advanced life forms did emerge from simpler organisms. Why consciousness escalates in living things? Where do thoughts come from?

Where does self-awareness come from? What is consciousness? And since no one can be located anywhere in one's body, why do we have out-of-body experience? Why are we potentiated to understand the magic of science, physics, mathematics, biology, botany, engineering, medicine, architecture, literature, philosophy, astronomy, art, music and so on? Why are we here, where did we come from, where are we going, what is our purpose in life? Science cannot explain these and with thousands of other abyss mysteries that science is not able to figure out by any scientific methodology.

The more intriguing question should be why the fine-tuning of the universe, why is our universe is so tailored for the emergence of life? We should delve into the infinite mysteries of the universe, like a daunting task as it is, but through human drive and perseverance, we can gradually reach the hidden wisdom and the blueprint of what life is all about.

The cosmological constant (A, Lambda) constant is a term in Einstein's theory of gravity that influences the expansion rate of empty space. It can be positive or negative (unless it is within an extremely narrow range around zero, the universe will either collapse or expand too rapidly for galaxies and stars to form).

25

THE BIG BANG

People cited a violation of the First Amendment when a New Jersey schoolteacher asserted that evolution and the big bang are not scientific and that Noah's ark carried dinosaurs. This case is not about the need to separate church and state; it's about the need to separate ignorant, scientifically illiterate people from the ranks of teachers.

— Neil deGrasse Tyson.

Is a cosmological model, a theory utilized to explain the beginning and how the universe has evolved? It states that the universe was in an extremely hot and dense position prior to expansion 13,.7 billion years ago. This theory is based on fundamental observations:

In 1920, Hubble detected that the distance among galaxies was increasing all over in the universe. should decipher that galaxies had to be closer to each other in the past.

In 1964, Wilson and Penzias found out that fossil-like cosmic background radiation emitted throughout the beginning of the universe when it was hot and dense, since the cosmic background radiation is observable everywhere in the universe.

The composition of the universe, for example, the number of atoms of various elements is consistent with the big bang Theory. The big bang theory is so far the only theory that can describe why we observe an abundance of primeval (pre-historical, primordial) elements in the universe.

I believe the mechanism of a huge volcano eruption should resemble, and perhaps give us an idea about the big bang, but with a colossally bigger magnitude in eruption. Geologists tell us that Volcanoes are made by eruptions of lava and ash when magma rises through cracks or weak spots in the Earth's crust. A buildup of pressure in the Earth is relinquished, by things such as a plate movement which forces molten rock to explode into the air causing a volcanic eruption. The scientist also tells us that Volcanic gases are harmful to health, vegetation, and infrastructure, but the most abundant volcanic gas is water vapor, which is harmless.

Either way, scientists also believe that significant amounts of carbon dioxide, sulfur dioxide, hydrogen sulfide, and hydrogen halides can also exude from volcanoes. Pyroclasts (a dense, destructive mass of very hot ash, lava fragments, and gases ejected explosively from a volcano and typically flowing downslope at great speed) also known as (tephra) are materials forcefully thrown to the atmosphere via explosive eruptions. When loose materials (like volcanic bombs, volcanic blocks, and gases, which are expelled during violent eruptions) are mixed with ashes, the so-called pyroclastic deposits are formed.

Therefore, after becoming aware of volcanic mechanism, logic should dictate two probable scenarios. First, either the big bang occurred out of nowhere, exhausted of any prior preparation, appeared out of nothing and without any evolutionary process, if so, it must have been a miracle, which certainly calls for the hands of God. Or, it must have happened because of the gradual accumulation of lava, the concentration of extremely hot ashes, volcanic gases, molten rocks, magma and because of other volcanic depositories, etc.

This should confirm matter, since matter should confirm motion, where motion demands space, time, direction and purpose, causing a build-up of intolerable pressure which eventually substantiated enormously huge explosion, namely the big bang beyond anyone's imagination, and if so, then, because logic dictates, it should remind any savvy-minded person to notice the prior existence of matter, certainly before the big bang explosion.

The further noticeable issue is that any explosion should bring destruction, chaos and disorder as big bang explosion must have brought, which on the contrary the big bang evidently must have resulted in an orderly, extremely intricate life, infinitely disciplined nature and magnificently organized, if so, again we need to see the undeniable hands of God in making of a masterpiece design, creating an awesome universe, which I am afraid is taken for granted by unmediated minds unreasonably denying the indisputable facts about a superbly dazzling (brilliant) creator. "It is either coincidence piled on top of coincidence, or it is deliberate design." Robert J. Sawyer, *Calculating God.*

26

THE MEANING OF LIFE

Humanity is potentiated with the gift of intelligence as everyone is blessed with the miracle of awareness which needs to be invigorated to give meaning to one's life, which no doubt is correlated with having the opportunity to grow in a decent environment free form societal ills and suppressing factors that can impact people for the worse.

It is true that some are more ambitious than others, but many are also equipped with positive variables that millions if not billions are deprived of in which they play a huge catalyst in their being successful.

Meaningful lives are for extraordinary people: teachers, scientists, philosophers, professors, saints, artists, scholars, doctors, surgeons, nurses, writers, poets, engineers, politicians, ministers, bankers, researches, musicians, activists, explorers, national leaders, and so on, and since life can become meaning with purposeful livings, then, there are those behaving idol without having a mission or a purpose in life, and not able to make sense of what they are here to accomplish.

"I don't believe people are looking for the meaning of life as much as they are looking for the experience of being alive." Joseph Campbell

People that are professionally engaged are more focused as they are more in tune with their lives. Meaningful living also is relatively linked with happiness that often materializes when one is on top of what one does for a living and has not lagged behind. As accountability is frequently an issue for so many as they care about their profession and the excellent work they are committed to doing.

When people's duty at work, with daily chores, weekly plans, monthly outlooks, even yearly agendas are intact as they feel orderly and not behind their responsibilities, it makes them less stressful and more relaxed without much anxiety or pressure for performing their daily tasks right, as many meticulously pursue what must be done daily, weekly, monthly, even annually, making them happy and with much less distressed. No doubt that stressful lifestyle and happiness are correlated, which will tremendously help, if one can disentangle oneself from doing what one does not love to do.

Either way, people should not be devoid of caring, attention, tenderness, connection, wanting to belong, sympathy, compassion, opportunity, education, intelligence, relationship, commitments, responsibility, accountability, honesty, reliability, love, devotion, dreaming, imagination, creativity, and millions of other things that we should have to collectively help give meaning to our lives, which without we would be much prone for not making it than when we do. Humanity should be bonded to a social contract not only among those living but also for the sake of future generations.

It is an undeniable fact that Godly societies are more in accord with morality, as millions believe in virtue, belief in destiny with purpose, as they believe in a creator, which no doubt is fueled with doing good. That I am certain is accordingly sealed with believing in some sort of divine reward or ugly punishment in people's mind, and rightly so, since no fool would believe in the same consequences for doing right and for acting wrong.

Either way, people should not be devoid of caring, attention, tenderness, connection, wanting to belong, sympathy, compassion, opportunity, education, intelligence, relationship, commitments, responsibility, accountability, honesty, reliability, love, devotion, dreaming, imagination and creativity, and millions other things that we should have to collectively help give meaning to our lives which without we would be much more prone to not making it than when we do.

Let's not forget that many people are frustrated with the word God, as I do not blame them. Innumerous charlatans and so-called preachers, priests, Mullahs, Rabbi, monks and so on with deep pockets have belittled the word God showing huge discrepancies between their words and their action for the worst beyond belief; which has apparently become an issue with the non-believers, atheists, agnostics, etc.

I rather say, Creator, to perhaps mitigate their reluctance approach to even discuss the sacred word of our God. The point is that discussing and talking or preaching about the creator demands sacrifice. What I mean is you are damned if you understand and are conscientious, and you are damned if you don't, an individual without conscious that is used to constantly feed the beast inside which is irrelevant to what is moral.

When you are enlightened, obviously you will not stand by and let what is not just to take place, as in one way or another you will get involved, even if it is to call for the law to intervene. That is of course if circumstances permit, if not so, then most probably you even might sacrifice your own life to avoid a tragedy of certain kind. I am sure you have heard about the phrase that says no good deed goes unpunished.

Well, when one is enlightened with having a sharp conscious, a compassionate heart, one will perhaps go to the extreme to save an innocent life, which should expect not only praise but sometimes punishment, if one is dealing with an emotionally unintelligent person or perhaps an immorally oriented individual. But overall human beings are of good nature, imagine if you are certain that an innocent female either of proper age or not is going to be raped, or you are sure that in a rubbery about to happen someone is to get killed, or probably of proper age to go to war for your country's sake, and might happen that a child is about to be drawn where you are present, or may be struck by a moving car or a truck, and when a terrorist attack of some sort is going to endanger many lives.

Experience has shown that many individuals volunteer to help by instinct and without any hesitation, sacrificing their own lives to save others, this is a fact. So when we hear the creator made human beings in his image, "Don't you know yet? It is your light that lights the world." Rumi

It should dictate that so many willingly pay a huge price and sacrifice time, money and even their own lives to avoid a tragedy, or to stop an innocent by-standard from not getting killed or even hurt. Because of the enlightenment, the wisdom and the compassion within you, you will not remorse your heavenly actions, no matter what punishment beholds you, which certifies the phrase that says what goes around comes around. This is when the law of karma makes sense.

This is why you should resist anyone trying to devoid awakening the heavenly giant within your heart to do good, and challenge those who perhaps plan to stop the infinitely potentiated cells and neurons in your brain from progressing and from living your full potential where the sky is the limit. One will awaken when one finally stopped agreeing to things that insult one soul. This ought to happen despite any system with corrupt motives or shortcomings imposed on you because of wrongful cultural upbringings and toxic environment.

You must try to belittle the beast within you and activate the spirit, the divine soul, the revered conscious that is waiting to become materialized. "The awakening of consciousness is the next evolutionary step for mankind." Eckhart Tolle

"Your vision will become clear only when you can look into your own heart. Who looks outside, dreams; who looks inside, awakens." Carl Jung

As Plato said, "good is its own virtue", and as the nature of good is "higher consciousness" so is the nature of evil which is "lower consciousness" embrace the fact that: You are your mind, your thoughts, you're conscious. If you see yourself as able as having strength and achievement you possess a conscious with reactive respond.

If you are frightened, where you are in survival mode, and your life is at stake, you possess a conscious of fight or flight. If you are progressing, growing and are in an evolution mode, your conscious is of intuitive response. If you are relaxed, calm and focused, yours is serenity of mind and awareness. If you are the dreamer, making your dreams a reality, you have a mind for creativity.

If you possess a visionary mind, you are potentiated with making miracles to happen. if you possess a mind of deity, yours is conscious of sacredness. The mystery which we need to solve is who is overseeing the above and millions more if not billions of organic responses which literally dictate who you are. You might say I am the one who makes my choices as I decide what to do, correct, but where are you truly located either in your brain or within your body. Let's both of us work on that since so far, the predominant finding is to do good and avoid evil.

When endowed with a good conscience, then all good deeds seem mandatory, as you see no choice but to help those caught in a helpless position, and since your high conscious will constantly remind you of yours being a reluctance to assist when you should have, but did not. As your awakened conscious will cause you tremendous pain, that is if you could have helped it, but did not. Hence, no matter if your kind intention and good work are appreciated or not, your reward is with an Omnipresent Creator.

27

IS IT GOD OR HUMAN GREED?

Then, a great deal of concern arises stating that even with a finely tuned cosmos and/or since the intricate life should remind us of a first cause/designer, there's too much suffering in the world to believe in God. That certainly is true as there exists so much pain in our world beyond anyone's imagination as it should not be denied. But the blame is wrongfully directed and not justifying so.

If honesty, truth, intelligence, decency, and courage should mean something, then, we should aim our anger towards the actual culprits and target the real source of the problems. Humanity should hold those accountable that relentlessly push for the well-being of the very few against the will of many.

Governments are in cahoots with the rich elites and the multifaceted corporations in an oligopolistic atmosphere to globally suppress the basic needs of billions of deprived people as they are struggling to barely live way under the poverty line, without any mercy from those controlling the world by policing and the military industrial complex; as God has nothing to do with it, because the atrocities are caused by our own kind as the fault should be directed at them.

It looks like global citizens are colonized by the moguls of our time where masses of commoners are exploited by surreptitious means forcing billions to leave below the poverty level, as the multi-national corporations have taken people's right and their freedom away by taking their resources and livelihood. The monumentally rich elite have the means to loudly trumpet freedom and human-rights, forgetting that no freedom and no right of any kind can exist without having the means to survive, as they are not in the same boat as globally billions of poverty-driven people are. Money is the worst discovery of human life. But it is the most trusted material to test human nature. Buddha

The point is that need and having freedom are attached at the hip, the more need one has the less free one can be, another word if you are needy, relatively speaking, you cannot be free. We by nature need to breathe, to consume food, must drink water, must rest, need to work, need be sexual, must reproduce to avoid extinction.

These factors are extremely essential for humanity to survive. But this naturally driven requirements should not be mistaken by artificially manufacture needs created by monumental corporations that keep millions out of work when they feel like it, or when they see it fit to maximize their profit. Hence taking millions of worker's freedoms away since workers can no longer afford basic living with being unemployed.

It is a no-brainer that economic bondage and forcing millions to unemployment can sure inhibit people's freedom no matter how much of empty rhetoric is hollered into people's ear with no substance. No one can actually feel free when one cannot feed one's family, not able to keep a roof over their head, not affording education, and not able to afford proper medical for themselves and their loved ones.

They have enslaved masses of global inhabitants through huge class differentiation, where extreme economic inequality has exhausted so many from any hope of recovery and for a better living. This is not rocket science to understand since it is deliberately formulated by big corporations, designed to keep the status quo, that is I believe a recipe for disaster, where the poor get poorer and the rich get richer. This occurs through the barrel of guns, as they immediately extinguish any fiery voice demanding justice, which instead they need to stop fueling the fire of poverty, as there is a limit to everything, including suppressing humanity. Hence, in our contemporary living, we are left with a clear-cut choice, a definite choice which must not be played with. Either to save capitalism and ditch the planet, or get to rid of capitalism and save the planet. Then Jesus said be aware! Guard against every kind of greed. Life is not measured by how much you own.

28

MORAL ABSOLUTISM

Further question branches out by the atheists that a moral life doesn't need God. Not so, true morality requires a transcendent standard God. Before elaborating on this rather imperative concern. We ought to know that Science affirms that the finely tuned cosmos was created out of nothing.

Life's order, design, purpose, the infinite complexity, they all demand an Intelligent Designer, as our response to pain and suffering is relative to our knowledge of right and wrong/good and evil in a fallen world. God has gifted humanity with conscious and a potentiated entity called the brain, that if just given a chance to grow. It will stop all the anguish and the sufferings of the world and will proceed to conquer the entire universe which with no doubt must believe it to succeed and overcome all the burdens in our lives.

As for morality, no human being can claim knowing it all, besides no human-being is free from making mistakes, as no one is absolutely perfect, referencing our behaviors human beings are relative to acting either good or bad, everyone as the saying goes everyone has skeletons in their closet. No man should be trusted with absolute moral laws. As we are all relative beings, as with no prejudice everyone makes mistake.

The sole absolute conscious is God which oversees the mind of the awakened universes with no flows.

Absolute morality is when universal standards of right or wrong apply to all people at all times irrespective of their culture or beliefs. Relative morality is based on the theory that truth and rightness are different for different people or cultures. Hence no man can morally be in a position to globally, universally be followed because of diversity in so many socio-cultural beliefs and what should define what is moral. Bottom line, what is crucial to the human soul, is to educate the heart as well as literacy for the mind. "Educating the mind without educating the heart is no education at all." Aristotle.

Absolute means any theory in which its rules are absolute: they cannot be altered as they are universal. Relative means any theory in which something is judged in relation to something else and thus is open to change. Absolute laws or rules of morality will never change. Moral Relativism (or Ethical Relativism) is the position that moral or ethical criterions do not reflect objective and/or universal moral truths, but in lieu (alternatively, instead) make claims relative to social, cultural, historical or individual circumstances.

Moral absolutism asserts that there are certain universal moral principles by which all peoples' actions may be judged. It is a form of deontology, in which deontology derives from the Greek words for duty (Deon) and science or study of logos. In contemporary moral philosophy, deontology is one of those kinds of normative theories concerning which choices are morally necessary, forbidden, or allowed.

The challenge with moral absolutism, however, is that there will always be strong disagreements about which moral principles are correct and which are incorrect. Moral Absolutism is the ethical belief that there are absolute standards against which moral questions can be judged and that certain actions are right or wrong, regardless of the context of the act. One should further bear in mind that we are partially instinct-driven animals with physical needs as we must satisfy our instinctual urges to survive. This often can compromise our judgments for the sake of bodily pleasures. or our spiritual and moral guide.

> I count him braver who overcomes his desires than him who conquers his enemies, for the hardest victory is over self."
>
> — Aristotle.

29

MULTIVERSE UNIVERSES

Multiverse universes are apparently raised in our contemporary life by non-believers to state their case. Science has realistically brought us a colossal amount of realization. It is understood that the sum total of human knowledge doubles approximately every couple of years or less. of physics and cosmology, we astoundingly know what happened to our universe as early as a tiny fraction of a second after the big bang. In chemistry, we understand the most complex reactions among atoms and molecules, and in biology, we know how the living cell works and have mapped out our total genome. But can this enormous knowledge base reject the existence of some kind of pre-existent outside force that may have launched our universe to be the way it is?

The scientific atheists have tried to describe this problematic mystery by offering the existence of a multiverse—an infinite set of universes, each with its own parameters. In some universes, the conditions are wrong for life; thus, by the sheer size of this alleged multiverse, there must exist a universe where everything is right. But if it takes a massive power of nature to make one universe, then how much more strength would that force have to be orderly for creating infinite universes? Therefore, the sole hypothetical multiverse does not resolve the problem of God. The incredible fine-tuning of the universe indicates the most powerful debate for the being of an imminent creative entity we may well call God. the fact is that we must have a powerful creator to essentially force all the parameters we require for our existence. "I believe we live in a multiverse of universes." Prominent physicist Michio Kaku.

What is fine-tuning? What is a multiverse? The multiverse is a hypothetical group of multiple universes including the universe in which we live. Together, these universes include everything that exists: the entirety of space, time, matter, energy, the physical laws and the constants that describe them.

In summary, the fine-tuning argument points out some of the physical properties of our universe that are meant to prominent the right circumstances for making atoms, stars, planets, galaxies, the universe, and life. If the outcomes were even a bit different, life could not form or survive in the universe. Any savvy mind would see God crafting and sustaining a universe to accomplish his purpose of making it just right for humanity to exist.

The multiverse shows a model where our universe is one of many universes, and each of the universes has a variety of physical properties. But this should not be so wacky to reject the omnipotent, omnipresent and the omniscient God, it should indeed manifest the infinite power of God beyond anyone's imagination, since the infinite God is the cause for the unbounded cosmos as mankind should expect more philosophical and scientific surprises as humanity grows to achieve more knowledge and information to discover more dimensions, and to further divulge the mysteries of the cosmos.

It is surprising that some high caliber philosophers and well known scientists would doubt God, knowing that human intelligence and awareness give rise to scientific discoveries that are often bound to be wrong, as this cannot be historically denied, since new things have consistently come along to replace the old, as many scientific ideas either had to be corrected, or previous founding's had to be improved to make sense.

The point is we are not flawless, as we do not possess the absolute wisdom and the utter intelligence, so is many of our findings. No scientific theory can be the answer for millions of complex questions to quench humanity's thirst for the answer to many curious oriented inquiries. Renowned physicist Stephen Hawking said, "A combination of quantum theory and the theory of relativity would better explain our existence than divine intervention."

It shouldn't be surprising if the next scientific Joe to show up next and say what I claim is the solution to all the puzzling question in which humanity is grappling with, that my so and so theory is the answer to all there is and no divine intervention would be necessary, because through modern history is not the first time such title is raised and wouldn't be the last. whenever the hypothesis on the multiverse universe become a reality for conveying life, then, the fine-tuning of those universes without any doubt must have occurred by a higher power to make them fruitful.

It is a fact that rigorous mathematical structures are behind the quantum theory, string theory, gravitational forces by the physicists and cosmologists tied up with the probabilities of multiverse universe. But no matter how advanced we become in our scientific discoveries we should never disregard the infinitely intelligent mind of our creator orchestrating the entire show. "String theory envisions a multiverse in which our universe is one slice of bread in a big cosmic loaf. The other slices would be displaced from ours in some extra dimension of space." Brain Greene

If scientists are correct, then all the stars and galaxies we can observe in the clear night are just a tiny fraction of an unimaginably huge assemblage that scientists call the multiverse. The whole universe may be just one element—one atom in an infinite quintet (combo) of heavens, a cosmic wonder. So far physicists have put forth three exclusive debate for the existence of the multiverse.

First is the big bang, the catastrophic event that made the universe into existence about 13.8 billion years ago. Some physicists believe the big bang happened by a random fluctuation which they call quantum foam The big bang is thought to have been triggered by a random fluctuation in what physicists call the quantum foam, a vortex (whirlpool) of virtual particles that pop into and out of existence. as many scientists claim that there could have been many such events leading to multiple universes. The second argument for the existence of a multiverse arises from string theory, in which string theory says that matter is eventually made not of particles but of unthinkably small, vibrating strings or loops of energy. Physicists believed that string theory might afford a theory of everything that is, a system of equations that could describe why our universe has the precise properties that it does. For instance, why is the mass of a proton 1836.15 times greater than that of the electron? No one has a convincing expiation.

String theory's equations seem to have an amazing number of probable solutions (that's a one followed by 500 zeros). Strangely enough, some string theorists debate that each of these solutions can explain a different universe, each with its own physical properties. String theory is a theoretical framework that tries the idea that the point-like particles of particle physics can also be modeled as one-dimensional objects called strings. String theory attempts to unite the four forces in the universe—the electromagnetic force, the strong nuclear force, the weak nuclear force, and gravity into one unified theory.

Physicists believe string theory is a potentiated theory for everything, perhaps able to unite all matter and forces in a single theoretical framework, which could explain the fundamental level of the universe in terms of vibrating strings rather than particles. In the meanwhile, superstring theory formally known less as string theory is occasionally called the theory of everything because it is a uniting physics theory that reconciles the differences between quantum theory and the theory of relativity to explain the nature of all known forces and matter which if so, it would be huge breakthrough for science and the scientist's mind behind it.

One imperative component of string theories is that these theories demand extra dimensions of space-time for their mathematical consistency. In bosonic string theory, space-time is 26-dimensional, while in superstring theory it is 10-dimensional, and in M-theory it is 11-dimensional. Spatial dimensions. Classical physics theories describe three physical dimensions: from a particular point in space, the basic directions in which we can move are up/down, left/right, and forward/backward. Time is often thought of as the fourth dimension. Time plays a key role as a dimension in mathematical formulations of physical laws and theories such as general relativity and string theory. The qualitative maneuverability of time as the fourth dimension is arguable.

The third argument for the multiverse arrives from quantum theory. even though it's has been around for more than a century now and has shown to be very successful in explaining the nature of matter on the smallest scale, quantum theory guides us to a number of existential probabilities that defy common sense, known as many worlds translation of quantum theory began in the 1950s, the universe necessarily splits in two each time there's a quantum event. Niels Bohr suggested the Copenhagen interpretation of the quantum theory, which indicated that a particle is whatever it is measured either to be for instance a wave or a particle, in which cannot be assumed to have specific properties or even to exist until it is restrained and measured. Quantum mechanics is the body of scientific laws that shows the preposterous (bizarre) function of photons, electrons and the other particles that make-up to the entire universe. Wave-Particle Duality of Light.

Quantum theory indicates that both light and matter consist of tiny particles which have wavelike properties linked with them. Light is made up of particles known as photons, and the matter is composed of particles named electrons, protons, neutrons. In our contemporary lifestyle the most exact clocks in the world, are atomic clocks, able to utilize the foremost behavior of quantum theory to measure time. They monitor the specific radiation frequency required to make electrons jump between various energy levels. Modern quantum mechanics came about in 1925 by German physicists Werner Heisenberg, Max Born, and Pascual Jordan generated matrix mechanics, and Erwin Schrodinger the Austrian physicist which invented the wave mechanics and the non-relativistic Schrodinger equation.

Some elementary notion of quantum mechanics is the Bohr theory which constitutes the idea of energy levels but does not succeed to divulge the details of atomic structure. It is the theory utilized for extremely small particles, such as electrons in atoms. Quantum theory is the theoretical fundamental of modern physics which explains the nature and behavior of matter and energy on the atomic and subatomic level. The nature and behavior of matter and energy at that level is occasionally indicated to as quantum physics and quantum mechanics.

30

ONENESS VS. NOTHINGNESS

As demanding as technology is, I am afraid it can be troubling too. It seems that industrialization and technology advance people's IQ while people's empathy for their fellow human beings and the environment keeps declining. We live in a progressive era which ironically violence and criminal conduct has rampaged as people's faith has deteriorated, even replacing God with science.

So many are losing sight, ignoring that scientists conduct scientific research to advance knowledge in an area of interest. In reality, they discover the truth by plying (draw on, exploit) facts; they act as gynecologists relentlessly pursuing new scientific ideas from the womb of mother nature. It seems they are probing for the Oneness, and look for the root causes of the infinite possibilities. Hoping that perhaps one day they could detect the point of singularity where Oneness resides.

Scientists are adamant to discover the mysteries of our universe, to find the real source of existence where they research for the absolute power of intention behind this extremely mind-boggling cosmos. Misinterpreting modernisms by millions and miss understanding science and technologies by lots of people, they have caused a lack of collective awareness, as often neighbors are completely cut off from each other as they do not exist. Millions are so individualized, they have become robot-like, mimicking mechanical routines like they have no soul. They relentlessly engage in electronic plays, incessantly pursuing cyber-oriented activities, often with sexual bearings, and so many are obsessed with diversified gadgets like there is no tomorrow.

People's priorities have changed, these days one is more concern with let's say a dead Raccoon in their backyard than a child dying because of hunger in Asia or in Africa. As if we live in the Paleolithic (periods of the stone age) era. We should know that spiritual and moral values gravitate humanity towards the culture of tolerance and understanding.

Compassion plays a decisive role in refuting cruelty, and being considered keenly draws on wisdom, while kindness, pursuing art, creativity, and beauty are to appreciate soul searching. the spirit does not work with the hand, there is no art. Leonardo da Vinci. Nations can resort to progressive cultures to collectively harness science, exchange art, and manifest civilized conducts to mandate freedom, glorify democracy and reach the pinnacle of human rights so that everyone can taste the sweetness of life as it is meant to be.

The principle of causality and the axiom of non-contradiction is to avoid ambiguities and dissension (discord, disharmony) in all propositions, which without nothing in the material world should actually work. since both doctrines not only apply to the tangible world but are certainly decisive in conceptually oriented phenomena for validating logic in philosophy, science, socio-cultural, socio-economic, socio-political and certainly for reaching God, spirituality and the existence.

Coherency in moral behaviors should be sought, to avoid hypocrisy in one's conduct, and not stray from the path of righteousness and what is just. Good and evil are not just nominal, as good is its own virtue, so as evil is repugnant, which if moral turpitude (degradation) shall somehow overcome, then human demise will be on the ballot.

The point is that all pluralities initiated from oneness, the entire cosmos started from singularity where everything in existence shall purposefully return to God the creator of heavens and Earth. Consider one's own place in the universal unity in which we all belong, and the Oneness of which we are all a part of, from which we all depart and to which we all return.

Many scientists, prominent philosophers believe that accidental behaviors will never verify unity, they so confirm that no accidental motion can purposefully reach unity, but in contrary, they generate chaos and disharmony. "Technology is destructive only in the hands of people who do not realize that they are one and the same process as the universe." Alan W. Watts

Further, let's put the search for traces of God to test. let's imagine that nothing exists. I often did so, but with no avail. I just am not able to delineate (portray, depict) nothingness. I mean to imagine no light, no darkness, an imagination barren of stars, planets and galaxies, no universe of any kind to dwell on.

I mean, can anyone imagine no space, no time, no matter, an idea devoid of any sentient life, to utterly imagine nothingness. I mean an absolute vacuity (void), just nothing. It neither is conceptually nor physically possible. begs the end-all question from curious minds? Why is there something rather than nothing? To envisage nothing is nonsensical (not sensible, absurd.) It is not practical to fancy nothing—not only no space, time, matter, energy, light, darkness or any aware beings, but no consciousness at all to perceive void, to behold nothingness. In this sense, the question is literally not probable.

Nothing, nil, naught, is something. A fallacy, a deductive paradox, inferential sophistry, a wrongful reasoning or non sequitur (Latin for it does not follow) is a flaw in the structure of a logical argument which renders the argument invalid. It obviates (preclude) balderdash (nonsense, bunk.)

The absence of all there is. Perhaps so many people think that how insignificant nothing is but far from it; the idea of nothing is primal to our universe. It is awkward to imagine absolute nothingness. If we are able to remove all there is from inside of a small container box: all the air, molecules, atoms, particles, until not a thing is left in it. At this stage, we should see and feel that there is nothing in this empty box since we have removed everything from the inside since the box literally looks empty. But what we know as emptiness is not corollary (by-product) to what we see, since such void arranges most of the universe; which are the atoms forming everything and not excluding us.

Hence, it is deductive sophistry (fallacy) to talk about nothing like it was a something that ceases to exist, is not. Here we are faced against the puzzling issue of describing what we mean by nothing and the exclusion that language intrudes on the problem. The very act of trying to dialogue about nothing makes it a something. Alternatively, (otherwise) what are we saying? should, in reality, be abjured (formally rejected) since contextually does not make any sense.

31

NOTHING WOULD HOLD GOD'S NONEXISTENCE

In the classification of nothing let's categorize some of the issues that perhaps can encompass something that would be contradicted by nothing: since in the material world nothing does attribute to anything physical, mental, moral, spiritual, platonic love and God, etc. If by nothing is meant no physical objects or matter of any kind, for example, there can still be energy from which matter may arise by natural forces guided by the laws of nature. Physicists, for example, talk about empty space as seething with virtual particles, from which particle-antiparticle pairs come into existence as a consequence of the uncertainty principle of quantum physics. From this nothingness, universes may pop into existence.

Nothing excludes creation ex nihilo. If by nothing is meant that there is no physical, mental, platonic or nonphysical entity of any kind, then there can be no God or gods, which means that there cannot be anything outside of nothing from which to create something.

This negates the Christian theologian argument that God created the universe ex nihilo, or "out of nothing," based on the English translation of Genesis 1:1 that "in the beginning, God created the heavens and the earth." This is misleading. Recent scholarship has suggested that the Hebrew word for "creation" in Genesis 1:1 is bara ()—a verb that more accurately translated means to "separate" or "divide." Genesis 1:1 should read, "In the beginning, God separated the heavens and the earth." Separated from what is not indicated.

Nothing is unstable; something is stable. Asking why there is something rather than nothing presumes nothing is the natural state of things out of which something needs an explanation. Maybe something is the natural state of things, and nothing would be the mystery to be solved.

In his sweeping narrative, *The Greatest Story Ever Told—So Far*, a sequel to his 2012 book *A Universe from Nothing*, Krauss notes that Einstein was one of the first physicists to demonstrate that the classical notion of causation begins to break down at the quantum realm. Although many physicists objected to the idea of something coming from nothing, he observes that this is precisely what happens with the light you are using to read this page.

Electrons in hot atoms emit photons—photons that didn't exist before they were emitted—which are emitted spontaneously and without a specific cause. Why is it that we have grown at least somewhat comfortable with the idea that photons can be created from nothing without a cause, but not whole universes?

One answer has to do with our discomfort with the Copernican principle, which holds that we are not special. We prefer religious and anthropic explanations that the universe was created and fine-tuned for us because they put humans right back in the center of the cosmos anthropocentrically—it is all about us. But 500 years of scientific discoveries have revealed that it isn't about us. From this fact, we may gain purchase on a perspective that engages both the religious and scientific impulse toward a sense of awe one gains from contemplating nothing.

32

MIND CONTROL

Human beings are potentiated to learn, to reason and solve problems. We're self-aware, and we're conscious of our surroundings, the presence, thoughts, and feelings of others. We make tools and practice the art of deception, we're creative. We think abstractly. We have language and use it to concoct complex ideas. All of these are relative signs of intelligence—we are highly intelligent beings. I say relative, since not everyone is endowed with great IQ, or born with golden opportunity to raise at the top. Even when one is highly intelligent one must be educated, trained and have the financial means to succeed in life.

Historically speaking, those at the top, the ruling class, the elites, do not easily let go of their power without a bloody encounter. They will resort to anything and everything to subdue and quell (end) any uprising, peaceful or none, either through force or by mind manipulation. The rich elites, the ruling class, the state, and the media work in cahoots to control the commoners, and fundamentally they have the resources and all the technological means to mentally exploit and control people's mind.

The authorities utilize propaganda and censorship to keep the population at bay (preventing them from reaching, attacking, or affecting) the status quo, to make certain that people are thinking in a proper way. The idea of overcoming and making the citizens subservient to the system is not new, but the modern approach in the technology of mind control is extremely sophisticated. The commoners cannot even fathom the tactics and the strategy that the system uses against them since the system buys the most intelligent and extraordinary minds to work for them often against the will of the people.

For instance, one of the techniques used to substantiate mind control was developed by Dr. John C Lilly, when he was working for the US National Institute of health. Dr. Lilly found out that certain wavelength format could control the water molecules inside the subject's brain which could intrinsically (essentially) alter the undertakers think and feel. Evidently, the technology utilizes frequency waves of 40hz, not needing the use of electrodes. According to Melissa and Aaron Duke of Truth stream Media, the Lilly wave is solely the tip of icebergs.

The couple believed that a man known as Hendricus G. Loos patented a grotesque (bizarre, unheard of, extraordinary) invention called Nervous System Manipulation via electromagnetic fields from monitors. Mr. Loos claimed that his invention when utilized can change human's emotional state by altering the electromagnetic fields around them through devices like a television screen and computer monitors.

Loos wrote, "It is, therefore, possible to manipulate the nervous system of a subject by pulling images exhibited on a close by computer monitor or TV set." Probably the most sinister part of this invention is that it can be exploited without the subject of the mind control ever being aware of what has occurred. Furthermore, Aaron and Melissa Dykes also have indicated brain mapping technology, according to Truth Stream Media brain mapping technology is enabled to decode human brain which means it can render the ability to the user to read thoughts of other people. It is literally a big problem since there are no laws against covertly monitoring people's trend of thoughts and the invasion of the inhabitant's privacy, as it is presently legal, although not ethical at all.

33

WHAT SCIENCE SAYS ABOUT THE MATTER AND AFTER WE DIE

If the matter can neither be generated nor obliterated, then how was the universe was hatched? Scientists agree that the entire amount of energy and matter in the universe stays constant, solely altering from one form to another. Further, $E = mc2$, an equation derived by the twentieth-century physicist Albert Einstein, in which E represents units of energy, m represents units of mass, and c2 is the speed of light squared, or multiplied by itself. Energy equals mass times the speed of light squared. On the most basic level, the equation says that energy and mass (matter) are interchangeable; they are different forms of the same thing. Under the right conditions, energy can become mass and vice versa.

Then it shouldn't make any difference to either say that matter can neither be generated nor destroyed, which you can say the same thing for energy too. $E=mc2$: Einstein's equation that gave birth to the atom bomb. It says that the energy (E) in a system (an atom, a person, the solar system) is equal to its total mass (m) multiplied by the square of the speed of light (c, equal to 186,000 miles per second). Therefore, if matter and energy are interchangeable, then it should really not matter. The first law of thermodynamics doesn't actually specify that matter can neither be created nor destroyed, and instead it says energy can neither be created or destroyed.

It should say either matter, or energy cannot be created or destroyed, since once again matter and energy are equivalent or better yet, are identical. It states that the total amount of energy in a closed system cannot be created nor destroyed (it can be changed from one form to another). It was after nuclear physics told us that mass and energy are essentially equivalent -this is what Einstein meant when he wrote E= mc2 that we realized the 1st law of thermodynamics also applied to the mass. Mass became another form of energy that had to be included in a thorough thermodynamic treatment of a system. Hence, the total amount of energy in the universe has to remain the same, from the beginning of the universe until the present.

The overall understanding is that total energy in the universe is constant, and scientists believe that the universe is expanding. There are infinite stars, planets, galaxies and with prevalent globular clusters, matter and energy seem to commute, rushing off everywhere in many directions. The scientists say that the expansion of the universe does not have to consume more energy as the universe expands, since the distance between stars or galaxies increases. Therefore, the gravitational energy between them decreases to compensate.

Further, thermodynamics does not know what value the total energy should carry, since the physicists believe that the amount can be colossal (huge), but constant that is known as an open universe, where the amount of matter/energy exceeds a definite so-called cut-off density level. in our universe. It is now believed zero which is called a flat universe, as many physicists agreed that the matter-density in the universe is equal to the cut-off density. It could also be negative, even an encircled, a closed universe where the amount of matter is less than the cut-off density.

Finally, they say it could be anything, but whatever the value is at the present, it was at the very beginning too. According to the science of physics, the entire matter and energy in the universe now existed in some form or shape at the big bang. Once again, the notoriety of the point to make shown through the image courtesy of NASA, stating that The expansion of the universe doesn't have to take more energy -as the universe expands, the distances between stars or galaxies increases, and thus the gravitational energy between them decreases to compensate. Quantum mechanics indicates that an extremely tiny scale and for an extremely short period of time, energy can be spontaneously being made and destroyed. Similar to boiling water, where bubbles spontaneously show up and burst, energy—in the form of particles—can very quickly appear from the void of space-time, exist for an immensely short amount of time, and disappear again.

Normal time and length scales average out to what thermodynamics indicated. It should hold true (that no energy is created or destroyed within the closed system of the universe). But eventually, what they mean is that if there was such a tiny fluctuation at the beginning of time, it could have made the total energy of the universe at creation a bit more than zero, and hence, the universe will always carry that total amount of energy, since such a fluctuation could have been what made the universe to begin in the first place.

The scientific field of cosmology, also the growing field of string theory, is trying to answer this ultimate question, how did the universe start? But so far, no one knows what occurred at the moment the universe initiated. The First Law of Thermodynamics (Conservation) states that energy is always conserved, it cannot be created or destroyed. In essence, energy can be converted from one form into another. The Second Law of Thermodynamics is about the quality of energy. It states that as energy is transferred or transformed, more and more of it is wasted.

The bottom line with infinite interactivities in stars, planets, galaxies, and in the entire universe, one should expect some type of lop-sidedness and imbalances causing energy shortage in some part of the universe, or energy abundant in other parts, even causing energy exhaustion in the heavens above. Instead, energy transferability is awesomely at work converting the precise amount of energy required to where is designated to go and vice versa without any malfunction, which should definitely alert us with the immense discipline and magnificent power of an infinitely competent designer overseeing everything in existence.

If we are also energy-driven, and an inseparable part of nature, then what happens to us when we die? We know we are here temporary which sooner or later we expire. Scientists say that after we pass on, the atoms in our body will forever remain here. but most of the atoms in your body are forever. Alternatively, we are either buried, embalmed (to treat a dead body with specials to prevent it from decay) or not, or buried. If so, then one's soft tissues are eventually consumed by bacteria and tiny organisms. Also if one is burned, one's soft tissues are consumed by oxygen and made into carbon dioxide, water, and sulfur oxides and nitrogen. The long-term effect is that we become food for other organisms.

The dead person's bones also will decay, but more slowly than the soft tissue, which then phosphorus and calcium in dead body's bones will end up into the soil and taken by the plants. Then, some plants will be eaten by animals, where eventually the animals die, some consumed by humans and cycle through biosphere redundantly, over and over again. So one wouldn't know how much of and which predecessor's body one has taken in. There are some radioactive elements, not many which few of them decay and turn into other elements before they can arrive into the biosphere.

Radioactive potassium will become calcium, small amounts of thorium and uranium will eventually turn into a lead, with most of this decay, the new elements made the stay here on planet Earth. In the process helium is also formed as Earth gravitational force cannot hold helium, hence a bit of it will take off into space. Some of it will get away from the solar system and shift to the stars, and some will be caught by Sun and other planets like Jupiter which is the fifth planet from the Sun and the largest in the solar system. It is a giant planet with a mass one-thousandth that of the Sun, but two-and-a-half times that of all the other planets in the solar system and Mars.

The point is that no matter what happens to you after you die, or how you expire, your atoms do not care since they just stay the way they are, and start a new life elsewhere doing the same job they did for you.

Most of your atoms commute and do their thing. Our body continuously dies and rebuild itself as it constitutes our genetic pattern as the atoms and molecules in changes. Most of the atoms that build your body today are not the same atoms that made your body a few months or years ago.

34

ENLIGHTENMENT; AN EXTREMELY POTENT AGENT

For this enlightenment, however, nothing is required but freedom, and indeed the most harmless among all the things to which this term can properly be applied. It is the freedom to make public use of one's reason at every point. But I hear on all sides, 'Do not argue!' The Officer says: 'Do not argue but drill!' The tax collector: 'Do not argue but pay!' The cleric: 'Do not argue but believe!' Only one prince in the world says, 'Argue as much as you will, and about what you will, but obey!' Everywhere there is a restriction on freedom."

— Immanuel Kant

An answer to the question: What is enlightenment?

There are two fundamental issues, one is that life is hard, so they say, which it is not supposed to be, life is meant to be good, and the second is that there are opportunities, but not available to everyone. These two troubling states are manufactured, they sure stem from people not getting their fair share out of life, and often for millions that are exhausted of any given chance. One might ask if so, why intelligent communities and savvy minded people do not do anything about it.

Historically speaking inhumane behaviors happened through the dark ages, force and savagery by the powerful and the mighty were the norms, and not so surprisingly common, that has caused beyond repair damages to mankind. Violence and exerting brute force was the key for the strong to rule and create masses of slaves and millions of subservient individuals to do as the violators and the tyrants desired. The point is that stupidity and ignorance played a big role in dwelling on (populate) atrocious behavior.

Perhaps not much of criticism should behold the culprits since civility of mind and manner were just simply absent. Societies were thoughtfully barren, and not mentally fertile enough to fight back, where most victims were not mindfully potentiated to realize their rights as a human being which they should not have been exploited, and lowered to the animal level. God or gods also did not mean much, again because of lack of human intelligence worshiping idols and man-made agents of some sort. As Immanuel Kant said: "How then is perfection to be sought? Wherein lies our hope? In education, and in nothing else."

Then, of course, there are those who believe that God will punish the evil doers, even so, they do not realize that the good God has endowed humanity with all the tools and the resources to live happy and free. The mind of man is not to be taken lightly, as God has made it possible for the mankind to conquer the universe in which far exceeds for solving the problems made by our own kind, and not wait for the creator of heaven and earth to save us from the torts (misdeed, felony) of bad characters. "Space and time are the frameworks within which the mind is constrained to construct its experience of reality." Immanuel Kant.

People should realistically confront abuse of power and injustice by the few and not wait for so long that one day Messiah, or any other faith-related Icon to appear from beyond the space and time to free us from the clutches of so much economic inequality and extreme financial transgressions by the moguls of time, which have resulted in people's suffering and despair, it just does not make any sense. "All our knowledge begins with the senses, proceeds then to the understanding and ends with reason. There is nothing higher than reason." Emmanuel Kant.

The violator's irrelevancy to God and acting far away from good conscious has made life miserable for billions, and unreasonably very hard for the global commoners, as they literally feel the horrific financial impact imposed on them, leaving so many destitute as the victim's cry for help do not reach those in position of power and fame.

The Persian poet Saadi Shirazi said that:

Human beings are members of the whole.
In the creation of one essence and soul.
If one member is affected with pain.
Other members uneasy will remain.
If you have no sympathy for human pain.
The name of human you cannot retain.

35

LIFE AFTER DEATH

Theories of where humans go when they expire have been the question since humans have lived. Many religiously oriented thoughts believe that there is a God and that heaven is where the righteous souls end up, and Inferno (hell) is where the evil souls go. Some are Polytheism (from Greek polytheisms) is the worship of or belief in multiple deities, which are usually assembled into a pantheon of gods and goddesses, along with their own religions and rituals.

As those gods have no control of where humans go. Some believe that souls are reincarnated. Some believe that nothing happens when people die. Others believe that after a person dies, they are gone forever. Some believe all go to the same place when they pass on. As far as the human soul, the overall understanding is that human soul or spirit is energy-oriented and runs through our vein and permeates brain waves, the nervous and so on, is any different than the energy that science says is never created nor destroyed?

Either way, it seems that the energy is being recycled in a matrix world which all things are conserved, which can shed lights on the idea of reincarnation that believes after death, reincarnation occurs depending upon the accumulated karma, rebirth occurs into a higher or lower bodily form, either in heaven or hell or earthly realm. No bodily form is permanent: everyone dies and reincarnates further. It is believed that some people remember past lives.

The data from their lives are still preserved within the soul.

36

INFINITY VS. FINITE WORLD

Infinity can only correlate with the infinite God.

Physicists have to deal with math to make sure their experimental assessments, either at the cosmological level, like the big bang model, or any other scientific hypothesis that they are working on makes sense before establishing a theory that assuredly can be relied on. Hence, if we should accept the big bang as our best accomplished cosmological model, then the big bang should be considered as the beginning of the universe, which initiated about 14 billion years ago. But then, realistically acknowledging this time period is not feasible, it can only be a prediction which seems not applicable to our actual universe because of scientist's findings based on relate to numbers.

But numbers do not exist, they are simply adjectives, which definition of an adjective is that it is a word that describes or clarifies a noun. Adjectives describe nouns by giving some information about an object's size, shape, age, color, origin or material. It's a big table (size). It's a (round) table, they are not nouns. If one says, round you should ask round what?. The natural numbers also do have a start, but not an end, they do not possess any finality.

For instance, if one says 100, then, you ought to inquire 100 what? Let's assume for an instant, we ask an accountant to show us 5 he/she perhaps hold up 5 fingers. But we did not inquire about showing us fingers. When he/she decides to withdraw the fingers, then the adjective five also vanishes.

Then, another accountant or mathematician writes a 5 when is asked to exhibit 5 but 5 is not a number, it is the symbol that represents a number. The Romans used the symbol V for five, and the roman symbol for 1 through 10 are as follows I, II, III, IV, V, VI, VII, VIII, IX, X.

We shouldn't be deceived by numbers since they only exist as concepts or thoughts in our minds, they truly do not have an independent reality of their own, Numbers must be attached some type of names for them to make sense. One cannot find a number not being attached to something to make sense. But they are concepts which we cannot do without.

Have you ever seen a number line? That is how a math teacher, a mathematician or any math student will describe a number line: In math, a number line can be defined as a straight line with numbers placed at equal intervals or segments along its length. A number line can be extended infinitely in any direction and is usually represented horizontally.

A number line can also be used to represent both positive and negative integers as well, but number lines do not exist in the real world. If one tries to draw a number line one can only draw a line that can go so far, can go a definite length, it will never be infinite. Some mathematicians, physicists or others in affiliated fields relate to space and indicate the line can go on forever, but in actuality, no line will go very far in the real world.

Infinity (symbol: ∞) is a concept describing something without any bound, or something larger than any natural number. In mathematics, infinity is often treated as a number (i.e., it counts or measures things: an infinite number of terms) but it is not the same sort of number as either a natural or a real number.

When used in the context infinitely small, it can also describe an object that is smaller than any number. It is important to know that infinity is not a number; rather, it exists only as an abstract concept. Infinity Symbol Meaning Revealed. Many utilize infinity for symbolizing its modern interpretation of eternity and everlasting love, or the infinite God.

However, occasionally infinity draws from its traditional understanding as the symbol of perfection, duality, and empowerment.

Further, Infinity is an invaluable abstract concept in mathematics, physics, and philosophy. Isaac Newton used the abstraction of infinitely small times and distances to formulate the calculus upon which all modern physics and much of mathematics relies. The question centers on whether

Infinity (∞) is a quantity or an amount. One can enjoy the symbolic infinity as a sign of limitless love, empowerment, and other positive affirmations.

No doubt that mathematics is the heart of many scientific discoveries, especially physics. What one should notice is that as meaningful as numbers are, they are a concept that we cannot do without, as they seem to be the language of God. Italian astronomer and physicist Galileo Galilei said:

Mathematics is the language with which God has written the universe. It is imperative to know that mathematicians do not operate in the real world.

They operate in the realm of concept which they have no physical reality, since numbers do not exist, they are not subject to the boundaries of physics. Numbers are not influenced by factors such as pressure, gravity, statics, hot, cold, humidity, light, dark, snow, rain, wind, heat, and so on.

That is why if an experiment is mathematically compatible and correct, can most probably be relied on to constitute a theory. It also should be noticed that no equation can fully regard every probable physical effect that is involved, the reality is simply too complicated than it looks.

There are many imaginary ideas in mathematician's view of infinity which can only be true in their minds. For instant when a math-oriented individual, a mathematician, an accountant or anyone in related field states that there is an infinite number of numbers or points between any two given points.

This can solely be true in their minds, where a point has no width. In reality, we cannot find a number thin enough, with absolutely no width to fit the infinite points between two designated marks, even as smallest as an atom, since atom also has width. There is just no way that one can fit an infinite number of the point between to marks or two points. yes, multi-millions of the atom, perhaps billions can be placed in a line that is one or two millimeters long, but nothing can ever come close to fitting infinite numbers or points between two indicated marks or points.

It is just not practical in the real world even electrons that smaller than atoms that are as close to having no width as we cannot know how small they are. So we could get possibly an infinite number of electrons into our millimeter line. But be also aware that electrons carry an invisible something called charge. Therefore, put two electrons close together and they will repel each other. I am afraid most people's judgment is in their eyes, they believe what they see, as it is often difficult for so many individuals to grasp abstract concepts.

The imperative point is that most concepts like, God, time, gravity, energy, universe, numbers, consciousness, sub-conscious mind, thoughts, ideas, memories, emotions, feelings, infinity and millions of other things are concepts that are just not tangible, in which without we cannot carry on, where they should be realized, if we are to present a make sense view of our world. As for making sense, do mathematicians not know we live in the rounded world, and no imaginary number line can go to infinity since our planet has no edge and what one imagines is to make sense, because what in our world goes around, comes around, obviously, they imagine otherwise.

Hence, In the real world, there is no infinity. Infinity can never start and never stop. As such, nothing in our real world is infinite. Anything that starts is limited by its beginning and thus cannot be infinite, not excluding how life started. Only something that never initiates can never terminate, as we cannot locate such a thing in the real world of three-dimensional physics. Everything in our world has a beginning, that is why we cannot practically relate to infinity; which with a beginning logic dictates to expect an end, at least in the materially based world.

Let's be clear that infinity can only be a property of higher realms, the spiritual domain with beyond grasp dimensions, an unimaginable concept that can solely be attributed to the almighty God.

37

WHO IS RUNNING THE SHOW IN OUR BODY AND MIND?

What we so far know is that through our senses we learn about the outside world, and become aware of our surroundings. Dynamic interactivities with our environment happen through our nervous system, via our five senses of seeing, hearing, smelling, tasting and touch impacted by the outside world. The information accordingly is taken by our nervous system to the brain, which our brains interpret, assesses and apparently re-arranges them sending them back again via the nervous system and our senses to our limbs, the same senses that delivered messages to our brain in the first place, now telling our limbs what to do.

Further, the outside world couldn't have been the same as what our brain interpreted afterward. The external world should be different and not the same to our brain before the human brain produces a subsequent translation and in making sense of them. what is imprinted in our senses as certain figures, shape, colors, sound, noise, smell, taste and touch are much different to millions of other creatures besides us. So, it seems that what we see, hear, taste, smell, and touch, what we experience in the so-called the real world is not the same as what we comprehend them to be, the external world is not as we know it to be.

Then, for the outside world what we know as matter is nothing but condescend energy, the same energy as our immaterial senses and the nervous system, otherwise, they wouldn't have been conductible, and transparent to our senses. Now, what our senses, our nervous systems including our brain are made of? The dynamics in more details are: The nervous system draws in information through our senses, processes the information and triggers reactions, such as making one's muscles move or causing one to feel pain.

The central nervous system (CNS) includes the nerves in the brain and spinal cord. Central nervous system: a part of the nervous system includes the brain and spinal cord. The parasympathetic nervous system, part of the human nervous system that unconsciously controls our organs and glands when the body is at rest. The brain is the body's main control center. The main function of the Central nervous system is the integration and processing of sensory information; it synthesizes sensory input to compute an appropriate motor response or output. The central nervous system is made up of the brain and spinal cord.

The peripheral nervous system is made up of the nerve fibers that branch off from the spinal cord and extend to all parts of the body, including the neck and arms, torso, legs, skeletal muscles and internal organs. Cerebrum: is the largest part of the brain and is composed of the right and left hemispheres. It manages higher functions like interpreting touch, vision, and hearing, as well as speech, reasoning, emotions, learning, and fine control of movement.

Cerebellum: is located under the cerebrum. The cerebrum, the large, outer part of the brain, controls reading, thinking, learning, speech, emotions and planned muscle movements like walking. It also controls vision, hearing and other senses. The cerebrum is divided into two cerebral hemispheres (halves), the left halves, and the right halves.

How does the nervous system usually communicate with the rest of the body? Peripheral nerves carry information to the central nervous system, which then processes the info and dispatches a message back telling the body how to react. While the function of the dendrites (which dendrites are components of neurons, the nerve cells in the brain, neurons are large, tree-like structures made up of a body, the soma, also known as the cell body with numerous branches called dendrites extending outward) of neurons is to pick up signals and send them to the cell body.

Emotions, like fear and love, are carried out by the limbic system, which is located in the temporal lobe. While the limbic system is made up of multiple parts of the brain, the center of emotional processing is the amygdala, which receives input from other brain functions, like memory and attention.

The nervous system has three main functions: To collect sensory input from the body and the external environment. To process and interpret the sensory input. It controls all parts of the body. It receives and interprets messages from all parts of the body and sends out instructions. The three main components of the central nervous system are the brain, spinal cord, and neurons.

The brain forwards messages by the spinal cord to peripheral nerves throughout the body that serve to control the muscles and internal organs. The somatic nervous system is made up of neurons linking the central nervous system with the parts of the body that communicate with the external world.

The central nervous system deals with the rest of the body by sending messages from the brain through the nerves that branch off of you. Muscles move on commands from the brain. Single nerve cells in the spinal cord, called motor neurons, are the only way the brain links to muscles. When a motor neuron inside the spinal cord fires, an impulse goes out from it to the muscles on a long, very thin extension of that single cell known an axon.

These messages go through specialized cells called neurons. Unlike most other cells, neurons have the competency to interact with other cells and transmit information across relatively long distances. Notice that such intricate transactions for making one aware of its surroundings through one's senses and the central nervous system happens very quickly. On average non-voluntary reflexes (which is actually information going to the central nervous system, being processed, and then going out to the motor neurons) take about 0.3 seconds. However, the average human can blink in about 0.1 seconds, which is probably a better measure.

But for instance, imagine one's sense of touch is lost known as hypoesthesia (also spelled as hypoesthesia) is a common side effect of various medical conditions which manifests as a reduced sense of touch or sensation or a partial loss of sensitivity to sensory stimuli. In an everyday speech, this is commonly indicated as numbness. Is part of the somatosensory system, the sensory system concerned with the conscious perception of touch, pressure, pain, temperature, position, movement, and vibration, which arise from the muscles, joints, skin, and fascial.

if one is to touch an extremely hot stove, one's safety is radically compromised, since the sense of touch is dead to immediately alert one of the killer heat. is applicable to other senses of vision, hearing, smell, and taste resulting in different kind of ills if not properly functioning. without our senses, basically the entire central nervous system can go obsolete because obviously they are awakening factors in linking us to the outside world and the central nervous system, they are as imperative as the spinal cord and our brain.

The point is that our senses and the central nervous system, our brain, work as mediators, or if you like, like a cell phone connecting us to the world outside. The more opening cells in one's brain the better connectivity to our external environment, just like an up to date apple cell phone, or any smartphone made of dynamic components, and with many ABS, and not a regular cell phone without having complex amenities, and exhausted of complicated functions.

Bottom line, consciousness, the mind, is managing our senses, and is running the central processing units (CPU) in our brain, denoting that it is our mind that is linked to the universal energy inclusively functioning as one, and as an inseparable part of what is permeating in all beings, and the entire creation. should make one wonder, who is running the show, if no one can be found inside of any one of us, except for a bunch of bones, muscles and nerves and other necessary affiliated parts.

What about having the outside of the body's experience. Why this conscious which is as real as one's breathing, and much closer than our aorta to us, cannot be located anywhere in our brain or any place in our entire body. Hence, before one should question God's existence, one should try to get to know oneself.

As Rumi said There is a candle in your heart, ready to be kindled. There is a void in your soul, ready to be filled. You feel it, don't you? Before doing so, one should shed bad habits and stay alive to do no evil and to uphold what is righteous. And as Rumi said: "Be like a tree and let the dead leaves drop." And in the road of cultivating your soul no one can help you; it is you that should feel the emergence of God within you.

Dig into your soul which is as deep as an ocean, which Rumi again said "I have been a seeker and I still am, but I stopped asking the books and the stars. I started listening to the teaching of my Soul." And be aware that: the most difficult things to do is to know yourself, before knowing God, so let silence to accompany you in that.

38

WHAT EXACTLY IS INSTINCT BEHAVIOR IF NOT SOFTWARE PROGRAMMING?

Growing up human is uniquely a matter of social relations rather than biology. What we learn from connections within the family take the place of instincts that program the behavior of animals; which raises the question of how good are these connections? Elizabeth Janeway

It is questionable how animals acquire the instincts that enable them with awesome innate behavior. It seems some behaviors are taught to animals by their parents and some traits are instinctual which animals are born with.

For instance, instinctive behavior in human-like Rooting reflex in babies is a primitive reflex that is seen in normal newborn babies, who automatically turn the face toward the stimulus and make sucking (rooting) motions with the mouth when the cheek or lip is touched. The rooting reflex helps to ensure successful breastfeeding. Originally when animals ascended out of the primordial sludge (muck, mud), and as our ancestors began to walk upright, the evolutionary process helped us to survive and reproduce.

If instinct is purpose-oriented and innate formats of action which are not the outcome of either learning or any experience. Then what other alternatives are left except believing in a magnificent designer which has programmed all there is in existence.

For instance, relating to instinct theory of motivation all organism is born with innate biological propensity (inclination, disposition) that assists them to survive. This theory suggests that instincts drive all behaviors,

Instincts are goal-directed and innate which are not the result of education or any experience.

If so, then what prominent psychologists like Sigmund Freud, Abraham Maslow, and other like William James are saying? Who orchestrated theories that supposedly are to resonate with the idea of behaving instinctual ambiguity since they say, quote instinct is a term used to describe a set of behaviors that are both unlearned, not experienced, set in motion as the result of some environmental trigger. Are they not saying that instinctual behaviors are caused by environmental trigger?

Therefore, when animals not excluding humans, mate, enjoy groupings, as social pleasure for humans, and as herding for the beasts, breeding, getting hungry, consume to survive, etc. Are they triggered by their atmosphere to function as such? Or are they natural agendas that we are born with?

Instinctual behaviors are often discussed in relation to motivation since they can also occur in response to an organism's need to satisfy some innate internal drive tied to survival. The question is that if instinctual behaviors are innately-driven, then what does environmental triggering has to do with it? since no experience, learning or triggering of any kind is basically required.

Referencing motivation again, if the initial conducts are innately maneuvered, then no outside force or cause is needed to motivate the animals to perform what they can so adeptly do because of their natural biological capabilities. This is not to say there are no learned behaviors, where environmental factors are sure decisive, but psychologist should make sure to prominent and discern (distinguish) instinctive actions from learned behaviors. What am saying if animals where exhausted of innate behaviors, and were not instinctually programmed, then, no outside forces of any kind could truly precipitate (prompt, provoke) them to do what they so naturally do.

> "Trust the instinct to the end, even though you can give no reason."
>
> — Ralph Waldo Emerson

As for mankind, this is what Charles Darwin believed: quote "The following proposition seems to me in a high degree probable—namely, that any animal whatever, endowed with well-marked social instincts, the parental and filial (particular blood relationship, avuncular, fraternal, maternal, paternal) affections being here included, would inevitably acquire a moral sense or conscience, as soon as its intellectual powers had become as well, or nearly as well developed, as in man. For, firstly, the social instincts lead an animal to take pleasure in the society of its fellows, to feel a certain amount of sympathy with them, and to perform various services for them."

— Charles Darwin, *The Descent of Man*

As for the human mind and man's psychological behaviors, there are some truth to Freud's role of mind that Freud redundantly disclosed, since he believed that the mind is responsible for both conscious and unconscious decisions related to drives and mental forces. The id, ego, and superego are three impressions of the mind in which Freud mentioned to make up a person's personality. Sigmund Freud emphasized the imperative of the unconscious mind, as the primary assumption of the Freudian theory, is that the unconscious mind rules behavior to a greater degree than people realize.

The focus of psychoanalysis is to make the unconscious conscious. The id is an important part of our personality because as newborns, it let us get our basic needs met. Freud believed that the id is based on our pleasure principle. In other words, the id inquires whatever feels good at the time, with no consideration for the reality of the situation.

Freud believed that events in our childhood have a great influence on our adult lives, forming our personality. Freud believed dreams represented a disguised realization of a repressed wish. He believed that investigating dreams indicated the simplest road to comprehending the unconscious activities of the mind.

According to the concept that Freud suggested, the dream is regarded as the guardian of sleep. According to Sigmund Freud, human personality is complicated and has more than a single component. In his famous psychoanalytic theory of personality, personality is composed of three elements. These three elements of personality—shown as the id, the ego, and the superego—work in concert to make complex human behaviors.

Further, the Freudian theory also segmented human personality into three major components: the id, ego, and superego. The id is the most primary part of the personality that is the source of all our most basic urges. Then, the superego comprises of two systems: The conscience and the ideal self. The conscience can punish the ego by causing feelings of guilt. For example, if the ego gives in to the id's demands, the superego may make the person feel bad through guilt.

Relating to Freud's psychoanalytic theory of personality, the id is the personality component made up of unconscious psychic energy that works to satisfy basic urges, needs, and desires. The id operates based on the pleasure principle, which demands immediate gratification of needs. In order to understand the role of the ego in one's life, one must first detect its purpose. The ego is the human consciousness part of you. It was designed to ensure one's security.

According to Freud, the unconscious continues to influence our behavior and experiences, even though we are unaware of these underlying influences. The unconscious can include repressed feelings, hidden memories, habits, thoughts, desires, and reactions. According to Freud, psychological development occurs during five psychosexual phases through a person's life: oral, anal, phallic, latency, and genital.

Latency Period: The period of lessened sexuality that Freud argued occurred between approximately age seven and adolescence. Freud believed that children went through a latency period during which we can notice a halt and retrogression in sexual development Latency is the fourth stage in Freud's Psychosexual theory of development, and it happens from about age 5 or 6 to puberty.

During the latency stage, a child's sexual impulses are suppressed. Freud believed that the nature of the conflicts among the id, ego, and superego change over time as a person grows from child to adult. Specifically, he stated that these conflicts develop via a series of five preliminary stages, each with a different focus: oral, anal, phallic, latency, and genital. Freud's structural model posits that personality consists of three interworking parts: the id, the ego, and the superego. The five stages of Freud's psychosexual theory of development include the oral, anal, phallic, latency, and genital stages.

During these stages, a person's id, ego, and superego develop, and each stage is dependent upon the fixation of the libido. Freud developed the psychoanalytic theory of personality development, which argued that personality is formed through conflicts among three fundamental structures of the human mind: the id, ego, and superego. According to Freud's psychoanalytic theory of personality, the superego is the component of personality composed of the internalized ideals that we have acquired from our parents and society. The superego works to suppress the urges of the id and tries to make the ego behave morally, rather than realistically.

In Freudian psychoanalysis, the pleasure principle is the instinctive seeking pleasure and avoiding pain in order to satisfy biological and psychological needs. Specifically, the pleasure principle is the driving force guiding the id. Sigmund Freud (May 6, 1856, to Sept. 23, 1939) founded psychoanalysis, a treatment technique that involves the patient talking to a psychoanalyst.

Even though Freud's ideas were disputes, he was one of the most influential scientists in the fields of psychology and psychiatry. Consistent with the psychoanalytic perspective, Sigmund Freud's theory of dreams suggested that dreams represented unconscious desires, thoughts, and motivations. According to Freud's psychoanalytic view of personality, people are-driven by aggressive and sexual instincts that are repressed from conscious awareness. Sigmund Freud's work and theories helped shape our views of childhood, personality, memory, sexuality, and therapy.

Meanwhile, the most reliable answer is that we do not yet understand the functions of dreaming, this shortcoming should not be surprising because despite many theories we still do not fully understand the purpose of sleep, nor can we gather the functions of REM (rapid eye movement) sleep, which is when most dreaming occurs. According to Freud's psychoanalytic theory of personality, the superego is the component of personality composed of the internalized ideals that we have acquired from our parents and society.

The superego works to suppress the urges of the id and tries to make the ego behave morally, rather than reality in which I am sure the environmental impact has a lot to do with triggering such human behavior like our dreams, and the functioning of id, ego and the super-ego. As far as for human instinctual behavior, we sure are programmed to eat when hungry, sleep and rest when tired, breath to stay alive, live in groups, defend ourselves, have the urge for having intercourse, and dream.

As for newborns, fetuses spend most of their time sleeping. At 32 weeks, your baby sleeps 90 to 95 percent of the day. During REM sleep, his eyes move back and forth just like an adult's eyes. Some scientists even believe that fetuses dream while they're sleeping. Further, a reflex action, also familiar as a reflex, is an involuntary and instantaneous movement in response to a stimulus. When a person accidentally touches a hot object, they automatically jerk their hand away without thinking.

A reflex does not require any thought input. Decided that it was not wisdom that enabled poets to write their poetry, but a kind of instinct or inspiration, such as you find in seers and prophets who deliver all their sublime messages without knowing in the least what they mean. Socrates

Instincts are innate complex patterns of behavior that exist in most members of the species, reflexes, which are simple responses of an organism to a specific stimulus, often triggered such as the contraction of the pupil in response to bright light or the spasmodic movement of the lower leg. Extensor spasticity is an involuntary straightening of the legs, which may also occur in the arms.

Instinct, or innate behavior, is an action that is impulsive or immediate based on a particular trigger or circumstance. Many scientists believe that most human behaviors are a result of some level of both instincts and learned behavior. other Reflexes normally solely observed in human infants are:

Asymmetrical tonic neck reflex (ATNR)

Palm omental reflex. The palm-omental reflex is a primitive reflex consisting of a twitch of the chin muscle elicited by stroking a specific part of the palm. It is present in infancy and disappears as the brain matures during childhood but may reappear due to processes that disrupt the normal cortical inhibitory pathways.

Moro reflex, also known as the startle reflex. The **Moro reflex** is an infantile **reflex** normally present in all infants/newborns up to 3 or 4 months of age as **a response** to **a** sudden loss of support, when the infant feels as if it is falling. It involves three distinct components: spreading out the arms (abduction), pulling the arms in (adduction), also meaning the movement of a limb or other part toward the midline of the body or toward another part.

Newborn **reflexes**. Newborn babies can become startled by a harsh noise, a jerky movement, or feels like they're falling, they might respond in a specific way. They might unexpectedly extend their arms and legs, arch their back, and then curl everything in again. This is an involuntary **startle** response called the **Moro reflex**.

Palmar grasp reflex. Palmar grasp reflex (sometimes simply grasp reflex) is a primitive reflex found in infants of humans and most primates. When an object is placed in an infant's hand and the palm of the child is stroked, the fingers will close reflexively, as the object is grasped via palmar grasp.

Rooting reflex. **Rooting reflex**: A **reflex** that is seen in normal newborn babies, who automatically turn the face toward the stimulus and make sucking (**rooting**) motions with the mouth when the cheek or lip is touched. The **rooting reflex** helps to ensure successful breastfeeding

Sucking reflex. The **sucking reflex** is probably one of the most important **reflexes** your newborn has. It is paired with the rooting **reflex**, in which a newborn searches for a food source. When he finds it, the **sucking reflex** allows him to **suck** and swallow the milk.

Symmetrical tonic neck reflex (STNR) is a primitive reflex found in newborn humans.

Tonic labyrinthine reflex (TLR) The tonic labyrinthine reflex (TLR) is a primitive reflex found in newborn humans.

Call these involuntary behaviors what you want, either instinctual or reflexes, the point is that they are not done by choice. Therefore, when psychologist Abraham Maslow argued that quote humans no longer have instincts because we have the ability to override them in certain situations.

He might have felt that what is called instinct is often imprecisely defined, and really amounts to strong drives. Otherwise, it is hard to gather what Mr. Maslow is actually talking about? As if, we can override breathing, as if, we do not have the natural instinct to protect ourselves, even when not triggered by the environment, or as if humanity can override propagation (procreation), or as if we can forego sleeping and rest, and so on.

All animals, including humans, are potentiated with innate instincts, as innate programming is the primary cause for their automatic actions; where the particular situation or certain environment can perhaps play as a catalyst for activating them, as their atmosphere cannot be the actual cause, or the primary reason for their instinctual mechanism, this naturally innate instinct are already endowed to them long before birth.

> "A young child can sense danger even if you repeatedly say, "I love you". There are those who can console a baby with their first touch and there are those who can make a baby scream, no matter what they try. Our basic animal instincts are suppressed by the subliminal messages fed to us by society. This leads to some surprising truths, such as this one: If the first kiss doesn't convince you, then nothing ever will"

> — Reham Khan

The mechanism of sexual intercourse, the interaction between the male and female reproductive systems results in fertilization of the woman's ovum by the man's sperm. These are specialized reproductive cells called gametes, created in a process called meiosis which can occur without any learning, they are often triggered by the opposite sex that is instinctual. When organisms that reproduce through asexual (without having sex) reproduction tend to grow in number exponentially. Thus, because they depend on mutation for variations in their DNA, all members of the species have similar vulnerabilities.

The beasts, for instance, the ambient behavior of ducklings, turtles, frogs, toads, seals and hundreds if not thousands of other animals, they are programmed since they are innately designed before even being born, like being able to live in water and dry land, where the Innate behavior comes from an animal's heredity.

An animal's instincts are examples of its innate behavior. For example, migrating birds use innate behavior to know when to incept their migration and the route they should take. Learned behavior arrives from watching other animals and from life experiences. Some birds even predict where they should be heading, flying for thousands of miles to reach climates contingent to their survival.

Birds can foresee the climate. Most birds have what's called the Vitali Organ, an exclusive middle-ear receptor that can sense an extremely small shift in atmospheric pressure. when you observe that birds are flying high up in the sky, the weather is most likely clear. An if birds fly low in the sky, you can be sure of that, a weather system is approaching. since bad weather is linked to low pressure.

Birds on a telephone wire predict the coming of rain. When the birds flew off, the storm was still hundreds of miles away, so there would have been few anticipated changes in atmospheric pressure, temperature and wind speed. Scientists think that this sixth sense that birds possess has to do with their power to hear sounds that humans cannot.

Furthermore, Rats, weasels, snakes, and centipedes reportedly left their abode and ran for safety several days before a destructive earthquake could occur. Also fish, birds, reptiles, and insects performing strange behavior weeks, days to seconds before an earthquake.

Certain behaviors, called instincts, are automatic, and they occur without the animal even noticing them. Instincts are inherited from parent organisms. Each year birds such as Canadian geese fly south for the winter. These animals know to migrate and hibernate because their instincts tell them.

Birds Learn to fly with not much help from their ancestors. It is true that birds learn to fly through practice, gradually refining their innate competency into a finely tuned skill. Thus, according to a psychologist, these skills may be easy to refine because of a genetically specified quiescent (dormant, shelved, temporary inactive, latent) memory for flying.

In addition to utilizing the Earth's magnetic field to orient themselves, some birds take advantage of the Sun and the stars to find their way. Whooping cranes, for instance, learn migration routes from older birds. When birds are migrating, they always know exactly where they are going, unlike us, when we're driving, we need a Sat-Nav, GPS, their sense of direction is dependent on a combination of three 'maps' of their own. Birds have a substance called magnetite, which is located just above their beaks.

Also, camouflaging is a physical adaptation in which the animal's body is colored or shaped in such a way that enables the animal to blend in with its surroundings. Like camouflage, mimicry discourages predators and improves the animal's rate of survival. Instinct is a behavior pattern that an animal naturally follows. Prey animals often use camouflage to hide from predators.

Camouflage is a way of hiding that allows an animal to blend in with its environment or otherwise go unnoticed by predators. Predators also sometimes use camouflage so as not to be detected by their prey. Have you not seen a bobcat, a cheetah, lion or a tiger in action, they act so cunningly when in hunting mode, as if they have earned a post-doctorate degree specialized in camouflaging trying to corner, and kill their prey from Stanford, or Berkley University?

There are four basic ways animals camouflage themselves. Most butterflies and moth protect themselves from predators by using camouflage. Some butterflies and moths blend into their environment so well that is it almost impossible to spot them when they are resting on a branch. Some butterflies are poisonous.

There are four basic types of camouflage:

Concealing Coloration. Concealing coloration is when an animal hides against a background of the same color.
Disruptive (uncontrollable) Coloration.
Disguise.
Mimicry.

Innate behaviors do not have to be learned or practiced. They are also called instinctive behaviors. Instinct is the ability of an animal to perform a behavior the first time it is exposed to the proper stimulus. For instance, a dog will drool any time it is exposed to food. Based on what one means by instinct, there is the breathing instinct, belief instinct, instinctive fear of snakes, among many others. Survival is our prime instinct which we will resume accordingly.

Like all animals, humans have instincts, genetically hard-wired behaviors that enhance our ability to cope with vital environmental contingencies. Our innate fear of snakes is an example. Other instincts, including denial, revenge, tribal loyalty, greed and our urge to procreate, now threaten our very existence. Hibernation is an innate behavior that is not learned after birth.

Animals that hibernate are born with an internal sense, or instinct, that tells them when they need to hibernate. During hibernation, an animal's body temperature drops, they take fewer breaths for a minute, and they do not need to eat. Some of the animals that hibernate include Hedgehogs, bats, snails, box turtle, garter snakes, bears, and so on.

The survival of 'the fittest of animal behavior and the awesome mechanism of how they are instinctually tuned to hunt. Like eagles, whales, cheetahs, lions, tigers, lizards, etc. and the speed in which they maneuver. Birds have something of an advantage when it comes to speed, for obvious reasons.

The peregrine falcon is particularly swift, capable of reaching speeds of up to 200 mph while at a dive, making it a fearsome hunter. The rest of the time it does not fly this fast, but that hardly matters to its prey. It is the fastest animal on the planet when in a dive. The eagle's eyes are very sharp and can see fish when the bird flies over the water. The eagle can look directly into the sun. As a test of the worthiness of its young, the eagle holds them up facing the sun.

In humans, the contemporary human brain (frontal cortex) is accountable for resolving problem, thoughts, memory, language, impulse control, judgment, and reasoning power. The primal brain (hindbrain and medulla) is responsible for survival instinctual mode, drive, and other instincts. When the primal brain is engaged (sympathetic response), one's modern brain is not active much. Learned behaviors, although they may have innate feature or foundations (motive, underpinning, cornerstone), they permit an individual organism to adapt to changes in the environment.

Learned behaviors are modified by previous experiences; examples of simple learned behaviors include habituation and imprinting (in psychology, imprinting is defined as a remarkable phenomenon that occurs in animals, and in humans, in the first hours of life. In humans, this is often called bonding, and it usually refers to the relationship between the newborn and its parents). Innate behavior comes from an animal's heredity. An animal's instincts are examples of its innate behavior.

For instance, migrating birds deploy innate actions to determine when to initiate their migration and the route that they should follow. Learned behavior comes from watching other animals and from life experiences. Behavior is decided by a combination of inherited traits, experience, and the environment. Some behavior, called innate, comes from your genes, but other behavior is learned, either from interacting with the world or by being taught. Examples of behaviors that do not require conscious will include many reflexes.

Examples of instinctive behaviors in humans include many of the primitive reflexes, such as rooting and suckling, behaviors which are present in mammals. further, there is not much that we know on how and why we laugh, except it bonds us via humor and interplay. It is a hidden language that we all speak, as it is not a learned collective or group reaction but instinctive conduct programmed through our genes.

Infant swimming or diving reflex. Most human babies exhibit an innate swimming or diving reflex from birth until the age of roughly six months, but babies this young cannot swim, due to their barrier of body features and strength. Survival instinct is present in all creatures with not excluding humans. Beasts such as dear, Gazelle, small mammals, and lizards often rely on their speed and quickness to escape predators, and many birds rely on the flight as their primary defensive strategy.

Some organisms, like a tortoise, armadillos, porcupines, and thorny plants, utilize armor, quills (any of the main wing or tail feathers of a bird.) and thorns to defend themselves against predators. In communal defense, prey groups actively defend themselves by grouping together, and sometimes by attacking or mobbing a predator, rather than allowing themselves to be passive victims of predation. Mobbing (to crowd around excitingly, to the multitude, to mass, to hoard) is the harassing of a predator by many prey animals. Other defensive mechanisms for some animals include:

live in groups (herds or shoals)
built for speed.
defenses such as poison or stings.
camouflage to avoid being seen by predators.
eyes to the side of the head to get a wide field of view (monocular vision).

39

HOW DO ANIMALS AVOID PREDATION?

Most animals face predation pressure and must avoid or defend themselves against predators for survival to successfully reproduce. Beside physical traits such as armor and camouflage, animals use behavior to avoid and survive predation; Prey detection is the process by which predators are able to detect and locate their prey via sensory signals.

Predators are an imperative part of a healthy ecosystem. Predators cull (select, choose) vulnerable prey, such as the old, injured, sick, or very young, leaving more food for the survival and prosperity of healthy prey animals, also, by controlling the size of prey populations, predators assist with lessening the spread of disease. Animals are far more intelligent than we ever recognized; the one thing that we've been educated within our research from the past is that so many species have much more going on inside their brains than we previously thought.

We know now that animals can solve puzzles, learn words, and interact with each other in complex ways. Crows can solve puzzles as well as five-year-olds. These remarkable birds are capable of constructing tools, using them and saving them for future use. Their cognitive abilities include problem-solving, reasoning and even self-awareness. Despite their relatively small brain, they have a good memory. They can remember other members of their own species and even recognize humans when they pose a threat.

A series of recent experiments exhibited crow's magnificent ability in troubleshooting and problem-solving with highly skill maneuverability. In one study conducted at the University of Auckland, researchers realized that when tubes of water that contained a floating treat were made ready, crows figured out that dropping other objects into the tubes would cause the water level to rise, making the treatment accessible. They also figured out that they could get the treats much fastest if they selected tubes with higher water levels to start, and if they dropped objects that sank, rather than ones that floated.

Other research, meanwhile, has shown that crows can intentionally bend a piece of wire in order to fish a treat out of a narrow tube. On the whole, researchers put their problem-solving skills roughly comparable with those of 5 to 7-year-old children. Researchers further experienced that cockatoos, like crows, can solve not so easy puzzles in order to get treats. In a research done in 2013 study, they required the birds to open a box (which contained cashew) by removing a pin, unscrewing a screw, pulling out a bolt, circling a wheel, and finally sliding out a latch.

Obviously, this takes a long time for an animal that doesn't have opposable thumbs. It took one cockatoo a full two hours, eventually solving the puzzle exposing that the birds are competent in striving towards goals that are much more distant than the researchers had previously believed. Other birds in the experiment, meanwhile, learned from the first bird and completed the whole puzzle much more quickly. when the puzzle was altered so that the five steps had to be completed in a different order, the birds seemed to detect this and responded accordingly instead of trying to replicate the previous solution.

Chimpanzees.

These are mankind's closest relatives. Chimpanzees are sociable animals and form elaborate communities. They are skilled at using different types of tools to carry out complex tasks, such as thin sticks to extract termites and rocks to open fruits. Combined with a powerful memory, these abilities make the chimpanzee the most intelligent (non-human) animal on Earth.

Dolphins are outstandingly smart in all sorts of ways. when captured, they can be quickly trained to complete tasks in exchange for treats and are known to mimic human actions just for the fun of it. In the wild, they've been seen to cover their snouts with sponges for protecting themselves against spiny fish while hunting and terminating spiny fish so they can use their spines to extract eels from crack (fissure, cleft, cranny, slot, fracture, crevices).

A dolphin's whistle seems to be similar to its name. It is interesting to know that each dolphin seems to own a characteristic whistle that represents itself, a dolphin's whistle sounds much like its name. Experiments show that dolphins swim towards the speaker emitting whistle of a family member much more often than an unfamiliar dolphin's, and when a mother dolphin is apart from her calf, she'll vent the calves' whistle until they're reunited.

Researchers also found that dolphins act differently upon hearing the whistle of a dolphin they'd last seen 20 years earlier, in comparison to a stranger's—they're much more tuned to approach the speaker and whistle at it redundantly, trying to make it respond back to whistle.

Dolphins are extremely sociable creatures with a highly developed ability to adapt to their habitat. They help one another when injured or ill and, thanks to their individually distinct calls, they're able to pass on their knowledge to others. In fact, the list of high-level cognitive abilities— including identification, differentiation, and behavioral control.

Elephants can cooperate and show empathy. Field researchers have realized that elephants cooperate in complex ways. Elephants have the largest brain of all land animals. Elephants notoriety is for their sociability and can express emotions, including happiness and compassion, as well as pain and grief. They show acts of altruism and self-awareness. With a greater memory than even us humans, an elephant truly never forgets!

Many families of related elephants travel together in clans, interact via low-frequency rumbles (finding out, come upon.) At times, they'll form circles around calves to protect them from predators, or carry out coordinated kidnappings of calves from competing clans (extended family, tribe) in the performance of dominance. Levels of coordination have been shown in controlled experiments, where pairs of elephants quickly learned to instantaneously pull on a rope to get a treat, and not to pull alone, as they would have risked ruining the chance of getting it.

Other studies, the researchers found out that elephants seem to show genuine empathy.

Contrary to many beasts that exhibit little interest in dead members of their species, typically, they either briefly sniff them before walking away or eating them. Elephants, however, show a special interest in elephant remains, lingering near them and in some cases becoming agitated as one can notice an ill-effect on their peace of mind. Field researchers have also noticed that elephants consoling, comforting each other—something seldom seen in other species. Typically, when an elephant becomes perturbed, it'll make squeaking noises and perk its ears up. often, other elephants from the same clan will come and stroke its head with their trunks, or put their trunk in its mouth.

It is a difficult task to study octopuses since they're aquatic, also a bit hard to keep them alive in captivity, and also because octopuses relatively live deep in the ocean. The imperative point to realize is that octopuses maneuver in an environment very different than ours, so basically their intelligence is directed at solving divergent (disparate, not the same) oriented goals. By far the world's smartest invertebrates, octopuses can manage intricate tasks, like opening a jar to get to its contents. They possess a good short- and long-term memory but also an outstanding ability to learn new skills from the moment they're born.

For instance, the mimic octopus (Thaumoctopus mimicus) can impersonate other species in order to save itself from predators.

Many scientists believe that they're smart in ways that are qualitatively different from us and the other species. They have the largest brains of any invertebrate, they also have more neurons than humans, sixty percent of these cells are in their arms, not their brains. Thus, their arms look like being individually intelligent: when the arms are cut off, they can crawl away, grab food items, and raise them up to where the octopus' mouth would be as if they were still linked.

Meanwhile, octopuses seem to have a keen sense of aesthetics, even though they're likely colorblind. Field researchers have observed octopuses gather Intelligence which is one of the prominent features of being human and it comes in various forms.

For example, there's verbal-linguistic intelligence (communicative ability), interactive ability. spatial intelligence (the competency to observe the world with the mind's eye), logical-mathematical intelligence (the power to solve mathematical problems) and potentiated with emotional intelligence (the ability to identify and manage your own emotions and the emotions of others), investigative ability. There are also other types of intelligence which, in the process of comprehending the workings of the human mind, we have tried to disentangle and define.

However, when we talk of animal intelligence, we talk in quite different terms. The study of animal intelligence has a long history. We can describe animal intelligence as the combination of skills and abilities that permit animals to live and adapt to their particular environments. Animals possess the ability to adapt to their surroundings by learning to change their habits and behaviors. Many species are also capable of forming social groups. All of these characteristics are based on the animal's capacity to process information and, by assessing this capacity.

Parrots

These birds have an incredible ability to know different human faces and have a high aptitude for communication, as can be seen by their aptitude (prowess, knack) for impersonating human voices. Parrots also possess an incredible memory, which assists them to solve complicated problems.

Rats

Rats dream in a similar way to that of humans. Thanks to their ability to process different sensorial cues, they can analyze situations and make their way out of mazes (confusing, labyrinth, puzzling) system. Interestingly, they have been found to display high levels of empathy, making sacrifices for other members of their species. Rats can even make calculations in order to obtain food from a trap without being caught.

Many animals depend on such a clock to maintain their circadian rhythm (If you've ever noticed that you tend to feel energized and drowsy around the same times every day, you have your circadian rhythm to thank). What is it, exactly? Your circadian rhythm is basically a 24-hour internal clock that is running in the background of your brain and cycles between sleepiness and alertness at regular intervals. It's also known as your sleep/wake cycle.

Animals that use sun compass orientation are fish, birds, sea turtles, butterflies, bees, sand hoppers, reptiles, and ants. While they usually use it together with other navigational methods, animals also use the Earth's magnetic field as their compass. While they use the sun and the stars to navigate, birds also use the Earth's magnetic field.

Loggerhead turtles can even sense the direction and strength of Earth's magnetic field soon after hatching, and later use this skill to navigate along their regular migration route. Other animals use land features such as mountain ranges and rivers, and dolphins use the shape of the ocean floor. The sun compass plays a role in homing pigeons which have the ability to return home after a great distance and may be used by birds that migrate during the day. Many songbird species, however, migrate at night. For many years' scientist suspected that birds take advantage of the stars for navigation.

Magneto-reception: The homing pigeon can return to its home because of its ability to sense the Earth's magnetic field and other cues to orient itself. Magneto-reception plays a part in guiding Loggerhead hatchlings to the sea. Some animals sleep for a long time in the winter, but they do not go into true hibernation. Their heart and breathing slow down, but often their body temperature does not drop as Bio-magnetism. Bio-magnetism is the phenomenon of magnetic fields generated by living organisms; it is a subset of bio-electromagnetism.

In comparison organisms' use of magnetism in navigation is magneto-reception, a sense which allows an organism to detect a magnetic field to perceive direction, altitude or location. This sensory modality is used by a range of animals for orientation and navigation, and as a method for animals to develop regional maps. the study of the magnetic fields' effects on organisms is magneto-biology.

Stimulus **modality** in humans also called **sensory modality**, is one aspect of a stimulus or what is perceived after a stimulus. For example, the temperature **modality** is registered after heat or cold stimulate a receptor. Some **sensory modalities** include light, sound, temperature, taste, pressure, and smell.

A **sensory modality is related to** sensing, like vision or hearing. **Modality** in someone's voice indicates a sense of the person's mood. In logic, **modality** has to **do** with whether a proposition is needed, possible, or impossible. In general, a **modality is a** particular way in which something exists.

Scientists who study whales believe the animals utilize a combination of senses to find their path, in a way that helps them observe the ocean floor, spot landmarks along the way and navigate in the proper direction. Enthusiasts have known for decades that whales use noises to communicate. When in search of food they circle around making a huge pond where they collectively make a horrifyingly loud noise which scares thousands of little fish as they pop up to the surface dead, and then are consumed by wales.

The point is that one shouldn't ignore the evolutionary impact of these marvelously disciplinary actions which ought to put any curiously inquisitive mind at awe. But why? Why should evolution, or any other force for that matter play such an active role in these incredibly complex procedures? One can use any lexicon which one desires, such as instinct, instinctual, or any other word to describe this magnificently awakened animal's maneuverability. But without considering a disciplinary awakened force, a magnificent designer implementing such intricate tactics and strategy in the animal kingdom, programming them for their survival must not make any sense.

Biology is the study of complex things that appear to have designed for a purpose. Richard Dawkins

Nothingness

We ponder on this controversial issue about if things are created from something, or perhaps are made out of nothing. But then, the proper question should be addressed as: Is nothingness impregnated with an infinite number of things or not? if not, then, quintillions of scientific discoveries which scientists and scholars have divulged and employed should mean fiction and no more. It should be harboring that our inventions have stemmed from nothingness and transmitted into actuality from the unknown; in which we either have already concocted or hope to excogitate in the future. if yes, then we should tirelessly dig into nothingness to further get closer to the truth.

We are conducive to perceive and define nothingness according to available human resources and competency. The term nothingness can be alarmingly deceptive since what we know as nothing, is actually everything; but since nothingness is incomprehensible to us at certain times, not realizing when and where, or by whom, nothing is going to give birth to our next scientific breakthroughs. Then we are deluded into believing nothingness as literally meaning being immaterial and barren to us which is based on our limited senses.

The consensus should be in accepting nothingness as the holy grail of creativity and where the real potential lay for things we persist on to decode and eventually conquer. if not, then, we have acted shortsighted in all of which we have discovered and hope to invent. We are faced with no choice but to delve into the reality of nothing and realize there is no such thing as void. Hence, it would make sense to switch and replace the word nothingness for the word unknown.

To say life came out of nothing is honestly an insult to reason since literally should mean God is in charge of the womb of what we know and grant as emptiness which in contrary is filled with propitious prospects. That gave birth to all there is and all of which there will ever be. Through the eyes of quantum physic which represent the world of unseen, renowned physicists like Niels-Bohr, and many of his colleagues accept and say quote: atomic uncertainty is truly intrinsic to nature: the rules of clock might apply to familiar objects such as snooker balls, but when it comes to atoms and quarks, and other subatomic particles, the rules are those of roulette. Many scientists believe these subatomic particles are being thrown around by an unseen ocean of microscopic forces.

It is therefore apparent that we must refuge to bounds of our senses to acquaint and to comply with the world outside of us, since as humans we cannot reconnaissance with what is beyond our ability and knowledge to decipher. should not mean that there is no magic in the air, or perhaps we need to quit searching for miracles, since the history of evolution should validate the human mind that progresses into dynamic stages of enlightenment where boundaries are magically torn and miracle like discoveries become the norm.

It seems beautiful minds are impacted with premonition and are mandated with a mission to seek and to perform gynecology into the womb of mother nature to give birth to yet another treasure, leaping into unveiling the mysteries of nature's obscurities to emancipate man from the clutches of ignorance.

Our curiosity into the realms of speculation and probabilities is fostered and potentially backed up by hidden agenda conveyed into the unknown ready to be exploited and burst into reality. of course it is inclined to action by passion, human drive, time consumed, and keen enough to feel and detect the maturity and the magnificent moment of delivery. That is encouraged with hope, perseverance, and bearing hardship through many trials and errors; and then occasionally bull-eyed into steppingstones for other miracles like disclosures. sometimes a huge leap into successful challenges where our struggle in bettering human life pays off generously.